"In *Cradling Abundance*, Maman Monique tells the good story of her calling to be an apostle for justice, truth, and healing in the church in Central Africa. What she describes is a woman's embodied theology of sacrificial service to 'the least of these' that leads us closer to the heart of Jesus. Her life gives us a glimpse of what the way of the cross looks like for our sisters in Africa."

Michèle Sigg, Dictionary of African Christian Biography (DACB.org), Boston University

"In this honest account, Mama Monique walks the reader through a diverse socioeconomic and political history of the Democratic Republic of Congo viewed through the eyes of one courageous woman. This is a beautiful story of life's complexities, traditional practices, gender relations, and the importance of education for Congolese women. It is also an account of human suffering and God's grace. This untold narrative needed to be told; it gives a window to the story of the church in Congo."

Médine Keener, coauthor with Craig Keener of *Impossible Love: The True Story of an African Civil War, Miracles and Hope Against All Odds*

"This biography of a remarkable woman, a remarkable place, and a remarkable people is all set against the shifting political systems of western Africa. Part engrossing novel intertwined with a history lesson, it reads like an intimate letter from a precious friend all sewn together with resilience that comes from faith. Like Jollof rice, there is a little bit of everything—but it's so delicious that you just cannot stop gulping it down. From the incredible opening scene where this defiant young woman armed only with her intellect and courage manages gun-toting military thugs until the final chapter, the reader is treated to a masterfully told encounter with another culture and continent. I just want to know which actor will play Maman Monique when the movie is made!"

Susan Brasier, ordained clergy with the PC(USA)

"Based on careful research, interviews, and personal engagement, this beautiful, poignant, and unique book narrates the life and witness of Maman Monique, a remarkable Congolese woman and world Christian leader. We hear Maman Monique's story of suffering, struggle, perseverance, and triumph in her own voice and the voices of her coworkers, thanks to the unobtrusive and illuminating editorial accompaniment of her friend, Elsie Tshimunyi McKee, Princeton Seminary professor, scholar, and teacher of the church who spent her first eighteen years in the Congo as the daughter and granddaughter of missionaries. The solidarity in God's mission shared by Monique and Elsie has generated a compelling 'grounded' account of the peoples of the Democratic Republic of the Congo as they moved out of colonial subjugation and through civil war, ethnic conflict, and poverty, then—thanks to courageous women like Maman Monique and her collaborators—toward a more just society where all children, women, and men are honored as equal recipients and agents of the 'cradling abundance' of God in Jesus Christ."

Thomas John Hastings, executive director of the Overseas Ministries Study Center at Princeton Theological Seminary and editor of the *International Bulletin of Mission Research*

Maman Monique speaking at the meeting of the Central Committee of the World Council of Churches, in Potsdam, Germany, January 2001. Her subject: "The Market Economy in the Democratic Republic of Congo."

Pastors John, Becca, Pauline &
friends at Doylestown,
Elsie Tshimunyi McKee

MONIQUE MISENGA NGOIE MUKUNA
WITH ELSIE TSHIMUNYI MCKEE

CRADLING ABUNDANCE

*One African Christian's Story of Empowering
Women and Fighting Systemic Poverty*

IVP
Academic
An imprint of InterVarsity Press
Downers Grove, Illinois

InterVarsity Press
P.O. Box 1400, Downers Grove, IL 60515-1426
ivpress.com
email@ivpress.com

InterVarsity Press® is the book-publishing division of InterVarsity Christian Fellowship/USA®, a movement of students and faculty active on campus at hundreds of universities, colleges, and schools of nursing in the United States of America, and a member movement of the International Fellowship of Evangelical Students. For information about local and regional activities, visit intervarsity.org.

Scripture quotations, unless otherwise noted, are from the New Revised Standard Version Bible, copyright © 1989 National Council of the Churches of Christ in the United States of America. Used by permission. All rights reserved worldwide.

This is a work of autobiography. The views and opinions expressed are those of the authors and do not necessarily reflect the viewpoint of any other person or institution.

Frontispiece photo of Maman Monique from the archives of the World Council of Churches. Taken Jan. 2001, Potsdam, Germany
Figure 1.1 map of the Democratic Republic of Congo from the Nations Online project, used with permission
Figure 1.2 map of the Democratic Republic of Congo © InterVarsity Press
Figures 2.1, 4.1, 4.2, 11.1, 12.1, 13.1, 15.1 personal photos by author

The publisher cannot verify the accuracy or functionality of website URLs used in this book beyond the date of publication.

Cover design and image composite: Cindy Kiple
Interior design: Daniel van Loon
Images: color map of Africa: © shuoshu / DigitalVision Bectors / Getty Images
       photo of Maman Monique: archives of the World Council of Churches, taken Jan. 2001, Potsdam, Germany

ISBN 978-0-8308-5298-7 (print)
ISBN 978-0-8308-5299-4 (digital)

Printed in the United States of America ♾

InterVarsity Press is committed to ecological stewardship and to the conservation of natural resources in all our operations. This book was printed using sustainably sourced paper.

Library of Congress Cataloging-in-Publication Data
A catalog record for this book is available from the Library of Congress.

P   28 27 26 25 24 23 22 21 20 19 18 17 16 15 14 13 12 11 10 9 8 7 6 5 4 3 2 1

Y   45 44 43 42 41 40 39 38 37 36 35 34 33 32 31 30 29 28 27 26 25 24 23 22 21

CONTENTS

ABBREVIATIONS

AACC   All Africa Conference of Churches

AFDL   Alliance of Democratic Forces for the Liberation of Congo, military alliance led by Laurent Kabila

AIC   African Instituted (or Independent) Churches

CCC   Church of Christ in Congo, federated Protestant denominations

CENEDI   The Center for Mentoring Children in Difficulties, Uvira-based nonprofit affiliated with Woman, Cradle of Abundance

CPK   Presbyterian Church of Kinshasa, part of CCC, partner with PC(USA)

FEBA   Femme, Berceau de l'Abondance = Woman, Cradle of Abundance

HAW   Hands Across the Water, youth club in New Jersey serving CENEDI, affiliated with Woman, Cradle of Abundance

INEAC   National Institute for Agronomic Study of Congo, where Maman Monique's father worked

IPN   National Institute of Pedagogy, the national university of pedagogy in Kinshasa, Congo

ISP   Institut Supérieur Pédagogique de Gombe / Higher Institute of Pedagogy, the Catholic university where Maman Monique studied

JMPR   Junior/Student MPR; see MPR

MNC   National Congolese Movement, Patrice Lumumba's party

MPR   Popular Movement of the Revolution, President Mobutu's party

PCUS   Presbyterian Church in the United States, 1861–1983, sending church for missionaries to Congo

PC(USA)   Presbyterian Church (USA)

PTS   Princeton Theological Seminary

SP   Security Police in President Mobutu's regime

UDPS   Union for Democracy and Social Progress, opposition party led by Etienne Tshisekedi

UN   United Nations

VEM   Vereinte Evangelische Mission / United Protestant Mission, German church aid organization

WARC   World Alliance of Reformed Churches, after 2010 World Communion of Reformed Churches

WCC   World Council of Churches

PROLOGUE

THE PLACE IS ZAIRE (now Democratic Republic of Congo), in the middle of Africa. The time is 1972, under the rule of General Sese Seko Mobutu.

I was just twenty, small and thin, a university student on her way home from the capital for the summer. After boat and train, the last leg of the trip was by truck. My brother and I and quite a lot of people were crowded in with all our baggage. Suddenly, we were stopped by a military barricade across the road. We had suitcases, I had bought clothes and things for my family. On the truck there were people from Katanga with their goods too. The soldiers ordered us to get out and let them search our suitcases or bundles. If we did not have sales slips for each item, they would seize it. I got out, but I was not having any of this theft. "If you want the suitcases, get them down yourselves!" The soldiers were astonished, and the other people terrified. "Maman, why are you doing that? You will get us arrested!"

"I will not get out my suitcase. Show me your orders. President Mobutu has forbidden barricades on the roads. People know where I am; if you hurt me, they will come and get you. You don't have the right to search people's belongings." We were speaking Tshiluba, but I switched to French. The soldiers hurried to their commander, in a brush hut. They said, "There is a girl here— she speaks Tshiluba, she speaks French. She is reprimanding us; she says that we don't have the right to put up barricades. They know where she is." The commander said, "Bring her to me."

They brought me to him. He said, "What! Why are you speaking in front of the soldiers that I sent?" I said, "Commander, can you show me your orders? If you do, I will obey what you say." He said, "What? You are impolite!" I said, "When the commander speaks impolitely, you answer him impolitely. If you are the commander, you should know that the supreme commander has given orders not to put up barricades. But you have put them here. You should know what awaits you. Even if you kill me today, you will also die. You won't last two days." The commander said, "Okay . . . good thing I called you over here. You must be some personage, but you should not speak like that when we are working." I said, "You are ruining what the president said. You should obey the president of the republic." He said, "Go!" They let all the passengers get back into the truck with their belongings, and we left.

When we got to the stop where my father would meet my brother and me, all the people in the truck told my father, "What a child you have, what a daughter! No, she is not a daughter; she is a man! She saved us." My father said to me, "That is good! You must always be like that." To them he said, "She is educated, she knows things, she is not afraid. Why were you afraid?" But they were afraid because they did not know how to defend themselves. The soldiers were going to steal all their things, but I was able to defend them. It was God's hand on me.

Later on, I founded a nonprofit called FEBA, which also took courage and has delivered many people from trouble. But that is part of the story to come.

PART ONE

BEGINNINGS

God created humankind in his image,
in the image of God he created them;
male and female he created them.

GENESIS 1:27

1

INTRODUCTION

Why This Book Matters and Where It Fits In

ELSIE TSHIMUNYI McKEE

MAMAN MONIQUE'S STORY

Muoyo webe = life to you! That is the common greeting in Tshiluba, the language that Maman Monique and I grew up speaking. I am Elsie Tshimunyi McKee, and I have the great joy and honor of introducing my best friend, Monique Misenga Ngoie Mukuna, "Maman Monique." My job is to set the stage for her and accompany you along the way. I will begin by telling you why I want to share Maman Monique's story.

First, Maman Monique is one of the most inspiring people I have ever met. She possesses a remarkable strength of purpose and has exhibited a lifetime of commitment to educating and serving women and girls and all "the least of these"—living her faith in ordinary life, day by day, year in and year out.

Second, Maman Monique is one of the most comprehensive models of a strong and compassionate woman that I know. She has never stopped learning and growing, initiating and creating, and then following through on a wide range of projects to improve life for the world around her. Gifted student and politically savvy citizen, farmer and expert tailor, talented school teacher/ principal and successful businesswoman, visionary social activist and smart networker, steadfast church leader and gadfly—all while being daughter, wife, mother, go-to person, and reluctant matriarch for her extended family. And for just about anyone else in need of wise counsel, a meal, a shoulder to cry on, a temporary roof, some frank speaking, a hospital or school fee paid, a biblical story of inspiration. With all this, Maman Monique is also one of the sanest people I know, with warmth and humor, grace and courage.

Third, I want to share Maman Monique's story because she opens a window on so many levels and aspects of life for women and girls in central Africa (and, I suspect, more widely in the Majority World). She tells other women's stories; she reveals the varied conditions of life as a girl or woman in that world. She also has brought other women and girls to tell their stories: this book includes many more voices than Maman Monique's. A significant number of her friends and associates and students graciously agreed to be interviewed, not all of whose first-person narratives could be printed here. This is their story, and its publication is for their joy.

Fourth, Maman Monique's story is worth sharing for its panoramic view of Christian women at work at every level of the church and community—from the local congregation through denominational and ecumenical women's groups to national and international venues. It demonstrates the engagement of laywomen (not just clergy or theologians) and provides clear evidence of women's strength of Christian faith, and the strength women draw from their faith, as well as the ways their faith can lead them to address injustice and discrimination in church as well as society.

Fifth, Maman Monique tells a good story.

To start off, you may want to know how this story came to be written. Every story has a story, and this one began about ten years ago, in 2010, when Maman Monique and I sat on the porch of her home in Kinshasa. This was my first visit back to Congo since she and I had met in 2008. We were both born in the large Kasai province, she in East Kasai, I in West Kasai, but her education was in Tshiluba and French, mine in English, so we did not cross paths at school. In fact, coming to know her as an adult, I was perhaps better able to appreciate how remarkable this sister is than if we had actually grown up together, though I am sorry for all the years of friendship that we missed.

When my husband, John, my sister Beth, and I arrived in Kinshasa in August 2010, Maman Monique was in the midst of a major crisis in her ministry, brought on by patriarchal jealousy (you will hear more about that later). While visiting her home, we met women and children whom she had rescued—and taken into her home. We heard their stories:

- The young girl in shock who fled from an abusive older husband: He already had a wife and grown children when he tricked her family into sending her to marry him, sight unseen. With counseling and education, she is now a confident and accomplished woman.

- The young widow whose in-laws stole her inheritance, who had nowhere to go with her infant daughter. After sewing school and her own further studies, she is now a self-sufficient and successful businesswoman, and her little girl happily visits her "grandmother" at Maman Monique's.

- The HIV-positive widow, victim of her husband's infidelity. She now has the medicines she needs, a microloan-based means of self-support, and a full and active life with her children.

- A family of orphans seeking help to survive. Food, school fees and supplies, and hope.

- All these and more.

We talked with Tatu Mukuna, Maman Monique's devoted husband and partner in faith, and with the colleagues who have for many years loyally followed her in her service to "the least of these." And we heard about FEBA, the nonprofit that is her brainchild, established to empower women and fight systemic poverty. Although Maman Monique has been engaged in various kinds of Matthew 25 ministry all her adult life, as an individual and through her church (informally and officially), the living embodiment of her spirit is the nonprofit Femme, Berceau de l'Abondance. The French acronym is FEBA or, in English, Woman, Cradle of Abundance. Inspired by the international Decade of Churches in Solidarity with Women, Maman Monique and some friends established FEBA in 1999. After challenges of various kinds, FEBA was relaunched by Maman Monique in 2010.[1]

The story I was hearing and seeing in Kinshasa in August 2010 began to take shape in my imagination. Who was this amazing woman? What else had she done? I wanted to know more. And the more I learned, the more I wanted to share the story of this remarkable Christian and her ministry. It is not just Maman Monique's work, though FEBA would never have happened or survived without her. She and those she inspires are demonstrating that those on the margins, "second-class citizens" of their world, can be instruments of "cradling abundance" (John 10:10) for others. This story is a window on the shared faith, deep prayer life, and sheer grit and guts of so many African Christian women who confront all kinds of challenges: human and natural,

---

[1]More information about FEBA, including additional photos of Maman Monique and her work, is available at womancradleofabundance.org.

political and economic, educational and spiritual, day in and day out. And they never give up, never stop caring, and never stop singing and hoping and working for life abundant in Jesus Christ, the Good Shepherd.

This book is Maman Monique's personal story, and the stories of her friends and students who offered me the privilege of hearing the words from their lives and hearts. It is not an objective collection of statistics about women and poverty. It is not a careful analysis of politics or culture. It is a personal conversation among friends, which English readers now can "overhear." The original conversations were taped (a few video, mostly audio) over the course of about seven years (2011–2018), primarily in French, with some in Lingala or Tshiluba with French translation. (Some of those I interviewed did not know French, the common language of educated Congolese; I do not know Lingala, and my Tshiluba is rather rusty for anything except reading the Bible, so Maman Monique and her colleague Maman Antoinette translated into French.)

Then the tapes had to be transcribed and typed. They produced about 679 pages of French (169,696 words, over twice the length of this book). Translating to English was not a problem. Cutting and editing was something else, particularly since the conversations had wandered over many subjects, as conversations do. (My most frequent interjection was *Quand?* [When?] to determine whether what she was saying came before or after the previous story.) Then it was necessary to make a chronological and/or topical order and decide what had to be cut to make a book of reasonable length. Maman Monique collaborated all along, but the structure is my contribution. She read and corrected different drafts, and we continued to add more miniconversations in the last several years, 2018–2020, to bring the story up to the present. We are both very grateful to my students at Princeton Theological Seminary, who read an earlier version in class; to our editor Jon Boyd; and to the anonymous reviewers for IVP Academic, whose good comments helped identify things that needed to be clarified for you, our readers. Some of those questions are answered in the historical and cultural overview that is presented here, and more information is found in my sidebars throughout the story. Before turning to the larger history, it is helpful to explain how Maman Monique and her friends are called.

Names are very important, and in African culture they also tell a great deal about a person. Traditionally, a child has a given name from the family, normally from the father's side. For Maman Monique, that is Misenga, for her paternal grandmother. The "surname" is the father's given name. For her that is Ngoie: Misenga <u>Ngoie</u>. (To help keep things straight, the "surname" will be underlined. However, it is not appropriate to call someone by the surname alone because that is in fact the identifying name of another person.) When a woman marries, her husband's given name is added or, more often, substituted. For Maman Monique that is Mukuna: Misenga <u>Mukuna</u>. Since Christianity came, most people have received a baptismal name, which is usually biblical or Western, though it can be Bantu. In this case, it is Monique. Sometimes an additional name (or two) signifies a particular characteristic. For example, Luba twins are called Mbuyi and Kanku along with whatever given name they receive; Maman Monique's maternal grandmother was Mbuyi Kaleka. Finally, a person who is outstanding for some specific character trait may have yet another name. That same grandmother was called Mutangila Nzambi, or "one who has seen God," for her close relationship with God.

In African culture, one never addresses an older person without some title, and often a title is used when speaking about any adult. Thus it is Mamu Misenga or Maman Monique (depending on whether the speakers are using Tshiluba or French), or Tatu Ngoie or Tatu Mukuna (for her father or her husband). *Tatu* or *Mamu* is a title of respect as well as a way of naming father or mother. *Maman* is the French equivalent but is often used also with the Tshiluba name.

To give an English example, let's use my name. My parents were Charles and Anne McKee; my father's parents were George and Elsie McKee. I would be Elsie <u>Charles</u>, my father would be Charles <u>George</u>, my mother's married name would be Anne <u>Charles</u>, and my grandmother's would be Elsie <u>George</u>. When missionaries came to Congo, they became part of the community. Their Congolese friends gave them Tshiluba names, and their children were baptized with Tshiluba names. My grandparents George and Elsie McKee were named Tatu Ntalaja (or Ntalasha) and Mamu Tshimunyi. Their older son, my father, was baptized Ngulumingi and known as Ngulumingi <u>Ntalaja</u>. I was baptized Tshimunyi and known as Tshimunyi <u>Ngulumingi</u>. In a happy reversal of expectations, my Christian name is Tshimunyi; Elsie Anne McKee is my American name.

To keep the naming as simple as possible, in this book usually a person will be referred to by the name she or he most often uses, along with the common title, e.g., Maman Monique / Tatu Mukuna. The list of those interviewed will provide a brief identifying phrase for each person, and the list of key people also identifies several people named in the text.

Maman Monique's story belongs in the wider horizon of African women writers, especially the Circle of Concerned African Women Theologians, often simply called the Circle. This organization was founded by Dr. Mercy Amba Oduyoye and friends in 1989.[2] The work of the Circle was initially a response to the fact that male and non-African researchers were effectively oblivious to African women's voices. The Circle has done remarkable work in changing that, opening doors to real conversations by African women, about their lives and religion—remembering that religion touches on virtually every aspect of life in Africa. In their pathbreaking book, *The Will to Arise*, Dr. Oduyoye and Dr. Musimbi Kanyoro gathered essays from a rich range of Circle voices. They affirm "the benefit of learning from the first-hand experiences of women,"[3] which I might call putting the stress on embodied theology, living witness.

> As women relate their own experiences, the church in Africa will be forced to listen to a people who have until now been denied a voice. The church will not only listen, but will be enriched by talents and gifts that have remained untapped until today.
>
> Women will gain more courage and respect. As they hear each other, East and West and South and North, African women will begin to see their stories as collective and corporate stories of God's people of faith.[4]

Oduyoye and Kanyoro say that "patterns emerge as African women search for wholeness and transformation of both the African culture and the church."[5] Tracing some of those patterns is one purpose of this book. The leadership of Dr. Oduyoye in the World Council of Churches' Decade of Churches in Solidarity with Women played a critical role in Maman Monique's own story, prompting the birth of FEBA. Words of wisdom from members of the Circle celebrated the launch of her other brainchild, Tumekutana, the continent-spanning network of African Presbyterian women.

---

[2]See Mercy Amba Oduyoye, "Introduction: The Girl Called Amba Ewudziwa," in *Beads and Strands: Reflections of an African Woman on Christianity in Africa* (Maryknoll, NY: Orbis, 2004), xiii-xiv.

[3]Mercy Amba Oduyoye and Musimbi Kanyoro, eds., *The Will to Arise: Women, Tradition, and the Church in Africa* (Maryknoll, NY: Orbis, 1992; repr. Pietermaritzburg, SA: Cluster, 2006), 1-5; quotation, 3.

[4]Oduyoye and Kanyoro, *Will to Arise*, 4.

[5]Oduyoye and Kanyoro, *Will to Arise*, 3.

Members of the Circle have normally been women with theological education, able to stand on the same professional ground as their male colleagues, correcting the inadequacy of the common interpretations of African Christianity. The Circle has broadened over its forty-plus years, and its members and publications have become more diverse. It is fitting that Maman Monique's story now joins the writings of so many gifted women, and brings its own distinctive contributions. Perhaps the most obvious difference is that, unlike the other Circle leaders, Maman Monique was not trained in theology. She is a laywoman whose formal degrees are in education although she has certainly learned from and led her full share of Bible studies. In fact, as with many African Christians, Maman Monique's life is permeated by the teaching of the Bible, so much so that she usually does not even mention specific texts, although Genesis 1:27 ("God created male and female in his image," author's paraphrase) and the FEBA foundation text, John 10:10 ("I came to bring life abundant," author's paraphrase), are favorites.

A second distinctive contribution of this book is that, while there are rich autobiographical essays by Circle members, these have been short.[6] Maman Monique presents here a full-length life story, the kind of case study that has space to show in rich detail the conditions and constraints, the creativity and determination, the joys and sorrows of African women's lives. Not just her own, but also those of family, friends, neighbors, and anyone she encounters, from illiterate child brides to highly educated professional women, from abandoned orphans to competent businesswomen, and more. Since Maman Monique's story will fit very well in courses on African women where Circle writers and other authors appear, a study guide is available from the publisher's website: www.ivpress.com/cradling-abundance.

Knowing where someone comes from and seeing what her world is like always make a story richer. Without cultural or historical or political context,

---

[6]For a few examples, see Oduyoye, "Introduction," n. 1; idem, "A Coming Home to Myself: The Childless Woman in the West African Space," in *Liberating Eschatology: Essays in Honor of Letty M. Russell*, ed. M. A. Farley and S. Jones (Louisville, KY: Westminster John Knox, 1999), 105-22; Musimbi Kanyoro, "Silenced by Culture, Sustained by Faith," in *Claiming the Promise: African Churches Speak*, ed. M. S. Larom (New York: Friendship Press, 1994), 1-4; Fulata Lusungu Moyo, "Singing and Dancing Women's Liberation: My Story of Faith," in *Her-Stories: Hidden Histories of Women of Faith in Africa*, ed. I. A. Phiri, D. B. Govinden, and S. Nadar (Pietermaritzburg, SA: Cluster, 2002), 389-408; and Sr. M. Bernadette Mbuy Beya, "Stand Up and Walk, Daughter of My People: Consecrated Sisters of the Circle," in *African Women, Religion, and Health*, ed. Isabel Apawo Phiri and Sarojini Nadar (Maryknoll, NY: Orbis, 2006), 208-20.

we can miss the point of a joke (and Maman Monique's humor is often understated). Or we may puzzle over the connection between statements (Why would it matter to Maman Monique's husband's job security where the leader of the opposition party was born?). Or we may be upset about something that seems extremely sexist in our context (How could it be praise to say that "my daughters will be men"?). The next section outlines the political and religious history of Maman Monique's world. More cultural comments will be found in the sidebars of the chapters to follow.

MAMAN MONIQUE'S WORLD

Maman Monique's Congo is a large and diverse world with a complex history. The nation known today as the Democratic Republic of Congo is a very big country (about 905,370 square miles) at the heart of the continent of Africa.[7] The region got its name originally from the people called the Kongo. Under European rule it was first called the Congo Free State (1884–1908) and then the Belgian Congo (1908–1960). At independence in 1960 it became the Republic of Congo and in 1964 the Democratic Republic of Congo. The name was changed to Zaire in 1971 by President Mobutu and then back to the Democratic Republic of Congo in 1997 under President Laurent Kabila. To simplify matters, in this book the name Congo or D. R. Congo or Congo-Kinshasa will be used for Maman Monique's country; its capital will be called Kinshasa throughout. However, to compound confusion, there are two contiguous African states called Congo. The other, smaller one had been a French colony; today it is called the Republic of Congo or Congo-Brazzaville (for its capital). Brazzaville and Kinshasa face each other across the Congo River.

Geography and languages. The Democratic Republic of Congo, a mostly landlocked giant, is the second largest country in Africa, set right in the middle, straddling the equator. It is more than one-quarter the size of the forty-eight

---

[7]Much of the following history is drawn from two sources: Georges Nzongola-Ntalaja, *The Congo from Leopold to Kabila: A People's History* (London; New York: Zed Books, 2002), esp. "Chronology," 265-78; and Emizet François Kisangani and F. Scott Bobb, *Historical Dictionary of the Democratic Republic of the Congo*, 3rd edition. African Historical Dictionaries 112 (Lanham, MD: Scarecrow, 2010). For chronology and overview of geography and history see Kisangani and Bobb, "Introduction," in *Historical Dictionary*; for specific details see individual entries, e.g., "Congo River Basin," "Luba," "Railways." Note that direct quotations will be consistently attributed, but matters that are more generally known (such as the various slave trades or the atrocities in the Congo Free State) will not receive specific footnotes. For further information, appropriate entries in the *Historical Dictionary* are the place to start.

contiguous states of the United States. There are mountains in the northeast, east, and southwest of the country and tropical rainforests along the Congo River and its delta. However, much of the center, including Maman Monique's region of the Kasai, is a plateau of savannah and forests. The single most important geographic feature is the Congo River, the second largest in water volume in the world (after the Amazon). With its major tributaries, the Congo River has always been key to travel in the country, and many cities are located on one or another of these rivers. The Congo River itself is broken by three major cataracts; the ones just below Kinshasa long formed an insurmountable barrier to the interior.

Over time the D. R. Congo has been divided into different numbers of provinces, from seven or eight to twenty-five or twenty-six. For practical purposes here, the major geographic regions are identified according to the divisions used in the early 1960s since those names are still fairly common, as is seen on the map (see fig. 1.1). There are six main regions:

1. Bas-Congo to the west of Kinshasa, reaching down to the Atlantic Ocean, partly heir of the ancient Kongo kingdom and well developed

2. Equateur in the northwest, in the Congo River basin, heavily forested and less densely populated

3. Orientale, in the northeast, the largest and most populous province, with rich agricultural resources but also somewhat inaccessible

4. Kivu, in the east along the lakes of the Great Rift Valley, mountainous but well populated and home to minerals like coltan

5. Kasai, rich in commercial diamonds, in the south-central plateau

6. Katanga in the southeast, the richest in many kinds of minerals, linked closely to southern Africa by history, economy, and ethnicity

The D. R. Congo is home to more than 80 million people, in hundreds of tribes speaking about 200 languages and 450 dialects of the Bantu family, which is the dominant language family in sub-Saharan Africa. There are four major trade languages: Kikongo, Lingala, Tshiluba, and KiSwahili. (The first three are Bantu; KiSwahili is a combination of Bantu and Arabic.) Kikongo is common in Bas-Congo; Tshiluba in the Kasai and Katanga; KiSwahili throughout the east: Katanga, Kivu, Orientale; and Lingala in Equateur and

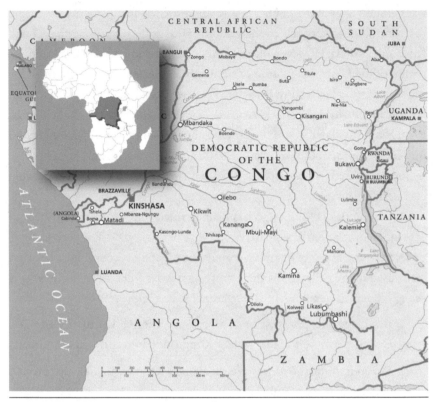

Figure 1.1. Map of the Democratic Republic of Congo

Kinshasa, and wherever the army is. Originally, smaller linguistic communities learned the languages of those who traveled for trade in their particular regions.[8] When walking is the primary mode of travel (there were traditionally no real beasts of burden; the largest domestic animals are goats), it takes determination to become a traveling salesperson. Maman Monique's people, the Luba, were the leading traders in the Kasai.

Political history. So how did all these different, widely scattered tribes—often traditional rivals, sometimes enemies, or entirely unknown to each other—get lumped together as one country? What did they have in common that would make a basis for a modern nation state? That is a complex, and historically fraught, question. The simple answer is, they were colonized by Europeans, specifically by Belgium. A brief glimpse back at history is helpful.

---

[8]For this and the following paragraphs, see Kisangani and Bobb, *Historical Dictionary*, s.vv. "Bantu," "Bas-Congo," "Equateur," "Katanga," "Kasai," "Kisangani," "Kivu," "Languages," "Mbandaka," "Orientale." Sometimes a fifth language, Lomongo, is included; this is spoken in Equateur.

In this place I will sketch the outline; more detailed notes about particular events will be added at appropriate places in the story.

In the centuries before and after AD 1500 a number of significant kingdoms and cultures—the Kongo, Kuba, Luba, and Lunda—developed in the western and southern parts of what would become Congo. It is important to note that this geographic region has its own rich history of empires and cultures. For present purposes, the main task is to outline how people who had lived in essentially homogeneous communities, without written vernacular languages or easy communications, have dealt with the (often involuntary) transition to a complex and diverse modern world, going from barter to a money economy, from tribal societies to modern nation states, in just a few generations.

The impetus for many of the changes that we call "modern" came from Europe or Europeans so it is necessary to trace the intersection of Europe and Africa. It began with trade, particularly the early modern European desire to find a water route to the wealth of the Far East. That led the seafaring nations (Portuguese, French, Dutch, English) to work their way south around Africa to reach India and beyond. Portugal led the way, arriving in Kongo in 1483 and India in 1498. Along the way these Europeans traded or settled in coastal areas of Africa, but until the nineteenth century they had virtually no contact with the interior. Trade included, of course, the horrors of slavery. Actually, there were three slave trades: war captives in African societies, European chattel slavery to the west, and Afro-Arab slave trade to the east. In local African practice, slaves had rights and some mobility. When captives were exported, the conditions of slavery were significantly different and usually much crueler.

There were some changes around the beginning of the nineteenth century. Europeans and North Americans abolished their slave trade, and later the practice of slavery. However, the industrial revolution meant that their economies were now more dependent than ever on finding large amounts of raw materials and new markets. Previously, the interior of Africa had been too difficult to reach, and industrialized countries had concentrated on easier sources, but the latter had become very limited, and the wealth of Africa's inaccessible interior developed a greater appeal. Parallel to this, nineteenth-century African empires such as the Luba and Lunda were beginning to collapse as their own trade routes across Congo were destablized by internal conflicts and European and Arab pressures (in the West and East respectively).

So began the European "scramble for Africa," which resulted in almost the entire continent being divided up among European colonizers. The Portuguese, Dutch, English, and French, who had already gained a foothold along the coast, pushed inward. Some European countries, however, came late to the scramble. Belgium and Germany were two that were determined to make up for lost time. King Leopold II of Belgium decided to commission the Welsh American Henry Morton Stanley to explore, make treaties, and claim land for the king. Stanley was internationally known as the man who had "found" David Livingstone so Leopold considered this journalist-adventurer the best person to stake his claim.

The Congo Free State. With Stanley's report in hand, Leopold and the German leaders put together a conference in Berlin in 1884–1885 to draw lines on the map of Africa to distinguish each European country's sphere of influence or colonial jurisdiction. In Leopold's case, this meant that the incongruously named Congo Free State became his personal possession. (In fact, the first nation to recognize Leopold's sovereignty was the United States, in April 1884.)[9] The Act of Berlin, February 26, 1885, was supposed to ensure that Leopold (and other colonizers) followed "certain principles: freedom of trade and navigation, neutrality in the event of war, suppression of slave traffic, and improvement of the condition of the indigenous people."[10] However, these principles were often neglected or even given only lip service, in Congo and elsewhere. The European lines both balkanized Africa, since they frequently cut across traditional linguistic or political boundaries, and unilaterally redefined traditional adversaries as one people, without regard to their own histories or desires.

Leopold alone could not personally exploit the Congo's many rich resources so he worked through corporations. For example, La Compagnie du Kasai was engaged in extorting as much rubber as possible from that area; African workers who failed to meet their quotas had their right hands chopped off. This scandal eventually came to international attention. An African American journalist, George Washington Williams, was the first voice in 1890, followed over the course of the next fifteen years by protests from Edmund Morel, a British writer, and American Presbyterian missionaries

---

[9]Nzongola-Ntalaja, *Congo from Leopold to Kabila*, 266.
[10]Kisangani and Bobb, *Historical Dictionary*, s.v. "Berlin Conference," 53.

William H. Sheppard and William M. Morrison. Their publications led to the end of the Congo Free State, and Leopold's private domain was handed over to the Belgian government to be run as a colony.

The new Belgian Congo was established with the mandate to adhere to the Berlin principle of "improving the condition of indigenous peoples." However, its administration was built on the basic legacy of Leopold's state.[11] It imposed control on the exploiting companies, greatly expanded means of transportation such as roads and railroads, and encouraged literacy but continued the imperialist or paternalistic attitudes, keeping power in the hands of Whites.

An important part of the mandate for "improving the condition of indigenous peoples" included Western education. Although it was perhaps the part of "modernization" that eventually enabled Congo to become an independent nation, new ideas of education were in their own way a challenge to traditional culture. All societies have educational practices determined by their own goals, whether these are the skills of hunting, farming, fighting, reading, cooking, childcare, carrying water, or any one of a number of other activities considered productive for the life of that group. Thus, it is important to distinguish between traditional education and literacy, especially when speaking of places like sub-Saharan Africa, where written vernacular languages came late.

Sub-Saharan Africans had many forms of traditional education, appropriate for their own social purposes, but they did not have written languages. That changed with the coming of world religions like Islam and Christianity, teachings grounded in books. West African empires that had become Muslim in the eleventh century acquired Arabic for religious purposes, but this did not lead to vernacular education because the Qur'an is not translated. Christianity, however, puts a high value on bringing religious faith into peoples' own languages, and, especially for Protestants, that means learning and writing down new languages in order to translate the Bible for their converts. So major Bantu languages became written vernaculars.

---

[11]Nzongola-Ntalaja, *Congo from Leopold to Kabila*, 26-27, sees the main purposes of the colonial period continuing "economic exploitation, political repression and cultural oppression in Central Africa" (p. 27). "Although these [racist] discriminatory restrictions had no legal basis, 'they were practiced just as effectively,'" (p. 39). Kisangani and Bobb, *Historical Dictionary*, "Introduction," liv, points out the importance of the extensive road and rail system. Different Congolese assess the positive or negative impact of the Belgian administration differently.

For European colonial rulers, education meant literacy, but there were different ways to organize this. The French and English set up their entire school systems in the colonial languages so all who learned to read and write learned French or English, though there was less effort to see that every child went to school. They also educated the brightest boys through university and some postgraduate professions, including physicians and scholars. The Belgian policy was the reverse: universal education was offered in one of the four major Bantu languages (Kikongo, Lingala, Tshiluba, Swahili); later, French was added as the medium of secondary school or university. This meant that everyone could in theory learn to read. It also meant there was a considerable divide between the great majority of the population and the limited number who could achieve a "Western" education in French, and this led to resentment on the part of some of the majority who did not have that opportunity. At the time of independence the Congo "boasted one of the highest literacy rates in Africa," but there were "less than 30,000 enrolled secondary students (2 per cent of total enrollment), fewer than 200 high school graduates, and only about two dozen Congolese [with] university degrees."[12] Most schools in Congo were initiated, run, and supported by Christian missions. Some government subsidies were available, but usually parents have also had to pay fees to supplement teachers' inadequate salaries or cover other expenses such as uniforms or supplies, so education has not been free.

After World War II the political situation began to change rapidly in Africa.[13] Soldiers who had fought with the Allies had encountered a wider world; across the continent there was a growing impetus among Africans to reject the colonial powers. One early sign of this in Congo was the appearance of new "higher ranks" for some Congolese in the paternalistic Belgian system. Those who were well educated in the Western ways and largely assimilated into a European social culture were called *évolués*, among the most obvious markers being that *évolués* knew French and were usually secondary school graduates. The legal term *immatriculé* referred to their position as "honorary" Europeans in the segregated society. (Maman Monique's father was an *évolué*, working for

---

[12]Kisangani and Bobb, *Historical Dictionary*, s.v. "Education," 149.
[13]This overview follows Kisangani and Bobb, "Introduction," *Historical Dictionary*, lxii-lxvii. See also *Historical Dictionary*, s.vv. "Evolués," "Kasai," "Katanga," "Luba," "Lulua," "Lunda," "South Kasai," and others.

a Belgian agricultural project.) In the 1950s members of these groups formed "associations" based on ethnic ties or as alumni of a common secondary school since political parties were not allowed.

The Belgian Congo came into the Pan-African independence movement rather abruptly and almost totally unprepared. Belgium had thought in terms of eventual and gradual autonomy, but significant international events sped up the calendar, beginning with Ghana's independence in 1957. Soon there were Congolese cries for "immediate independence!" Associations became a basis for political parties when Belgium accepted that local elections might be held in 1959, but some parties boycotted. Fighting along ethnic lines broke out in October in the Kasai and the Katanga as tensions between Lulua and Luba escalated into massacres, huge destruction of property, and many thousands of people driven from their homes. (Maman Monique's family members were Luba living in the Kasai. In the next chapter she tells several stories of this time.) In January 1960 a Round Table Conference of Belgians and Congolese agreed that the Belgian Congo would become the Republic of Congo on June 30, 1960, with a temporary constitution. Elections were held in May, and the top two vote-getters (from different parties and completely different political philosophies) became the new heads of state. Joseph Kasavubu of the Alliance of Bakongo became president, a largely ceremonial office, and Patrice Lumumba at the head of the National Congolese Movement (MNC) became prime minister.

Congo's Independence: June 30, 1960. There were big parades and flags flying. A few days later the army rioted for a raise in pay, and foreigners left or were evacuated. (Elsie's family was evacuated. Her father returned a few weeks later to stay with the church in the Kasai, but the rest of the family could not return until early in 1962.) At the request of Congo's government, the United Nations sent troops to help with police and administrative needs, but the country was soon faced with multiple secessions by regions possessing mineral resources that would make them viable stand-alone states. On July 11, 1960, the State of Katanga seceded, a separation that would last until early 1963. Lumumba's party, the MNC, split, and on August 3 the breakaway region led by Albert Kalonji also seceded from Congo to form the "Independent Mining State of South Kasai" (where Maman Monique's family lived). The fighting between Lumumba's and Kalonji's armies continued for months, and thousands of Luba and Lunda died. Famine was widespread.

Meanwhile, the national government was also separating along party lines. To complicate matters further, the Cold War between the United States and the Soviet Union played a significant part in the conflicts within Congo. President Kasavubu (supported by the West) and Prime Minister Lumumba (aligned with the Soviets) mutually dismissed each other, and Lumumba was placed under house arrest. In the upheaval the young army chief of staff Colonel Mobutu took control on September 14, 1960. Lumumba escaped and tried to flee to Orientale Province, where his supporters held power and planned to secede. When he was captured and assassinated on January 17, 1961, Orientale Province and some of Kivu seceded. In February 1961, Mobutu returned control of the national government to a new civil administration, and both the Kasai and Orientale secessions ended as their leaders joined the central government.

Congo's political situation remained very difficult in the early 1960s.[14] After the Katanga secession ended in 1963, its leader, Moise Tshombe, went into exile but returned the next year when President Kasavubu appointed him prime minister. In October 1965, Kasavubu dismissed Tshombe, who refused to leave, and the army took over on November 24, 1965, making General Mobutu the head of state. Mobutu announced that he would lead for five years and then elections would be held, but he soon set about centralizing power in his own hands and in the Popular Movement of the Revolution (MPR), which he established in 1966. With the army coup d'état its presence became much more marked everywhere. In 1967 Mobutu began the program of "authenticity" intended to draw people together as Congolese by diminishing tribal allegiances and centralizing power in the presidency. He took the name Sese Seko (instead of Joseph-Désiré). The country was renamed Zaire, and all its inhabitants were told to drop their European names and European dress. In time Mobutu's MPR became the only legal party, and in 1974 the party became the state. International powers generally turned a blind eye to Congo's human rights abuses until the end of the Cold War. In 1997 Mobutu was forced from power by the military alliance led by Laurent Kabila, who ruled until his assassination in January 2001, when his son Joseph Kabila took over the reins of government. Congo experienced its first peaceful transfer of power in January 2019 when Félix Tshisekedi became president.

---

[14]This summary follows Kisangani and Bobb, "Introduction," *Historical Dictionary*, lxvii-lxxxvii. See also *Historical Dictionary*, s.v. "Tshombe," "Mobutu."

History of Christian influence. Christian missionaries first came to Congo near the end of the fifteenth century with the Portuguese.[15] The peoples they met were at least partially receptive, and a Christian church developed in the Kingdom of the Kongo, mostly south of the Congo River along the coast. (Some of the slaves brought to North America from this region of Africa were already Christian.) The interior of the continent was not affected by this coastal movement so both Roman Catholic (favored by Belgium) and Protestant missionaries (tolerated) came to Maman Monique's Kasai only in the late nineteenth century.

Although this was certainly not the initial purpose, missionaries brought with them Western medicine. This has often—though not always—been the most welcome aspect of modernization. The Western split between health of mind and health of spirit does not apply in African culture. Religion and well-being are tightly intertwined in traditional societies so introducing "new medicines" was a significant challenge to traditional religious ideas and practitioners. However, the effectiveness of new treatments of old diseases, especially in terms of addressing infant mortality, could be a very important factor in winning a hearing for the Christian word. Today about 70 to 80 percent of the country is Christian, divided among various communions: Roman Catholic about 50 to 60 percent, Protestants about 20 percent, Kimbanguists about 10 percent and some other African Instituted Churches. Approximately 10 percent are Muslims and 10 percent follow traditional religions, although the influence of the traditional ideas is still widely felt.

The first Protestants—English, American, and Swedish Baptists—had begun to arrive in Congo in 1878, working near the coast. In 1890 Samuel Lapsley and William Sheppard were sent by the Presbyterian Church in the United States (southern) to Congo. They stayed with the Baptists briefly and then moved inland. (All the Protestants cooperated, and those already settled would help each new mission get oriented before it set out to evangelize new groups in the vast interior.) For the Presbyterians, going inland meant getting beyond the first big falls on the Congo River, at the site of what was then Leopoldville, now Kinshasa. Sheppard's account of the journey around the falls

---

[15]This summary follows Kisangani and Bobb, "Introduction," *Historical Dictionary*, liv. See also *Historical Dictionary*, s.v. "Christianity," "Islam," "Kimbanguist Church."

and upriver is a remarkable, graphic—and sometimes terrifying—adventure story, complete with hundreds of hippos, which can be quite dangerous.[16]

So in 1891 Lapsley and Sheppard made their way about eight hundred miles up the river system, first by the Kasai River (the Congo's largest tributary), and then the Lulua River, to Luebo (see fig. 1.2). This was situated where rapids marked the end point for navigation on the Lulua, at its juncture with the little Luebo River, where a Belgian stock company had a small station. The Americans received permission to lease land across the Lulua, in an open space in easy walking distance of several villages. There they established Luebo-Mission (so called to distinguish it from the commercial station Luebo-Etat).

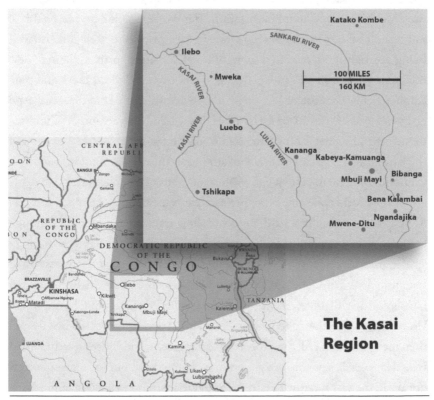

Figure 1.2. Map of the Democratic Republic of Congo for Maman Monique's story

[16]William H. Sheppard, "Presbyterian Pioneers in Congo." First published 1921; various reprints exist, including in *Four Presbyterian Pioneers in Congo*, Presbyterian Church in the United States, 1965. For much of the following, see Ethel Taylor Wharton, *Led in Triumph* (Nashville: Presbyterian Church US, Board of World Missions, 1952), 16-32, 70-74, 78-82, 111-12, 130, 144.

The first task was to learn the language(s). The African porters whom they had hired from the Baptists could help with a smattering of words, but most of the study had to be conducted by the old method of point-and-name. And Bantu languages have a completely different structure from Western ones so this was a considerable feat of cooperation by Africans and Americans. Preaching and teaching began as soon as the missionaries could speak Tshiluba at all. A dictionary, grammar, and a Bible followed as quickly as possible, mostly the work of William Morrison, while Althea Brown Edmiston's dictionary and grammar successfully tackled the Kuba language.

The Americans were a small, "seed-planting" group. Lapsley, a Caucasian, died of tropical disease less than two years after he came to Luebo, but the intrepid African American Sheppard carried on. New colleagues joined him, many recruited by him. In the first twenty years, about half were a remarkable group of African Americans, including Sheppard's wife, Lucy Gantt; Althea Brown; Alphonso Edmiston; and an amazing elderly woman named Maria Fearing, who promptly opened a home and school for young girls (a program that was the forerunner of Maman Monique's ministry). Along with preaching and translating, the missionaries were active in attacking injustices. As noted above, Sheppard and Morrison were major players in the public battle to bring conditions in Leopold's Congo to international attention and force the king to hand over his private domain to Belgium. They also freed slaves whenever possible.

The main work of spreading the faith was in the hands of Africans. The people closest to Luebo-Mission were the Kete, clients of the neighboring powerful Kuba people among whom Sheppard and then the Edmistons worked. Response to the gospel among Kete and Kuba was slow, but the Luba and Lulua tribes were soon drawn to the new teaching; the first convert was baptized in 1895. The Lulua lived to the south and east of Luebo in what came to be called West Kasai, and the Luba further to the east, in East Kasai. Some were part of the workforce the Belgians imported to Luebo and compelled to build railroads beginning in the 1890s. Some were brought by slave traders such as the Zappo Zaps and bought and freed by the missionaries. Others came to Luebo-Mission because they heard about the new religious teaching, either through the small handful of missionaries themselves, as they walked to villages at a distance from Luebo, or more often from Lulua or Luba who had come to the little schools at Luebo and returned to their own villages to share the news.

In the first years, those who became Christians, whether they originally came to Luebo for that reason or not, moved to Luebo-Mission and established their own flourishing new village around the growing Christian settlement. Already by 1906 several thousand Luba and Lulua had come. By 1911 there were probably about ten thousand Congolese gathered in Luebo-Mission, mostly Lulua and Luba, including over seven thousand baptized converts. The Reverend George McKee, Elsie's grandfather, who arrived in 1911, remembered that the largest groups were from Bakwanga (Mbuji Mayi), Ba Kua Kalonji, and Bena Kalambai, all Luba from East Kasai, the original homes of Maman Monique's ancestors (see fig. 1.2).[17]

The movement of Presbyterian evangelization south and east was strong, starting around 1912 with the establishment of the station called Mutoto among the Lulua, 160 miles southeast of Luebo. George and Elsie McKee helped begin this new educational center. Many tribes in other parts of the Kasai were also asking for missionaries, who brought Western education and medicine along with their preaching. In 1917–1918 the McKees and another couple established a new station at Bibanga, 180 miles southeast of Mutoto. This was the land of Mutombo Katshi, chief of over forty thousand Luba, who had for some time been requesting a mission station within his territory. (Elsie's father was born at Bibanga, which would become the site of the first Presbyterian secondary school, Maman Monique's alma mater.) Evangelization continued to extend south, often along the railroad that now linked the Kasai and the Katanga with Kinshasa and the Atlantic coast. Among the missionaries was Maman Bitshilualua (Virginia Allen), who came through the city of Ngandajika, Maman Monique's birthplace, and taught her grandmother Mbuyi Marthe to read and write.

Maman Monique Misenga's paternal great-grandparents were probably among the first Christians in West Kasai, and her maternal grandmother was one of the early powerful Christian voices in East Kasai. Now that we've set the scene, let's hear her tell her story.

---

[17] Oral memoirs of George McKee recorded for his children.

2

My Family and Childhood

For my maternal grandmother, Mbuyi Kaleka Marthe, in every problem you had to pray. If she came to pray, the illness was finished. That impressed us! For all of us children, if there was sickness, we said, "We must call Kaku (Grandmother)." She had a strong faith and believed firmly in Jesus Christ.

She was also very hospitable. She never wanted to eat in the house as many families did (to be private). She wanted to eat outside so that she could call other people passing by to come and eat also. My grandmother lived with her oldest daughter, who sold smoked fish and other things at the market. Grandmother helped my aunt—and she would "adopt" poor children. When a child came to market to buy something, my grandmother would ask him, "How many people are there at home?" When the child answered, she would give him what he had paid for and then add some more, in order to provide enough for all the family. She might even give him back a little of the money and tell him to go and buy tomatoes and oil to go with the fish. My aunt would ask, "Maman, why did you do that? You are eating up all the profits." My grandmother would say, "There was not enough for the family." And my aunt said no more because she was also very generous.

In Africa, our families are the way we define ourselves. The single most important influence on the person I have become was my father. His Christian character and energy in making a good life for his family and everyone around him and his vision for educating his daughters as well as his sons gave me both model and opportunity. My mother was his partner in faith, and she and her mother were the patterns of prayer who taught us how to be women.

My Father's Family

My father was Ngoie Tshiamanyangala Kazadi Moses. He was born in 1918 at Luebo-Mission in West Kasai, the son of Kazadi Ngoie Philip (added name

Nsenji) and Misenga <u>Mudile</u> Marthe; he was named Ngoie for his paternal grandfather. His paternal grandparents, Ngoie <u>Kayumba</u> and his wife Mujinga, came
from East Kasai, the Bena Kanyuka section of the large village Bena Kalambai
(see fig. 1.2). Like other Christian converts, they had settled in the growing village
surrounding Luebo-Mission and built their little house on a street named according to their family's village of origin. Each street had a little chapel where the
people prayed together in the evening when there were no services in the big
Luebo church. The home of my father's family was on the Avenue of the Bena
Kanyuka, and their house was very close to the chapel where they prayed.

My paternal grandmother was named Misenga <u>Mudile</u> Marthe, the
daughter of Mudile <u>Tshyombo</u> and his wife Nzeba. She was born at Luebo-
Mission about 1902. There is no birth record, but her age can be figured from
the date of her first child's birth in 1915; girls were often married by twelve
(fourteen was considered late). Her parents also came from East Kasai, and
her family's street was called the Avenue of the Ba Kua Kalonji. Both my
grandfather and my grandmother retained the memory of their families' villages of origin, but neither of them had ever been there, and my father was
always identified by Westerners as coming from Luebo.

My father was the oldest son of the four surviving children of Kazadi Philip
and Misenga Marthe. He had an older sister, Kambia Mbombo Léonie, and
two younger brothers, Nsakadi Jean and Ilunga Paul. Kambia died in 1950
before my birth so I never knew her. When I was born, people said that I re-
sembled her very much—and she was a strong woman and helped raise her
younger brothers. When their father, Kazadi, died, she was about nine or ten,
my father was six or seven, and the other boys were younger. Grandfather
Kazadi had had a small business, and before he died he placed a symbol of
commerce on my father's body, to indicate that he would earn his living by
commerce. He gave his second son, Nsakadi Jean, the power to work in the
mission, but he did not say anything about the third son. Nsakadi studied to
become a nurse and always worked in the mission hospital, but the youngest,
Ilunga, did not have much schooling. When our grandfather died, his widow
married his brother, according to the tradition: the brother "inherited her."
They had a daughter, Musuamba, but later our grandmother left this second
husband. We knew our uncles, but we did not get to know our father's younger
half sister until we were grown.

Widows and Children

Traditionally, a widow would be married to one of her late husband's "brothers." This was intended as a form of security for her and her children, but it could also be a form of control.

By tradition, a father determined the paths of his children. He might endow the boy with a symbol of his career, as Maman Monique's grandfather did for some of his sons. This was taken very seriously, and the omission of the symbol was considered significant for the child's future.[1]

My father grew up at Luebo-Mission, in the Presbyterian church. He studied through the ninth grade, the last year of regular schooling at the time. He may have started working at Luebo-Etat, across the river from his home, and there or in Kananga he came to the attention of Belgians. They saw that he was talented and wanted him to work for them as a nurse, so he continued his studies at Kananga. Then he was hired by the directors of the National Institute of Agronomy Study of Congo (INEAC) at Ngandajika in East Kasai. When the Belgians saw his abilities, they trained him as a veterinarian because INEAC had a large herd of cows. He taught another man to help at the infirmary when he had to go to tend the cows. My father did his work well. When his Belgian boss left Congo in 1958, he gave my father his property: auto, refrigerator, rugs, tablecloths. When all the Belgians left at Independence, they put my father in sole charge of INEAC to take care of everything.

Before continuing with the story of my mother's family, I want to add what our father told us about the missionaries. He said that they came from the United States, far away, to Luebo. They did not know Tshiluba, but they learned it. They lived in the same conditions as we did, but they showed us that we do not have to live in such conditions. That inspired the Congolese people with the spirit to transform, to build, so that they rose up against the slave trade, colonization, and exploitation. In that time, Congolese themselves practiced the slave trade, stealing or buying children to sell. With the coming of the missionaries, that was prohibited. People began to go to church. The missionaries preached, and people who heard the preaching saw that those who traded in

---

[1]For more information on these and other cultural background topics, see the study guide on the *Cradling Abundance* book page at IVP's website, www.ivpress.com/cradling-abundance.

slaves were doing wrong. They pointed out those who were selling enslaved children, and the missionaries bought the children to free them.

The missionaries provided a lot of education. They created schools and began to teach people. They helped them cultivate various fruits and coffee and oil palms. There were oranges and lemons, but especially grapefruit. There was lots of coffee at Luebo; lots of people drank coffee, and that made Luebo important—that is the only place I learned about coffee. There was palm oil; they had a market, and people came to Luebo to buy oil so those who produced it could earn a living. People also farmed, so there was food, though they did not do animal husbandry.

Traditional Foods and Malnutrition

The basic traditional food is bread made from the cassava root, the main product of rural women's subsistence farming. Both farming and preparing cassava are labor intensive, all done by hand with short little hoes that required workers to bend over as they worked. As a food, cassava is almost entirely starch, which fills the stomach but does not provide any significant nutritional value. Babies may be fairly plump as long as they are breastfed, but then they begin to eat the same food as the rest of the family and malnutrition is often the result. Missionary doctors introduced a recipe mixing one part corn flour with three parts cassava flour to make a more nutritious basic diet.

Another part of education was construction and cleanliness. The missionaries built with durable materials and showed how to build and organize a house. They taught the mothers how to organize the household and take care of the health of their children, feeding them nourishing food and practicing good hygiene so they would not get diarrhea. They showed them how to care for clothing—that helped me when I was working with women. When I trained the women and brought them together, I could ask one of the older women who had learned in the early days to rise and show her clothes so the women could see how clean they were. "See what they learned and how they remembered it." You have to keep the house clean, the clothes clean; it does not cost much money to keep things clean. When you have money, you buy what fits with that amount of money; if it is well sewn and clean, that shows its value.

And health—there was no hospital in the region; the missionaries built a hospital that cared for people and created jobs. My uncle who worked in the hospital had a good life, and lots of people knew him. The missionaries brought baby clothes for newborns and even things for older children—nice clothes. When I visited my uncle's family, I saw that the poor children around there had good clothes. So the missionaries showed people it was necessary to share what one has. That was the truly positive side. But there were other Congolese who thought that the missionaries should bring everything: food, clothing, everything. Instead of making an effort, those people would work only to win praise from the missionary. But people like my father remembered many things. When my father wanted to build a house, he built a beautiful one. In our childhood we lived in good conditions. I never knew a life of poverty, lack, because my father raised chickens, ducks, rabbits, goats, and cows and farmed all kinds of food crops. We drank fresh cow's milk; we never experienced famine.

MY MOTHER'S FAMILY

The family of my mother, Bitota <u>Mbaya</u> Rosalie Bitshilualua, was from Ngandajika in East Kasai. My maternal grandmother was named Mbuyi Kaleka <u>Mbaya</u>; her husband was Mbaya <u>Tshibalabala</u>. He died young, in 1939; we never knew him. My grandmother told us that he was a slave trader. At that time one could buy someone's child in one place to sell to people somewhere else. Our grandparents became Christians about 1937 because the Presbyterians came there to evangelize. There were already Catholic missionaries in the area, but my grandparents were converted by the Presbyterians and received the baptismal names Simon and Marthe. Later, because of her faith, we called my grandmother Mutangila Nzambi—"she who has seen God."

Domestic Slavery

Historically, slaves were normally war captives. However, into the twentieth century children might be sold at a time of family crisis, to pay a debt or to buy food in a famine. When bought, the slave would become a kind of indentured servant. One of Maman Monique's colleagues, Maman Henriette, was the daughter of a slave; see her story in chapter fifteen.

When she was widowed, my grandmother had only four surviving children, one boy and three girls. There had been a number of babies between the son and the much younger daughters; my grandmother said that it was only after the missionaries came that her children lived. The boy Kalala was born about 1918 and the first girl, Tshijuka Louise, about 1929. My mother, Bitota Rosalie, was born in 1934, and her younger sister, Bishola Sarah, about 1936. When my grandfather died, his family decided that my grandmother should marry his brother and return to their village, but she refused. I was surprised to learn that already at that time my grandmother could say no to the customary ways. She said, "I must stay with my children" at Ngandajika. The relatives took my mother, Bitota, to Lubumbashi in the Katanga—she was about five—and she grew up there. They sent her to school, and she learned to read and write, though her sisters did not really have a chance to study. Then when she was thirteen, my mother came back to Ngandajika.

You have to understand my grandmother's faith. When the Presbyterians came to Ngandajika, she became a Christian. My grandmother named my mother Bitshilualua; it was the Tshiluba name of the missionary who taught my grandmother to read and write. She named my aunt Sarah for another missionary. My grandmother devoted herself to the church with all her heart. She was an ardent and faithful woman. She supported the children's choir, and she rejected all the traditional customs, something I still find astonishing. In Congo when children are ill the traditional treatment is to apply the powders of certain herbs to the sores. My grandmother rejected all of that. She said, "God is the one who treats. You must not rely on traditional customs, but just pray."

All of us grandchildren stayed with our grandmother, and we always felt at home. She made no distinction among us, and we thought we were all brothers and sisters, one family. She helped all of us children come to know Jesus. She prayed a lot and taught us to pray with great faith, believing that we are actually talking with God and that we hope for healing. My mother prayed the same way. And God has done many things in answer to those prayers!

OUR FAMILY

It was at Ngandajika that my father met my mother, Bitota Rosalie. My father saw her and married her, even though she was very young. People said, "How can you marry a girl of thirteen?" He was twenty-nine. When they were married, my father took my mother to Luebo to live with his mother for three years. Then she came back to Ngandajika to be with my father and started our family. My older brother, Tshimenga Joseph, was born on April 19, 1950, and I was born on April 21, 1952. After me there were ten more girls and two more boys: Mujinga Marie, Mbuyi Therese, Lusamba Mélanie, Kambia Mbombo Léonie Titine, Bitota Rose (bébé), Tshiana Jeanne, Nzeba Chantale, Ndaya Pauline, Musawu Philomène, Mbaya Tshibalabala Simon, Tshijuka Tshitshi, and the last, Kalala François Tonton, who was born in 1979. (See fig. 2.1 for a picture of some of Maman Monique's siblings.)

Figure 2.1. Maman Monique with her parents and some of her sisters and brothers. Ngandanjika, c. 1972. L-R: back: Lusamba Mélanie, Mbuyi Therese, Misenga Monique, Mamu Bitota Rose, Tatu Ngoie Moise. L-R: front: Tshimenga Joseph, Mbaya Tshibalabala Simon, Mujinga Marie.

My father wanted all of his children to be educated so he paid the school fees for us. All of us completed primary and went on to secondary, and seven girls and two boys finished secondary school with the state exam and diploma. One of the boys, Tshibalabala, and four girls did not complete secondary school, and my father was disappointed. My older brother, Tshimenga, went to university, but he had some problems and did not graduate. My youngest brother, Kalala, and I were the only ones who completed university; he studied economics and I did pedagogy. My father was very happy with me because I was intelligent and I loved my studies and devoted myself to them. (Kalala was only three when my father died so he did not live to see his youngest child go to university.)

In our village, people thought that girls were not really people because they leave the family when they marry; only the boys were considered people. They said that my father did not have children because he had so many girls. But he said, "My daughters will one day be men." They said my father should not send us to school, and they were especially opposed to his sending me to university, but he said that all of us, girls and boys, were able to learn and work. All my sisters went to school; they know how to organize their affairs and defend themselves and work, so as not to be rejected in society. Our father also taught us vocational activities. I learned to sew at home, not at school. My father created a spirit of initiative in me. He said, "I do not want you to be unhappy or enslaved in life. I am teaching you vocational activities so that, even if you do not have a job from what you learn at school, you can work." That is what has always motivated me.

Girls are close to their mothers, and they always talk with them. I learned how my mother felt. She was a victim of violence from the people around us because she had so many daughters. When she gave birth, they would ask if it was a girl or a boy; if it was a girl, that was shameful in their eyes. However, my father did not reject her for bearing daughters. My mother loved all of us, but she always warned us not to do anything that would shame her. When I went to university, people thought I was going to be a prostitute, and my mother said, "Please, don't shame me; it is good to behave the right way." My mother was our friend because we were always together and we talked with her about everything. She was a good mother, and all her grandchildren loved her.

My father was always very hospitable. Even before the births of all my sisters and brothers, our house was always full. My father welcomed everyone who came, first the children of his brothers and sister and my mother's family, but also his friends' children. That was especially important after Congo's independence in 1960.

Education

Schools in Congo are of very uneven quality so the only nationally recognized standards are the state examinations at the end of primary and secondary school. Those who pass at the secondary level earn a diploma, which for many years was the highest rank of education. It is about the equivalent of the North American associate of arts.

Location and language are important determiners of the quality of schools. Rural ones are normally less well equipped than urban, and Bantu-language primary does not lead neatly to exclusively French secondary. There has also been considerable change over time, from a country almost entirely rural to one with many medium and a few very large cities, from a school system wholly in the Bantu languages to one that also began to include French after World War II. Bantu-language primary schools were and are widespread and usually not too expensive because missions or churches have supported them, sometimes with government subsidies. Secondary schools were for a long time very limited in number so they had to be boarding institutions drawing from a much wider region. It was physically impossible to attend unless one lived within walking distance or in the dormitories. Secondary education also cost much more than primary, both for tuition and especially for board and room. With more cities, urban students now have better opportunities to access secondary education although it still requires money and fluency in French.

Given the patriarchal culture, girls were much less likely to be able to attend school regularly if at all, and for many years it was uncommon for them to go to secondary school. Maman Monique's father gave his daughters the same advantages as his sons, but even so not all absorbed it the way she did. It was also still natural for him to measure social status in the traditional way: by comparing his daughters favorably to men (the highest rank).

LIVING THROUGH INDEPENDENCE AND WAR, 1958–1961

About 1958 people began to struggle for independence. In October 1959 war began between the Luba and the Lulua, fighting and killing. We are Luba, and my father wanted to bring his family who were at Luebo (in West Kasai, which was mainly Lulua territory) to East Kasai. After he got permission from INEAC to borrow a vehicle, he and a chauffeur drove to Luebo to collect his mother, his son, and two nephews. His brother Nsakadi Jean said he wanted to remain at Luebo because he was working at the mission hospital.

The return to Ngandajika was difficult because there were barricades at various points. My father was wearing his nurse's uniform, and the chauffeur was in military uniform, which enabled them to get through. The back of the vehicle was completely enclosed, and the family hidden there could not cough or budge for fear of alerting the soldiers at the barricades. At home we were anxious about this trip. I was a little child, but I remember that my mother was very worried. When the vehicle neared INEAC, the chauffeur began honking the horn to let us know they were coming. Everyone was happy. Lots of people came to welcome my father and the family from Luebo. That was when my paternal grandmother, Misenga, for whom I am named, came to Ngandajika.

In the context of fighting, there were not only tribal issues but also economic and social tensions. Congolese who had more Western education and had developed skills and jobs were called *evolués*. This could be meant in a good or bad way, but there were people who resented these "foreign-identified" men, and they incited the youth, who then pointed to people and said, "Those people are the *evolués*; they are in (Lumumba's) MNC." The youth came to each house to say, "Show us your card" (of your political party). My father was educated and worked at INEAC (the Belgian agricultural research center) so he was in danger. One day they took him and another man and killed the other man. When my father came back, he made my mother and me each carry a little sack with money in it. He said, "If they kill me, you can keep that and it will help you go on with life." I did not understand what he meant (I was only about eight).

One day the fighting came to our village. There was a great deal of firing, guns going off everywhere, Lumumba's soldiers coming; we were locked in our houses. Lumumba's forces killed many people. Then Kalonji's men came, firing lots of guns, and Lumumba's fled, except for one man who had been shot in the stomach. When the shooting was over, Kalonji's soldiers told all the men in the village to come out of their houses. Then three soldiers came toward our house, and everyone was afraid because they thought the men would kill my father. But my father and one of the soldiers began to hug each other and to cry; the man was my father's cousin, and he said, "Don't cry. I came to see if you were alive." Just then someone came to tell my father, "There is a soldier in the infirmary; his intestines are coming out, and he wants the nurse to come care for him." My father was going to go, but his soldier cousin said he could not go alone. The cousin took his gun, loaded it, and said, "Let's go." When they got to the infirmary, the cousin saw that the wounded man was wearing Lumumba's uniform, and he got ready to shoot him. My father said, "No, no, no. Don't do that, don't do that!" But while he was speaking, his cousin shot and killed the soldier. He said, "No, we can't leave him alive; he is the enemy. I can't let you take care of him—he has killed lots of people on our side." From that time on, the youth in our village who were killing people began to respect my father. They killed many people, but they said, "No, his cousin is in the military who came to save us. We can't kill him."

There were also conflicts within the large Luba tribe between people from different clans. The director of INEAC at that time was a Congolese named Nyanganda Tshen. He was from Kabeya Kamuanga, the wrong clan, so the local people wanted to kill him. My father heard about this, and he took the director and disguised him during the day. Then at night my father hid the man a long distance away. Very early in the morning my father left the house and went to show the director the various paths where he could find transportation to take him back to his people. Later that morning people came to look for the man and asked my father where he was. My father said, "How would I know? He was at his house. Do you want to come in and search? Where would I hide him?" They came and searched our house, but they did not find the man. They went to my father's friends and still did not find him. God saved this man, and he was very grateful for what my father had done.

MY FATHER AND THE EXTENDED FAMILY

After this time, we stayed at INEAC, and my father was able to protect it. When some Belgians came back, they recognized his work and promoted him and said that he should move from the workers' village to a house in the

Belgian area. We moved there in 1962, and so our life was a little different from the other children at INEAC.

When my father first came to INEAC, he saw that the Congolese workers' salaries were not adequate. He was a man who knew how to organize in order to support his family, and he also helped the other workers organize. He set up a rotation system for the workers to farm the unoccupied fields. They cultivated corn—lots of corn. They could sell it and pay for school for their children, buy clothes, buy food. My father also made big fields for himself; he grew everything: rice, corn, beans, cassava, peanuts. My father knew how to do business with his harvest; he kept the corn until the off-season so that he could sell it at a better price. I learned that there are two seasons: when there is food and when there is not. When you keep your harvest, you can make two parts: one to eat and one to sell when the prices are better. My father also did animal husbandry: chickens and geese and rabbits. We had lots and lots of chicken eggs. He also made a fish pond and raised fish. When they matured, we had lots of fish and sold a lot. Even during the war, when people were starving, we always had the food that came from our fields and our animals. All of our father's activities to support his family and feed other people taught us that we must always work.

At our house there were always a great many people to feed: not just our family but the children of my father's friends and also of poor people. At that time, in 1962, the Luba were chased out of the Katanga after the war with the Lunda. That is why two of my "uncles" and their families came to us as refugees; one was my father's cousin who was also a nurse, and one was his youngest brother, Ilunga. The house was full of the children of these uncles and of my maternal aunt and of my father's friends. My father paid their school fees, and they ate with us. Food was cooked three times a day for three groups; first for the boys, then for the girls, and then for the adults. So we all grew up together.

My father bought a property for my uncles and his mother and built houses for all of them, so they moved out of our house to their own places. His youngest brother, Ilunga, was one who always discriminated against us girls. He said to my father, "You don't have children, you have frogs." When my father sent me to secondary school, this uncle said, "Why? What is she going to do?" He was always opposed. He told his sons, "You have to go to university; you can't let those frogs get ahead of you." He did not have the will to work; he kept coming to my father to make demands, as if he had the right to come and get what he wanted.

My father's other brother, Nsakadi Jean, was the opposite. When I went to Luebo for vacation, he always received me very well. When I was thirteen, I went to visit and lots of people came to welcome me. He loved me, and he bought nice clothes for me. He also talked about my marriage. He pointed out certain villages, "If someone from there asks to marry you, you must refuse." And for other villages, "If someone from there asks you, you can marry him." When I got home, I told my father about that, and he said, "No, if you love someone, even if he comes from one of those villages which your uncle didn't like, you can still marry him." Some of the children of this uncle lived with us. He wanted them to be educated, but only one boy did well at school and none of the girls. We always had good relations with him and his children, but we were much closer to my mother's family.

Arranged Marriages

Traditionally, marriages are arranged by families, with the father having the deciding power. In this Christian family, Maman Monique's uncle Nsakadi Jean was ready to imagine her having a choice but restricted the possible suitors. Her father, however, was prepared to accept her choice, without regard to traditional tribal constraints.

I have already mentioned my mother's sister, Maman Tshijuka, who was so generous in feeding people by her business. She married and had three children, but her husband beat her a great deal and abused her. My grandmother said, "You can't live with that," and my aunt divorced the man. She did not learn to read or write until she was grown, but then she could read the Bible in Tshiluba and did so until her death in 2014. Her younger sister, Maman Bishola, did not go to school, but she married and had many children. She died young, before her brother and sister. She was a good woman, but she did not have the courage to defend herself from constant pregnancy and traditional total subordination to her husband.

Faith, the Church, and Primary School

My father was Presbyterian, but the people at INEAC were Catholics. He was friendly with the Catholics, but he wanted to worship in his own church and he wanted us to remain Presbyterian. So he asked the Belgians at INEAC, and they agreed to give him a house to be a Presbyterian church. There was another Presbyterian man there; with him and our family, we made twelve and we started worshiping there. My father wrote to the presbytery to ask that the church be recognized as a congregation of the Presbyterian church and for them to send us a pastor. The Belgians also gave a house for the pastor. My father and the other man began to evangelize, and people started to come to the church.

For primary school I first went to the Catholic school at INEAC very close to our house. After third or fourth grade my father sent me to the Presbyterian school at Ngandajika, which was about nine kilometers (5.5 miles) away. For that we had to get up very early in the morning (at 4:00 a.m.), wash the supper dishes, sweep, bathe, and go off to school. Sometimes we got a ride; some days we had to walk. When there were a lot of us, we ran and sang as we went and came home.

When I was in sixth grade, I became very ill. I was sick for a month. I got very thin. This occurred at the time when I needed to take the admission exam for secondary school. The Presbyterian secondary school at Bibanga was very good. Representatives of the school came to Ngandajika to administer the entrance exam, but the place was nine kilometers (5.5 miles) away from our home and I was very ill. My sixth-grade teacher sent a message, "Even if she is sick, bring her so that she can take the exam because it is only given once. If she misses this time, she won't be able to go to Bibanga." My father took that seriously. He asked me, "Are you willing for us to take you there to do the exam?" I agreed, though I was weak. So they gave my older brother the bicycle, and he took me to Ngandajika on the bike. There I was, propped up in a corner with my back to the wall so that I could sit up. More than four hundred of us took the entrance exam, and only two of us succeeded. I was the only girl, and I had been sick at home for a month.

When I finished the exam and came home, my aunt Tshijuka prepared food for me, but when she got back to her home in Ngandajika, she told my grandmother, "Look, Misenga could die; she is very sick and they took her to do the exam." My grandmother left Ngandajika that night and set off on foot, by herself, at night. At this time there were crazy folks in the forest who were attacking and killing people on the road, but she was determined. She arrived at our house about 2:00 a.m. When my mother opened the door, my grandmother said, "Where is Misenga?" She came into the room where I was and began to pray. She said to God something I have always remembered: "*Nzambi, katuvua bunvuangana nebe nanku to. Nzambi, hatoka mpaha. . . .*" "God, we did not make our agreement with you like this. No, no. You are God, you have the strength and the power on earth as in heaven. I belong to you. We already made our agreement. I do not want this. We did not agree that my grandchildren would be sick or die. No! I want to see Misenga get up and eat." My grandmother prayed with authority; she prayed through the night. In the morning she asked them to prepare eggs for me. They did, she gave them to me, and I ate. My grandmother said that at the end of the week I would be recovered and I was. She was with me, she was praying. This is the reason we called her Mutangila Nzambi, "Who has seen God," because she believed firmly.

3

Student Days

It was not easy to be a girl at school, but my father helped me a great deal. When I was in primary school, I was the first in the class, ahead of the boys, and the boy in second place said, "She has a fetish." (He meant that I had been given a magic charm to make me succeed.) My older brother was at school with me, though not in my class, and he said, "Yes, it is true; they made a fetish for Misenga when she was little." I cried! My eyes were red and swollen. My father said, "What is wrong?" When I explained, he said to me, "Don't cry. When they say that you have a fetish, say, 'Yes, come see the person who made it for me' and bring them to me. I will correct them." (He did not believe in magic, but he knew that the boys did, and they would leave me alone if they had to face him.) My father's support gave me a lot of courage.

When I was growing up, everyone in Congo was supposed to go to primary school, but secondary school was expensive and it was not common for girls to attend. My father was determined to give his daughters that opportunity, but this was against the culture, and other people often made things difficult for us. In the course of my education, I learned firsthand some of the ways that girls and women suffer violence when they challenge male dominance.

Challenges at School

Graduation for primary school was July 2, 1965. Then I went to secondary school at Bibanga. It was a long distance from Ngandajika, 84 km (a little over 52 miles). At Bibanga, boys went directly to the first year of secondary, but girls had to do a preparatory year. But that was unjust. We studied, so how could the boys go ahead? While I was at Bibanga, I saw the situation evolve (partly through my experience). One day during the preparatory year our math professor brought us a problem that the second-year students had not been able to solve—and I worked out the right answer. I finished that year with a grade of 90 percent; sometimes I had 40 correct answers out of 40 questions, or 60/60; occasionally it was 35/40. When the professors graded my papers, they were very pleased.

Girls, Work, and Education

Although all children were supposed to attend primary school, girls were frequently unavoidably absent. Traditionally, they were expected to work from early childhood. By the age of three or four they were responsible for younger siblings. When they were a little older, they normally spent a significant part of every day carrying water for the household from the nearest stream. There were also challenges when they reached puberty. Because there were no regular hygiene products, menstruating girls stayed at home. Boys were the favored children. They were not expected to do chores like their sisters. They had free time for play so they rarely missed school. Consequently, when entering secondary school, most girls would not be as well prepared as boys and would need a remedial year. Monique's father ensured that his daughters were not taken out of class to do housework so she had the full benefit of her primary education.

At the end of the year we were getting ready for vacation while the professors marked the exams. Mr. Eric Bolton, the principal, said to the others, "This girl is very intelligent. We should count that she has done the first year (the same as the boys)." Maybe he was remembering that math problem. The other professors agreed, and they sent someone to find me but did not explain why. The messenger added his guess, "You'll see; they are going to send you away." I said, "Oh. . . ." I went to meet with all the professors where they were sitting together with the elders of the church. I asked why they had called me. Everyone was looking at me. I was trembling. Principal Bolton said, "All the professors here have testified for you and all the elders. We the directors have decided that you ought not to have to do the first year, but you should go directly to the second year. But we wanted to ask you your opinion. Would you like to go to the second class?" I said, "Yes!" I was very happy. It was the first time that this had happened: for a girl to go ahead just like the boys. The professors congratulated me, but when I got back to the girls' dorm, the other girls were angry. "They let her skip a grade. They left us behind and only took her."

So I entered the second year of secondary school. Exam time was coming—only two weeks left. Then I found all my notebooks torn up—all of them. "Eek! Someone has destroyed my notebooks." It was difficult to figure out who had done it (we later learned that it was the jealous girls), but I thought that person would have a problem with God. They did it so that I would fail. The professors said that I could borrow their notes to study, but I did not accept the offer because I have my own way of taking notes and I could not adapt myself to theirs. There we were. From memory I made a summary of what I had learned to use to study for the exams. And I was successful in the first session. (Students have two chances to take exams, one at the end of the academic year and the other at the start of the following year. If you fail the first session, you can study over the summer and take the fall exam.) Even without my notebooks I was able to pass in the first session.

Studying with boys was difficult. They bothered me a great deal with their threats to hinder my studying. They said, "You think you can get ahead of us. You have come to compete with us—just you wait and see." I was not the only girl in the class, but they did this because they thought at first that I was going to fail, and then I skipped a grade. When I succeeded, they were angry. But I did not do it in order to compete. I loved studying, and God gave me grace. I studied, and I came out second in the class, or third, or sometimes first, year by year, so I finished secondary school without difficulty. I was good at math so at the end of the third year the Bibanga teachers offered to send me to the Presbyterian-Methodist school at Katubue (in West Kasai), which was very strong in math and science. However, my father did not want me to go so far away so I stayed at Bibanga to complete the humanities course.

One special memory of my years at Bibanga was the time during my second year when I was chosen to have a part in a play called *Topaz* by Marcel Pagnol. After we put on the show for the school, everyone knew who I was because I had mastered my role and played it very well. I received lots of presents; then everyone began to call me Miss Muche, the name of my character in the play.

At the end of secondary school there are state exams, and this again showed my troubles with the boys. At that time there was a system of certificates: if you did not do well enough to earn a diploma, you were given a certificate, and if you

> ## *Possibilities for Post-Primary Education*
>
> Western-style schools in Congo began with basic primary education and then added various other forms, first vocational and then university oriented. In the Belgian Congo, the primary and vocational schools like Bible institutes, industrial arts, and teacher-training institutes were first established in the Bantu languages. After World War II, education in French was added, including formal secondary schools and normal schools, theological seminaries, and a very few universities. Secondary education in Congo began to expand after independence in 1960, but high-quality schools were still very limited in number and many were still run by churches. Bibanga, the first Presbyterian secondary school, was established in East Kasai in the late 1940s to specialize in the humanities. In the mid-1950s Presbyterians and Methodists jointly established a secondary school in West Kasai to specialize in math and science. Temporarily located at Mutoto, it settled at Katubue in 1957. Graduates of these two institutions became notable leaders throughout the Kasai region and beyond. Note: The European educational system does not grade on the curve; it is a strict assessment of total possible points, and a passing mark is 50 percent.

failed both of those, you got nothing. The day of the math exam, when we finished, the boys were talking about their answers and asked me what I had written. I said, "I did not write that." They said, "Oh, you will fail." I cried. But Mr. Zerker, our math professor, came looking for me. They told him, "Oh, Monique is there; she is crying because she failed the exam." He said, "Who told you that she failed? You are just trying to discourage her." He told the boy, "You must not say that. It is not right." Mr. Zerker liked me because I was often the first in the class. I said to myself, "I will study to be sure; if God helps me, I will succeed. I only want to continue with the exams." So I kept on to the end, and I did not cry any more. First was a written exam and then an oral. When they announced the results, I had 59 percent. At that time, it was a very good score, and I received my diploma. One of the ones who mocked me got a certificate, the other nothing.

When we were at Bibanga, the American church was giving a scholarship each year for a student to go to university in the United States. The professors asked me if I wanted to do this, and I said, "I am young. I do not want to go so far away from my parents for so many years."

UNIVERSITY

Next came university! My father paid the ticket for me to go to Kinshasa where my older brother, Tshimenga Joseph, was studying. I was supposed to live with the family of one of my father's friends; their son Jean-Etienne had lived with us and was like a brother to me. I wanted to study pharmacy at the University of Lovanium; they admitted me but said I would have to wait a year to begin because the entering class was full. Jean-Etienne was determined to help me start university so he found a way for me to enroll at the Institut Supérieur Pédagogique de Gombe (ISP), a teacher-training university run by Catholic nuns.

But where would I live? I was supposed to stay at his parents' home, but that would mean crossing the city every day—a long distance, expensive and risky. Jean-Etienne knew that wealthy men tried to seduce women students when they came out the gate of the university so he found a clever way for me to get a scholarship and become a boarding student. The nun in charge of the boarding department was very strict. So Jean-Etienne told her, "This is my little sister. We are twelve children. Our father has been transferred, but we are at home. We are all boys, and she is the only girl. Our friends come over to our house, and it is not a good situation for her." The nun heard that, and immediately she gave me a place. (Jean-Etienne's story was imaginary, but the danger he was working to avoid certainly was not, and getting a place in the dormitory was his way of protecting me. I have always regretted his early death; he was a good and intelligent young man.)

A (DANGEROUS) GREAT ADVENTURE

In 1972, at the end of my first year at university, I had a great adventure. At ISP we had a scholarship to pay for our return home in the summer. It was 35,000 Congo zaires—a lot of money at that time, plenty for one plane ticket but not enough for two. My older brother, Tshimenga Joseph, was in Kinshasa. At first he lived with one cousin, then with another. He was not happy there, and he had not passed his state exam to receive his diploma. He was very intelligent, but something went wrong. I wanted him to go to Bibanga as

I had. I thought Tshimenga and I should travel home together. My scholarship was not enough for both of us to fly so we would have to go by boat from Kinshasa to Ilebo, then by train to Mweka, then on to Kananga and Muena Ditu (see fig. 1.2). The train would continue to Lubumbashi, but we would get off at Luputu to take a truck to Ngandajika. We sent a message to our father to say when we would arrive and got on the boat. It was difficult. After that I said, "Never again by boat."

On the boat there were lots of police and the young girls they were using for prostitution. But I was already at the university; at that time, to be a university student was a big deal. The captain said, "I want that girl," and he sent men to me to say, "The captain wants to talk with you." I said, "No. I am not going there to talk with him; he can come here if he wants." When I went to the shower his people came to take away the door. However, there were students from the University of Lovanium onboard with us; as university students we had a kind of solidarity. When they saw what the captain was doing, they made trouble. "She is a university student. You may not annoy her." They made a kind of protective cordon around me.

At Ilebo we took the train, and that also was not a good trip. At Mweka a man who was out of his head boarded the train and began to bother me. The students helped me a lot; they blocked the man from coming into my compartment. Some went to the conductor and asked him to stop the train. He did, and they made the man get off. We went on to Luputu and then got off to take a truck for Ngandajika.

When the truck had gone about 30 km (18.6 miles) from Luputu, we came to a military barricade. I told this story in the prologue so you have already heard how God's hand was upon me. After I confronted the captain of the soldiers, they let all the passengers get back on the bus with their belongings and we started off. When we had gone about 5 km (3 miles) the driver stopped the truck and said to me, "*Maman, udi musomba bimpe?* Are you comfortable?" The people said, "Maman, you have saved us!" They hugged me. They wanted to give me a better place, but I said, "I am staying here; let's just get going." We arrived near the place where my father worked; he had come with my sisters to meet us at the road. They hugged me and my brother.

As you have heard, the driver and all the people in the truck came to tell my father, "What a child you have! She is not a girl; she is a man! This girl saved us." They told the story to my father, and he said to me, "Yes! That is good. You must always go on like that." He said to the others, "She is well educated, she understands things, she is not afraid. Why were you afraid?" But they should have been afraid because they did not know how to defend themselves. The soldiers were going to steal all these people's belongings, but by God's grace I could defend them.

A FESTIVAL IN BERLIN AND ENCOUNTERS WITH VIOLENCE

I studied at the Higher Institute of Pedagogy (ISP) from 1971 to 1974. In this period Mobutu's party, the Popular Movement of the Revolution (MPR), which became the state party in 1974, had ideological seminars in all the universities and institutes of higher education. These were called the Junior (Student) MPR, or JMPR. The purpose was to get students involved in the party. When I came to ISP, I did not belong to the JMPR (or any party), but in the ideological seminars I asked lots of questions and people remembered that.

In 1973 there was a world youth festival in East Berlin, and Congo was invited to send delegates. The government chose students from all the universities in Congo: Kinshasa, Katanga, Kisangani, and the institutes of higher education. (Institutes are university level but teach one discipline rather than many as the universities do; in Congo we had institutes for pedagogy and for business.) Oddly enough, the officials picked me, though I was not a member of the JMPR. There were students who wanted to go, and they asked, "Why did you choose her? She is not in the JMPR; she doesn't like the MPR." The answer was, "She is intelligent; she is able to express herself well, to ask questions, to give answers." There were about twenty men students, including my "adopted brother," Jean-Etienne; we were only six women. There were government officials with us: the Minister of Youth and Sports and associate governors of the provincial subregions, all men of course.

It was on this first trip outside Congo that I experienced some new forms of sexual violence against women. There were several receptions at which the government officials tried to kidnap the women students for sex, and the men students protected us. One was a Pan-African gathering; there were Africans from all the countries. We females were there, and so were the officials. But they forbade our male students to come. The latter were outside, but they said, "We will keep watch. The moment they try to kidnap you, we will act and the

German government will be able to deal with the matter." After the lecture, we were told to invite the officials to dance, and they began to touch (fondle) the female students. Suddenly, a Cameroonian came up to me and asked me to dance; I went with him. The Congolese girls were dancing with men from all different nations instead of our government officials who wanted to paw us.

Then those who had organized the dance stopped it and said, "Let's go upstairs." This invitation was for us girls, not everyone. We got into the elevator to go up to the thirtieth floor, where the officials were lodged. They had set up a fine table and all kinds of drinks. We, the six female students plus three women who worked in some of the embassies, were seated there with the officials of the eleven provinces, the government ministers, and some of the JMPR. They brought us alcoholic drinks, offered toasts, and expected us to drink. They wanted to get us drunk so they could do as they pleased with us. I put my glass to my lips, but I did not drink anything. But the male students who had stayed below began to ask, "Where are the Congolese girls?" They were told, "The girls have been taken to the thirtieth floor." So they revolted and created trouble: "Bring down the Congolese girls immediately." The Germans were very angry with the male students until they heard, "They have kidnapped our girls." Then the Germans were angry because it was a dishonor to them for us to have been kidnapped so they insisted that we be returned. We got away, but I became ill with a fever after all of this.

But it did not stop there. The assistant governor of the subregion of Bandundu told me that he loved me. One day when I was sick, all the rest of the group were going out, leaving me alone in my room. This governor said, "I do not see Monique. Where is she?" When he heard I was sick, he found a means to get into my room. Someone told Jean-Etienne, and he followed the man. I was sleeping, but I woke up when the door opened. The governor said, "Ah. Now I am going to see if you can find a way to run away from me." I was trembling on my bed as he approached. Suddenly the door opened again, and there was Jean-Etienne. He pushed the official and began to hit the man, and hit him again and again. I begged him to stop. But if he had not come, think what would have happened to me. The man left, and Jean-Etienne asked me, "What did he do to you?" I said, "Just at the point when he wanted to touch me, you came in." From that day on, I could never be alone. I no longer enjoyed the trip. We girls were not at ease; when we went out, the male students were always with us. When we went to our rooms, they went with us and waited until we had gone in and closed the doors. By the time we returned home I had become very thin with all this violence.

At the end, the government ministers gathered us together to instruct us not to tell what had happened. They said we had come to represent our country and we had no right to say bad things to dishonor the authorities; we must forgive. They wanted to intimidate us.

A LETTER AND AN OPEN DOOR

The Berlin trip was not the end of my encounters with the government. In fact, President Mobutu's office wanted to hire me after I finished university. It began with a student fete.

In their final year, university students at the national institutions had the tradition of organizing a ball. We did not do that at ISP because it was a Catholic university, but one of the students at ISP was a girl named Marie-Jeanne Mawelu. She was from President Mobutu's home village, and her brothers worked in the presidential office. They told her that if she wrote a letter to the president, he would give the JMPR money to hold a ball. Fine. Marie-Jeanne was studying geography, but she knew I was doing French and history, so she came to see me and said, "I have to write a letter to the president to ask for money for a ball, but I don't know how to do it. Will you help me?" So I did. When she sent the letter, her brothers asked her, "Who wrote this letter? It was not you." She explained, "It was a student called Monique who is studying at ISP with me." They said, "We want to see this girl. You will get the money, but we must see the girl." That semester, my last before graduation, I was doing my practice teaching at Kimwenza, a distance from Kinshasa. I would come back to ISP on Thursday afternoons, go to class on Friday morning, and then return to Kimwenza for the next week of teaching.

One Thursday when I got back to ISP everyone was excited and afraid. "They came to look for you. It was the security forces of the president." (They were called the SP. If the SP came looking for you, it was serious indeed.) Marie-Jeanne Mawelu went on, "But don't be afraid. It was because of the letter you wrote. They read it and said it was very well written, and they want to see you. I thought it was better to see you and tell you first, and then go to the SP." I said, "Okay." So the next morning the SP sent for us. When we got to the SP building, only Marie-Jeanne and I were told to go upstairs. When we came into the room—it was incredibly luxurious—we met Makolo wa Mpombo, the principal counselor to President Mobutu. He said, "Mademoiselle Monique, is it you?" "Yes, it is I." He stood up to greet me: "Sit down." The chair . . . it was so luxurious. It was extraordinary. He said, "Mademoiselle, we have read your letter; it is really well written. Where did you learn French?" I said, "At the Presbyterian secondary school at Bibanga. Now I am at ISP, and I am doing French. I am in the third year." He said, "You have asked for money for the ball. We will give it to you, but since the letter is written in the name of the JMPR, we invited the whole committee to come. But we wanted to see you especially because you interest us. The president's office will engage you when you have finished your studies. You will come to work with us." I said, "Thank you."

They asked the other students to come upstairs. Then the president's adviser said, "Mademoiselle Monique wrote a letter asking for 300,000 zaires." (At the time it was a great deal of money, about $150,000.) "Since we can't give you the money officially, it was necessary for you to be here." Then I said, "Yes, Mr. Counselor. I said 'at least 300,000.' I think that the president's office, that is the state committee, could give us more than 300,000. I said 'at least 300,000.'" He said, "See how she talks; she speaks very well! She knows how to choose her words well. She said 'at least.' She is intelligent." Well—they gave us 500,000 zaires. He wrote a check, which we had to go to cash at the Bank of Zaire. We said, "Thank you." He said, "Mademoiselle Monique, when you have finished university you will come back."

So ISP had its ball. I returned to my studies, finished university, and graduated, but that was not the end of this story. Just after graduation I married, as I will tell in the next chapter, but I was still invited back to government headquarters. When I went upstairs to the office of the director of Mobutu's Security Service, he said, "Mademoiselle Monique, will you sign the contract? The president is going to China, and you will go in the delegation." That was President Mobutu's first visit to China. I said, "I can't travel; I have just married and among our people a married woman cannot do that." He said, "You will be rich; we will pay you well. Okay, go and reflect on it; consider it well." I said, "No, if you want to give me a job, yes, but not that job to travel with the president." He said, "No, no, no. Go reflect. You will be rich, very rich." Then he held out his hand, "See, there is lots of money." He took some money and gave it to me to show that he was very rich. "Go, reflect; we will call you back."

In the elevator going back down there were people who said, "She has a lot of luck." "She could go to China with the president, and she refuses." "She says that she has just married and can't go—she is not smart." "She could have lots of money." But there was one man who was listening, and when we exited the elevator he remained behind. He was turned toward another person and pretended he was talking to that person and not to me; he did not look at me, and he told me not to look at him. I just listened. But he said, "You must not accept this job. It is a bad job. They will see that you are intelligent, they will begin to give you missions to follow people and inform on them, and they will kill the people. You can only come in; if you leave, they will kill you. You must stay firm, don't accept, don't come back." I was terrified. When I left, the doorman said, "Mademoiselle Monique, there is a car to take you home." I got into the car with my cousin's husband who worked there, and they took us home. I was so afraid. I told the family what had happened. My cousin's husband said, "But you could do a single trip, and then you could quit." I said, "No. I cannot accept. I was told that 'if you enter and leave, they will kill you.'"

And it is true. Many of the students who went with us to Europe are dead. They went in, they got rich, they are dead. It is a world that has its own lifestyle. But I did not follow the money. God helped me remain absolutely sure; I refused. They called me a second time, and I went to talk with them. I said, "But give me another job; I don't think this job is for me." At that point they recommended me to be the inspector of the palm oil department for the country, but I said to myself, "As inspector I would have to travel a lot, all the time, in all the provinces of Congo." So I said, "No. I must only teach." I avoided all political positions; I could never accept that for the sake of money. So God was gracious to me to be able to say no and stick to it. I always say that God gave me grace in many things.

ꞱATU MUKUNA AND OUR FAMILY

CHILDREN ARE THE WEALTH AND JOY of an African family, and traditionally a woman's value is primarily defined by the children she bears. My life has been richly blessed with Tatu Mukuna and our nine children, and I am deeply grateful to God. Yet what came before marked my soul and gave me a heart to reach out, to understand how to be with those who mourn. Infant and maternal mortality are high in Congo. Women often die from childbirth complications, and there are very few families which do not lose babies, at birth or before the age of five. Nothing prepares you for the sudden death of your first precious infant, as I know from experience, and when you are also newly widowed, the world seems to end.

MY FIRST MARRIAGE AND FIRST CHILD

When I finished university in the summer of 1974, I married Katuku Paul, a medical student. My husband and I had both the legal and religious ceremonies; the church wedding was held in August at my home in the Kasai. Then we returned to Kinshasa. My husband was doing his medical residency at the university clinic, and I was teaching. I got pregnant immediately, and in July 1975 our baby son was born; we named him Ngoie for my father.

My husband completed his residency and began work as the night doctor at the clinic. One night he fell. He only told me, "Monique, they are going to hospitalize me." I said, "Why?" He said, "For some little tests." At that point our baby was only two weeks old. My husband was hospitalized, and they operated; there was something wrong with his liver.

Forms of Marriage and Divorce

In Congo there are several kinds of marriage: the most common form is the traditional one arranged by the families, which usually includes a dowry given by the man's family to the woman's family. This may be returned under certain circumstances. This contract is somewhat parallel to the European civil or statutory marriage and legally recognized. However, since Congolese now live on the bridge between tradition and Western practice, many people do both of these legal ceremonies to establish full state protection. A third kind of marriage is a church wedding. As is the custom in French-speaking Europe, this is separate and legally optional. Christians usually complete the official forms with the religious one, although the different ceremonies may be held at different times for practical reasons: it requires time to save up money for each one. By statutory law polygamy is illegal, but by traditional law it is not. However, a second (or later) wife does not have the same legal status in the courts, and a man who marries a second wife cannot reclaim her in the courts if she leaves him.

The type of divorce follows the type of marriage. A traditional divorce is as legal as a traditional marriage. For a European-style civil marriage, a civil divorce is necessary. When a traditional divorce is contested in court, it may be upheld by a civil decree.

Then he died. It was terrible. I was young, and it was a shock. I had never been present at such a death. I was in Kinshasa, and my parents were in the Kasai so I was far away from my family. At ISP, the university where I had studied, the nuns mobilized the students, and busloads of them from there and IPN, the other pedagogical institute—many students—came to comfort me. It was so sad: we were young; we had just finished our studies. It was so hard. I loved my husband very much, and he loved me very much. We were at the beginning of our marriage and had had no problems; it was the time when you are truly happy. And death came—after only eleven months of marriage.

We buried my husband. One of my husband's brothers was at our house. He was always at the window watching me. He was a soldier. Already during the funeral, he had the idea that he would marry me—"inherit me," according to the tradition. "Oh, you know, to take care of the baby. You should accept to

Mourning Traditions

The traditional way to comfort those who are mourning is to go and "sit" with them—like Job's friends did. Friends, neighbors, relatives, and the community at large make a particular effort to visit the bereaved, as with these busloads of fellow students. Normally, the community also takes up a collection to help with funeral expenses.

be your brother-in-law's wife." He brought his father to propose this marriage, without telling my parents, who should have been part of the conversation. His father said, "No, stay here, you will live well." He wanted me to marry his son. I said, "I can't do that. I came into your family, and I have just lost the one who loved me. I cannot stay in your family." It was very difficult.

My parents were informed of my husband's death by his older brother, who was at Lubumbashi. When he found out, he came directly to Ngandajika to tell my parents; he said that my husband's death was related to a family medical problem. It was as if he came to ask pardon. My father said, "You should have explained; we could have helped." But my father returned the dowry, because he said, "I do not want there to be any ties with my daughter." When my parents heard about my husband's death, they sent my older brother to Kinshasa to get me, and I went to the Kasai with my baby. However, I could not stay there because the baby had been born with a harelip and we had an appointment at the clinic for the surgery.

We returned to Kinshasa for my baby's operation, and for six months he was well and grew. Then suddenly he died. At midnight on December 31, 1975, the baby began to cry and cried all night. We went to the clinic in the morning, and his father's physician friends took care of him. I could not eat; I was with one of my sisters, at the hospital, day and night. Then they said the baby was doing well and could come home. We were ready to leave, and I was doing the final paperwork. But suddenly doctors began coming and going frantically. I was immediately very anxious about my baby. "What is wrong?" They kept reassuring me, but they would not let me see him, "No, Madame, everything is okay." "But my baby!" "No, Madame, it's okay." A neighbor had come to visit us; I said to him, "The doctors don't know you. Go in there and see the baby and come back and tell us what has happened." He went in and came back out, crying. When I saw him—I don't know how I did it, but I leaped up and snatched up my baby. I did not cry; I had lost my head. Then they took the baby to the morgue. I was stunned. They wanted to give me medication. Other people cried; I simply sat there and watched with a fixed expression—I was in shock.

After that, I lost weight; I could not sleep. This went on for a year. When I was a young girl, a young woman, I was a coquette. I liked to dress well. After this, I lost my taste for that. I gave away all my clothes. I could not work normally; I did my teaching, but it did not go well. Often I went home to Kasai; I could not stand being in Kinshasa more than three months without visiting my parents. At school they understood and allowed this since I was a good teacher. My heartbroken parents suffered with me. Many people accompanied me with prayer, and my father helped me very much. I was just praying; I asked God to give me peace. Finally, I began to recover. For many years, I could not talk about this terrible time. It is because I have had these experiences and because I have overcome them by prayer that I can comfort others.

When I was alone in Kinshasa, I took three of my younger sisters to live with me: Mbuyi, Mbombo, and Bitota. We rented a house in Lemba. I also had them with me to help my father because I was working and could pay their school fees. It was during this time that I became acquainted with Tatu Mukuna.

Old and New Customs in Competition

Traditional marriages require both families to be involved. Maman Monique's brother-in-law and father-in-law wanted to reclaim the tradition of a man inheriting his brother's widow, while silently avoiding the tradition that her family should be involved. They were appealing to Maman Monique to act without regard to her parents, something that was legal by European standards but contrary to African ones. Playing the old customs and the new ones against each other is one way that people (mostly men) have developed for making a widow's life more difficult. See the similar story of Maman Mado in chapter six. When Maman Monique's father returned her dowry, he was going beyond what the tradition required, but he was acting to sever all her in-laws' claims on her.

MUKUNA TSHILOBO LUKUSA CONSTANTIN

The family of Mukuna <u>Lukusa</u> Constantin came from the region of Kabeya Kamuanga, in East Kasai (see fig. 1.2). When Mukuna was young, his family moved to West Kasai near Luebo, but because of the fighting in 1960, they returned to their village, Tshatshatsha, in East Kasai. Mukuna's father, Lukusa <u>Tekesha</u>, married twice. With his first wife, Kabata <u>Mpanya</u>, he had many children but only three lived to adulthood. Mukuna, the oldest surviving son, was born on December 28, 1942. His younger brothers were Kalala Gaston and Kanda Kaja. Their father remarried and had one daughter, Nzeba. Mukuna did not have much contact with his half sister, but he was very close to his two brothers and their families and helped rear some of their children.

Education, work, and faith. There were Presbyterian evangelists in the region where Mukuna's parents lived, and the whole family became Christians when Mukuna was a small boy. He attended primary school close to home, in the regional schools, which had nine grades and were run by the Presbyterians. To continue his education, Mukuna had to go to Luebo. Because his family lived too far away for him to walk to and from school, he had to live with a family there. He spent two years studying to be a preacher, but the host family forced him to work hard and gave him limited food. He could not go to university as I did because he came from a poor family and lacked people to help him. But he was a courageous person; that is the reason he was given the name Tshilobo, which means "hero." This courage made him an autodidact; he learned so well that he seemed to have a full formal education. After his studies at Luebo, he returned to East Kasai, where his family lived, and got a job as a policeman. He did well and was sent to West Kasai for further education; his eagerness for study is why he was able to advance. Then he decided to move to Kinshasa, where he had many cousins.

In Kinshasa Tatu Mukuna got further training as a traffic policeman. However, he also had another office job in the motor vehicle department, as the person who dealt with lost licenses. As a policeman he had a small regular salary, but the office job was a much more responsible position and was paid accordingly—ten times as much as the salary. Because Tatu Mukuna was truly honest, his superiors trusted him, and that enabled him to have this kind of responsible job and earn a good income. When we married, he had two cars, which he had bought new. His relatives drove them as taxis.

Tatu Mukuna worked in the police department almost all his life. Around 1982, the government of President Mobutu accused him of being a supporter of Mr. Etienne Tshisekedi because they both came from the village of Kabeya Kamuanga. The government took away Tatu Mukuna's office job, leaving him only the traffic policeman's work with its tiny salary. For many years Tatu Mukuna did not have any other job. Finally, after the coming of President Kabila in 1997, Tatu Mukuna received training to be a police court judge, but he was too honest and could not tolerate the corruption. Around 2003–2004 he asked for early retirement on the basis of his health (asthma). But to the day of his death the state never paid his pension.

Ethnicity and Politics

Because ethnic loyalties are often the basis for political alliances, anyone who comes from the same village or tribe as an opponent is suspect, whether or not the person has ever had any contact with the political figure. President Mobutu's dictatorship had begun fairly benevolently in 1965, but it became increasingly restrictive, especially with regard to any political opposition. It was a one-party state, with growing repression; all members of the government had to pledge allegiance to him, so their positions were dependent on obedience to his will. In 1980, thirteen members of parliament demanded a multiparty system, but Mobutu refused. In 1982, led by Etienne Tshisekedi, the thirteen founded the Union for Democracy and Social Progress (UDPS). Mobutu accused them of treason and put them in prison. Tshisekedi was in and out of prison or detention many times for his determined nonviolent opposition.[1]

Tatu Mukuna's first marriage. As a young man in the Kasai Tatu Mukuna married a woman name Marivale according to the traditional forms. Then he moved to Kinshasa, and when he got a job he sent for her. She was very young, and she did not immediately begin to have children. Behind his back she started to tell the story that her husband was impotent. Finally, she had a girl

---

[1]Emizet François Kisangani and F. Scott Bobb, "Introduction," in *Historical Dictionary of the Democratic Republic of the Congo*, 3rd ed. African Historical Dictionaries 112 (Lanham, MD: Scarecrow, 2010), lxvii-lxviii, lxxi.

named Kabata for Mukuna's mother. Five years passed before Marivale conceived again. During this time she made fetishes (fertility magic), and she misbehaved: maybe she hoped to get pregnant by another man. Eventually, she had two more children, a girl, Mbombo, and a son, Mukendi. Marivale told her in-laws that Tatu Mukuna had given her the green light to go with other men, and she denied that these children were his. His cousins did not tell Tatu Mukuna what his wife was doing, but they advised him to take a second wife. They wanted to see if what his wife was saying about his impotence was true.

Other relatives from the Kasai visited, and then the whole story came out. Marivale denied it: "Oh, no, I did not say that." As proof, they called the cousin's wife to whom she had told this. Marivale had nothing left to say. Tatu Mukuna returned her to her family and divorced her in the traditional fashion. Later, Marivale took Tatu Mukuna to court—maybe she wanted him to buy her a piece of property or something. Even in front of the court she had nothing to say for herself, and the traditional divorce was reaffirmed.

My Marriage with Tatu Mukuna

When I became acquainted with Tatu Mukuna I was still grieving for my husband and baby. I did not know if I could bear to remarry; I was afraid of love. Family and friends worked with me a long time to accept the idea.

This is how it happened. I had studied at Bibanga, and the Bibanga alums in Kinshasa organized a choir. Tatu Mukuna had friends among these alums, and he became an honorary choir member to support us. Since he saw me singing there, he became interested in me. He asked for my hand; the first time he asked I did not accept. He continued his efforts, waiting because he knew I had lost my first husband and was afraid. Lots of people loved Tatu Mukuna— my sisters, my cousin. They said, "He is serious. It is good to accept him; you will have a good life." That is how I remarried. Tatu Mukuna was good for me; it was the marriage God had planned for me.

Tatu Mukuna's family were Presbyterian. Several cousins and relatives became pastors. When his father died, he told Tatu Mukuna, "In the face of all problems you must only pray to God." The whole time we were married, before work Tatu Mukuna would get up early in the morning to go to church to pray. Our eldest son, Eddy, has followed in his father's footsteps; he is truly very much involved in the church and supports me in my ministry.

My dear husband did a lot to support our parish. He organized; he visited people and prayed for them. When there were conflicts, he tried to resolve them. When he died, people said, "Now that Papa Mukuna is dead, our parish will not go on." He was also treasurer of the presbytery of Matete. When he died, people were surprised to see that everything was in order. They said, "It isn't possible" (in comparison with other treasurers who line their own pockets). They testified to his honesty. Even the vice president of the whole denomination said, "We have never seen that. Now that he is dead, we see that all the money is there—nothing is missing—along with all the reports." They were astonished and said, "Truly he will see God." I say that to show the level of his Christian faith. His parents brought him up to be a Christian, and he kept the faith. Even at home he encouraged me when the children were ill. Sometimes I was afraid, but he would say, "No, we must just pray." But I am getting ahead of my story.

When I accepted Tatu Mukuna, I told him to talk with my parents. I had given my parents a condition, "Do not accept the dowry until I know that I am stable, until I see how we live together." (I was afraid, and a dowry binds you into the other family.) We were married at the end of 1977. At first I refused to go to live in Tatu Mukuna's house so he rented a house for me in Lemba. But when our first son, Eddy, was born in December 1978, Tatu Mukuna insisted that I come to live in his house. He gave the dowry to my older brother (who was in Kinshasa), and after a time we had the church wedding.

When we married, Tatu Mukuna already had a household, including his younger brother and five children. There were his older two daughters, Kabata and Mbombo; Tshiela Benda, the ten-year-old daughter of his cousin; and two children of his niece. I also brought two of my younger sisters, Bitota and Mbombo, with me so we were a big family. Tshiela and I became close; we already had a tie because her mother had been a student at Bibanga several years ahead of me. Her parents had left her with Tatu Mukuna when they went to study in the United States. I regarded all of them as my children; there was no distinction. When I bought clothes, I bought the same for everyone. I taught all the children how to knit, to crochet, to make doughnuts. They learned how to support themselves and appreciated what I had done for them.

Tatu Mukuna and I had nine children together, four boys and five girls. Our first was a boy, Lukusa Tekesha Eddy, who has the name of his grandfather,

Mukuna's father. Our first daughter, Bitota Nelly (1980), has my mother's name. The third was named Mukuna Tshilobo (1981) for his father. Our second daughter, Katanda Nana (1983), was followed by our third son, Kanyinda Trésor Isaac (1985). Then we had two more daughters, Kambia Judith (1988) and Mwanji Sarah (1989). Our fourth son, Ngoie Moise (1991), was named for my father. The youngest is our fifth daughter, Nzeba Gracia (1994). (See figs. 4.1 and 4.2 for pictures of family members.) At home we spoke Tshiluba or French—but mostly French. Tshiluba, the language of the Kasai, is what Tatu Mukuna and I had grown up speaking, but in Kinshasa the common language is Lingala so that is what the children heard and spoke with their friends. Tatu Mukuna and I also had learned Lingala when we came to Kinshasa, but I wanted our children to keep their heritage so I insisted that they must speak either Tshiluba or French at home. Our niece, Tshiela, had learned Tshiluba as a small child in the Kasai, but our children were more comfortable in Lingala or French.

We brought up all our children and sent them to school—the girls as well as the boys—not just primary and secondary but also higher education.

Figure 4.1. The marriage of Maman Monique's eldest daughter. South Africa, 2007. Maman Monique (L) and Tatu Mukuna (R) at the wedding of their eldest daughter, Nelly Bitota, and her husband, Lyn Massamba.

Lukusa Eddy did economics at university and also got his master's. Bitota Nelly studied computer science, and she also got a master's. Mukuna Junior wanted to go to Europe for university, but I could not afford that, and he did not want to do university in Kinshasa so he only has the secondary school state diploma. Katanda Nana majored in sewing at school but then went to the United States to study nursing; she earned her CNA and AA and is working on her BS in nursing. Kanyinda Trésor did computer science. Kambia

Figure 4.2. Maman Monique with one of her granddaughters, Monique Blessing. Kinshasa, 2015.

Judith graduated with a degree in nursing. Mwanji Sarah and Nzeba Gracia went to live with their oldest sister in South Africa to continue their education; both studied tourism. Ngoie Moise did accounting. The three youngest children have now finished their university educations. Five of the children are married now, and I have ten grandchildren.

Through the years we suffered a great deal with our children's illnesses, sometimes very serious ones. The first very difficult time was with the children of Tatu Mukuna's first wife.

Early in our marriage the first two daughters who lived with us ran away to their mother, hoping to get their parents back together. But she could not take care of them, and both of them and their younger brother were terribly malnourished. When I learned about it, I was determined to save them. The boy Mukendi: his stomach was swollen, his legs were shiny, he had almost no blood. He had a terrible case of malnutrition and also a fever. The two girls, Kabata and Mbombo, had become very thin since they had left our house; their skin and hair showed signs of malnutrition. First, I took the boy to the clinic, and they treated the fever. I got soy flour to mix with corn flour and made a soup to feed them. I prayed for them. I prepared food and nursed them.

The boy was at the clinic only one day; the rest I did myself with nourishment, love, and prayer. A week later the children's health had improved, and after two weeks they were back to normal. The children stayed with me and grew up in our house. They were my children just as much as the babies I had with Tatu Mukuna.

Sometimes the illness was more severe. Our son Kanyinda was extremely sick when he was five years old. He had fevers. We gave him medicine for malaria, but that did not help so he was hospitalized. My mother was at the hospital with him, and I visited every day, but I had baby Moise at home. One day when I was there a nurse did a procedure with a syringe and drew out pus. She said, "Eek!" She hurried to tell the doctor, he came and cried, "It is septicemia." Only God saved Kanyinda. He was in the hospital for two months— and it was an expensive hospital, but at that time I had a lot of money. But I told God, "I can lose money, but I must have the life of my son." Later, after Tatu Mukuna's death, Sarah and then Eddy were very seriously ill; friends stood with me and always God helped me.

My Father's Death and "Ilunga Mbiya"

In his later years my father had diabetes because he smoked cigarettes. I was living in Kinshasa and teaching, but I would go to the Kasai to look after my father and mother. I bought medicine and presents for my father. He had his own things, but if I brought him anything—for example, a washcloth—he was very happy. He said, "See the washcloth that Monique brought me." Because I studied well and was intelligent and had completed university, my father loved me very much.

My father began to suffer seriously in 1980, but he was worse in 1981. I did not have money to visit him, but I started sewing. I made blouses and sold them, sewed and sold, sewed and sold, and got the money. When I got home I found my father very sick. I wanted to take him to Kinshasa for treatment, but I did not have any money. My mother and I began to do business; we sold the corn we had at home. Then we went outside the city to INEAC (the agricultural project where my father had worked) to buy more and bring it back to sell until we had enough money. When we arrived in Kinshasa, my father was very weak. After some examinations he was hospitalized. He began to get a little better, but then he went back into the hospital. I did not have any money; I took what little I had and went to buy corn and sell it, buy and sell, buy and sell. I did the business during the day and came to visit my father afterwards. Then he needed intubation and maybe that injured something, but along with the diabetes it was too much. My father fell into a coma and died. It was terrible.

Before that happened, one day when I got to the hospital my father said that he wanted to talk with me. "I have considered all my children, and it is you who can be my heir. I want to leave you all the responsibility, all my possessions." I said, "No, Papa. It is good to leave them to your sons because if you leave them to me they will kill me. Already they say, 'In all the problems, Papa only wants Monique, he only loves Monique.'" He said, "No. I don't see that my sons can do it." We argued. Finally he said, "Okay, if you do not want it, I will leave it to Kalala (my youngest son). But I will tell you something. You say that you are a girl. In the tradition of our village, a woman can be chief of the village. *Kuetu kudi mukelenge mukashi ba mubikile Ilunga Mbiya.* If she does not want to direct matters, she can give her power to her brother, but the brother is not the chief. He works and comes and gives an accounting to his sister. They call this woman 'Ilunga Mbiya'—a woman who is chief. So you cannot say that it is only boys who can direct; you can." After my father's death, maybe his words had an impact because for all the family I am the one who takes care of the problems. Whenever something happens, they come to me for help. When I am not there, they say, "Monique is not here. How can we do things?"

But what about a woman chief? I think about what my father said; if he were still alive I would talk with him more about it. He was talking about the Luba of the Bena Kanyuka village in East Kasai, my father's paternal grandfather's original home, the Luba Lubilanji. There are clans among the Luba who do not accept that a woman could be a chief, but there are some that do. I have heard people where I grew up say, "Ilunga Mbiya" or call someone "Ilunga Mbiya" but I did not know that there was any importance to the words—until my father told me about it. So the idea of a woman chief exists in the history, but in limited areas. At least in some places it is recognized that even a girl could take the power; it is known that there have been women who have directed the village. But I did not have time to ask my father more.

5

My Professions as Educator and Entrepreneur

ONE OF THE THINGS MY FATHER impressed on us was the importance of work. He prepared us to have a modern kind of career based on formal education and the ability to support ourselves through more traditional means such as farming and commerce. For many years I worked as a secondary-school teacher and principal. For most of my life I have been an entrepreneur and businesswoman, part time or full time.

There are many challenges to earning a living in Congo. Several years after I began teaching, they introduced computers to mechanize payment. For a while things went well. However, the checks were sometimes printed 00 instead of naming the amount of the salary; the months when the checks said 00 you did not get paid. That caused lots of difficulties. You could follow the process to claim the money: going up and down the system, up and down. You would be paid that month, maybe the next, or sometimes you went two months without salary. It was hard. After some years, I decided that I needed to find other ways to earn a living.

THE TEACHER AND PRINCIPAL

At school I had done the literature section; then I studied French and history at the Higher Institute of Pedagogy (ISP). I graduated in 1974, married in August, and returned to Kinshasa in September. I had two job offers, but both were too far from Kinshasa for me to commute. Then in January 1975 I found a teaching post at the Lumumba Institute in Kinshasa; it was a good school then. I taught French and history in the first and second classes of the six-year secondary program and used methods that helped the students understand things. When my students went to take exams elsewhere, they all succeeded. When the school inspectors came to observe my teaching, they always gave me high marks. I taught at Lumumba from January 1975 until 1982. In that year the government organized examinations that could lead to promotion; those who did well could become principals. I did well. But there was a problem: to be assigned to a good school, candidates often paid money. I did not have the money so it took a long time to find an appropriate placement. I worked temporarily in administration in the City Division of Education.

Then I got a place in a large secondary school for girls, the Kasavubu Professional High School. Part of my job was pedagogical oversight; I would go to a class where a teacher was giving a lesson and sit at the back and observe. For example, some teachers would come into the class and give a student a copy of the day's lesson to write on the board. The teacher did not explain; the students would not understand—they simply wrote what was on the board. The one at the board could make mistakes, and the rest would copy the errors. Afterwards, I would meet with the teacher to offer corrections. I explained to them, "These children are your children. Put yourself in the place of their parents. If you sent your child to school and afterwards he did not know anything, would you be happy?"

Teaching Customs

Schools are very poorly equipped, and normally students do not have textbooks. Instruction is given by the teacher, copied, and memorized, then repeated back by the students. At the university level, professors may prepare the instruction as a fixed text that students must buy.

The work as a teacher was good, and the salary was okay—when it was paid regularly. My school was a distance from our home, and you had to pay transport out of your salary. Even though I was farming as my father taught us, and doing small animal husbandry to provide food, we did not have enough for a good life for a growing family. When I saw how difficult the situation was, I decided to quit teaching and work in business—that was about 1983–1984.

BUSINESS WOMAN

My business began with sewing, and at first I worked close to home, in Kinshasa. In the market I saw baby clothes for sale; a merchant asked if I could make crocheted baby booties because they sold well. I took the model home and did not sleep until I had figured out how to make the shoes. Every day I got up very early, washed the dishes, and swept; then I would crochet. About 11:00 a.m. I would take the booties and bonnets to market to sell; there I would buy food and more thread and come home. I had mastered the work and was able to produce a lot. In the afternoon I would do more housework and then in the evening begin crocheting again. I stayed up even after the rest went to bed, and sometimes I worked until 11:00 p.m. or midnight. I began a sewing atelier at my house. I rented a sewing machine, and when I had some money, I hired a girl to help and rented a second machine. Then I had enough money to buy a machine, then a second one. I hired more helpers. I also created new models of baby clothes and began to make baby bed sheets. Mine were 1.5 meters wide (5.5 feet), which made them very useful for carrying the baby on her mother's back (instead of using the mother's second wrap). That was larger than the style being sold at the time, and lots of people bought mine because no one else was making them the way I was. For a while I had a monopoly.

I expanded to Brazzaville (across the Congo River), where my large baby sheets were popular. My cousin's wife did business in Brazzaville, and she took me with her. There I got acquainted with the markets and some businessmen. When I had sold my items, I would buy their models of layette. I looked at their linens and then came home and began creating different things. I tried to improve the styles, and I developed a big clientele in Brazza. I was selling more in Brazza than in Kinshasa. Sometimes they paid me in money, sometimes in merchandise that we did not have in Kinshasa, such as booties imported from Bangkok. At that time, I did not have a table or a shop (a regular place to display and sell retail goods) in the Kinshasa market so I sold to other merchants. At first I went back and forth between Kinshasa and Brazza three times a week, but later I made the trip every day because I had so many orders. I liked doing business and was respected. I did not have problems; in fact, people helped me, even with customs. By 1990 the business was really going well, and I had lots of money.

Then I ventured further from home. In Congo now everything is imported. During the colonial period there were some industries that produced cloth and other things, but most of those were owned by Belgians. When the Belgians left at independence, we did not have such industries, so now we import. When my local business was going well, in 1991, I decided to expand to South Africa. Baby shawls made there sold well in Congo. My first attempt to trade in South Africa did not work out well because I tried to partner with another woman who was talented but not honest. When she made a purchasing trip, she did not bring back what I had ordered and did not pay me back my investment.

So then I went to South Africa myself to purchase. We have a practice called a *ristourne*, which allows a small business owner access to a larger amount of money at one time, for a particular project. As a group of thirty women, we organized to take turns pooling our money. Each week each person would put in $100, and at the end of the week all the money would go to one member of the group. The next week the same thing happened, but the money would go to a different person. Once the members completed the whole circuit and started around again, it was done in reverse order, so the last person became the first to receive the collected amount. At the time, business was good and we made profits. I could put aside $300 a week. When it was my turn to have the *ristourne*, I could get $3,000 at once. And since I went last, when it came my turn, I would have another $3,000 at the end of the next week.

To travel to South Africa we just asked for information at the embassy and from people who had been there, and off we went. Doing business there I discovered an important thing: they have a sales tax that does not apply to foreigners. When you present your purchase receipts at the airport, they will reimburse you the 14 percent you paid as tax, but at the airport it is too late to use the money. The secret is to do business where they mark the sales tax clearly. We talked with those factories, and they refunded the tax to us so that we could buy more merchandise. I made a lot of trips to South Africa. Then China began pirating the South African styles and selling at a lower price, and the South African factory went under.

I also went to Morocco, to Casablanca. I had seen that West African–owned shops in Brazza offered articles from Morocco that sold well. I found an address, went to the embassy, and asked questions—the same as for South

Africa—and it worked out. I went twice with two of my sisters. When I was elected associate director of the women's department of our denomination, I had no salary so I had to continue to make baby linens and sell them. I also taught my daughters Bitota Nelly and Katanda Nana to sew the sheets. When I had to be away from home on church business, they continued the work and took the sheets to the merchants in Kinshasa, and so had money to buy food for the household.

THE DREAM OF A NEW HOUSE

With my commercial success I could afford to buy a piece of property and build a new home. We were living in Matete, one of the major divisions of Kinshasa, a city of about ten million or more. Within each urban division there are a number of communes or local political entities. Tatu Mukuna's house was in Kinda, one of the poorest parts of Matete; the property I bought was in Kunda, a somewhat better-off commune. When Tatu Mukuna's oldest daughter, Kabata, divorced her husband and came back to us, she made a lot of trouble in the house. She said that it belonged to her. According to tradition, it is the children of the first marriage who inherit; my children were in second place. I said to myself, "Given the way Kabata is behaving now, if I died my children would not have a home." I prayed as I did my business, and God truly blessed me.

Before the first "Pillage" in 1991 I had enough money to buy a property. I always kept a little money ($10) with me. The rest I saved; I kept it in our house, the way many people did because even if you had a bank account it was difficult to withdraw money. I kept my money in different currencies that I could not easily spend: sometimes Congo-Brazzaville francs, sometimes US dollars, Swiss francs, German marks, Belgian francs. When I wanted to use the money, I converted it all into dollars. At the time houses cost 200,000 zaires; a zaire was two dollars. However, the government had just devalued the currency and issued new zaires. I told Tatu Mukuna, "We can look for a house to buy." The first one he found was too far from Matete; so was the second. I said, "How can we get the children to church from that place?" I prayed that God would give us a property very close to the church. But Tatu Mukuna insisted on this house, and I said, "Okay." We got our cash together and started off to the make the purchase.

"The Pillages"

President Mobutu's reputation with respect to human rights was not good. By 1990 he was coming under increasing pressure, both at home and abroad, for his dictatorial rule and especially his abuse of power to enrich himself. Previously, he had benefited from the Cold War because he aligned himself with the West, but after the fall of the USSR he was no longer important. So in April 1990 Mobutu announced the end of the one-party state, and soon political parties formed and registered, including the Union for Democracy and Social Progress (UDPS) led by Etienne Tshisekedi (father of Félix Tshisekedi, the new president in 2019). In April 1991 Mobutu accepted the idea of a national conference, which finally began in August. However, it only lasted a week, and when it was dissolved the people were very disappointed. This was the situation when unrest broke out. (Colloquially, this is called "The Pillage" since it had a significant enough impact to become a temporal marker in the local culture.)

On the night of September 23, 1991, members of the armed forces began rioting because they wanted a salary increase and to be paid on time. They started at the Kinshasa airport, but the looting spread into the city, especially the better residential areas, all through the next day. After the soldiers had done, the local people joined in. Altogether it lasted about thirty-six hours, more than one hundred people were killed, and property destruction was estimated at $1 billion. French and Belgian soldiers came to evacuate foreigners. Then, through the month of October, similar riots erupted in other big cities of Congo, and about one hundred fifty more people were killed.[1]

IN THE MIDST OF THE PILLAGE

It happened that this was the first day of the Pillage, but we did not know that when we left home to buy our new house. As we were driving out of Matete (our district of Kinshasa), the people we saw told us that there was rioting and

---

[1]Emizet François Kisangani and F. Scott Bobb, "Introduction," in *Historical Dictionary of the Democratic Republic of the Congo*, 3rd ed. African Historical Dictionaries 112 (Lanham, MD: Scarecrow, 2010), lxxiii-lxxiv.

we should return home. We did not know how serious it was, so I said to Tatu Mukuna, "Okay, drop me off in the city. I have lots of merchandise there, and if they steal that, we are finished." He drove back home, and I went on with other people on foot. It was terrible—much worse than I had imagined. We were in danger of death. We would run, then hide when shots were fired. When they stopped shooting, we got up and went on. At the market I first had to get past the soldiers. But inside—it was terrible! There were corpses underfoot. I ran quickly to our place and found my sister; she had left in a taxi very early in the morning before the shooting began. She cried, "Eek. Yaya (big sister), how did you get here?" We knelt down and began to pray.

We were behind a big store where there was a lot of space to keep merchandise. The store had toilets and showers in the back. I asked my sister, "Where are the packages?" They were big packages and lots of them—almost forty. They belonged to me, my three sisters, my cousin, and his wife. My sister said, "There in the toilets and showers." When she had arrived, she had given money to the guard and the sentry at our place; they put boards across the toilets and showers and piled the packages of merchandise on top, and then closed the doors to hide the goods.

There were also big trucks behind the store, and we hid under them and began to pray because there was a lot of noise of gunfire. Bang-bang-bang-bang. The whole day the military and the civil guard looted and broke into shops; toward evening the populace began. We planned to stay through the night, but the guard and sentry said, "No, go back home. Give us $100, and we will guard your things." My sister had $100, and she gave it to them. My cousin's wife had also come: the three of us were there. We got down on our knees and prayed; then we left the market on foot to go to Matete. We saw people with their loot, the military in their vehicles plowing down the streets. When I finally got home, Tatu Mukuna called all the children and we prayed. Next morning we got up very early to go back to town and move our merchandise.

BUYING A NEW PROPERTY

After the Pillage, people were selling the things they had taken, but we did not buy any of the loot. Then, when the situation was truly calm again, we brought out our merchandise to sell. We were worried that it was not safe to keep our cash, so we said, "We must buy the property." My husband went looking again.

"I have seen a house in a very good place, but it is expensive." It was. I borrowed the last 50,000 zaires from my sisters. We bought the property, and I paid for all the documents. We went to the city hall, changed the names on the deed, and followed all the process to obtain ownership papers for the property. Then it was necessary to give notice to the people living on the land. They delayed for almost a year because of a conflict in their family, but finally they left.

God has always helped me in my business. To build this house I spent a great deal of money because the foundation was very deep. I made a *ristourne* with the other women and asked if I might have the collected money for three weeks in a row; they agreed and I paid them back. That gave me enough money at one time to start building. (I also bought a Volkswagen car-bus for my business so that Tatu Mukuna would not have to keep driving me places.)

BANDITS IN THE OLD HOUSE

We bought the new property at the beginning of 1992 and were in the process of building, but we had to move before we finished our new house because bandits attacked us in the old house. While I was doing business, I had money, I wore gold jewelry, and we had a good life. However, in the difficult situation of high inflation, gangs of thieves became an increasing problem. Though we lived in a poor neighborhood, our house was nicer than most because we had improved it and built an annex where our sons Eddy and Mukendi and Tatu Mukuna's younger brother, Gaston, and his son were living.

The gang came one night at 2:00 a.m. They began to shoot, and the neighborhood was paralyzed with fear, so no one went outdoors. Tatu Mukuna and I were in our bedroom. I said, "We must not be afraid. Just cry 'Help!'" Tatu Mukuna tried to go out, but I stopped him because if he had left our room the thieves would have killed him. The bandits came into the house. I saw Eddy and the others come from the annex, but Gaston stayed near the door of the house and the thieves shot him. I was at the window and could see him fall and told Tatu Mukuna. He said, "I must go out." But I held him back; he was a heavy man at that time, but God gave me strength to hold him back and block the door of our room. I watched from the window, and the thieves did not shoot there.

When we cried "Help!" a choir came. I had the habit of inviting our choir to come to our house and sing as a thanksgiving to God, and I gave money to support their work. This choir was on a retreat close enough to our house to hear my cry. They said, "Oh, it is the voice of Maman Monique." The neighbors had stayed in their houses for fear of attracting the thieves' attention, but the choral group came running. The thieves ran away; the choir did not chase them because they saw a man on the ground, bleeding, and they hurried to try to save him. When I had checked to see that the thieves were gone, I let Tatu Mukuna go out, but I put all our children in a room and locked the door so they would not see these terrible things. (The children included Eddy, the oldest at eleven, down to Moise, who was not quite one year old.) Tatu Mukuna began crying when he saw his brother. Gaston was not dead so I said, "No, we must take him to the hospital." But Gaston died on the way to the hospital.

It was God who saved us in all this experience. He saved my husband, he saved my children, he saved me. The thieves did not take my things; I had my money and my jewelry. But after that I sold my jewelry. I no longer wore gold jewelry, and I understood that when you live in a poor context it is better to be like everyone else.

THE MOVE TO A NEW HOUSE

We were still living in Tatu Mukuna's house, but the children were afraid. They could no longer sleep. Our new home was not ready, but there were two small houses on the property so we moved there for the children's safety. We continued work on our home, but we never were able to complete it because in 1995 I began my ministry at the church's Department of Women and Families, and I did not have much money any more. We had finished the children's part with a living room, three bedrooms, and a shower. The other part was not finished; it included a living room, our bedroom, and a shower, but the kitchen, dining room, storerooms, and other things we had planned were not done.

From 2003 on, Tatu Mukuna began wanting to sell a part of the property in order to complete the house. I thought we could rent out one part of the property. In 2004 I agreed to sell one of the little houses on the edge of the property. Then he wanted to sell the whole thing and buy somewhere else, but I said, "No. Don't you dare." But later, in 2010, after I was fired from the department, he was so upset that I agreed to sell part of the land because I thought it was better to sell property than cause him so much distress. He was afraid . . . maybe it was a sense of his coming death that made him so anxious. So we sold part of the property, but the money was not enough to pay for completing the construction of the part we kept. Then Tatu Mukuna died, and the house was still not finished. I would like to be able to finish it properly, but we still live there, and we share the space with others in need.

PART TWO

GROWTH

A capable wife who can find?
  She is far more precious than jewels.
The heart of her husband trusts in her,
  and he will have no lack of gain. . . .
She rises while it is still night,
  and provides food for her household
  and tasks for her servant-girls. . . .
She opens her hands to the poor,
  and reaches out her hands to the needy. . . .
She makes linen garments and sells them;
  she supplies the merchant with sashes.
Strength and dignity are her clothing,
  and she laughs at the time to come.
She opens her mouth with wisdom,
  and the teaching of kindness is on her tongue.
She looks well to the ways of her household,
  and does not eat the bread of idleness.
Her children rise up and call her happy;
  her husband too, and he praises her. . . .
  A woman who fears the LORD is to be praised.
Give her a share in the fruit of her hands,
  and let her works praise her in the city gates.

PROVERBS 31:10-11, 14, 24-28, 30-31

INTERLUDE

*An Introduction to Women in the
Tradition and the Church in Congo*

MARIE BALENGELA WAS FOURTEEN; her groom was thirty. She came
from the rural Kasai and had only a primary education (she did not speak
French); he had a university degree in economics and lived in Kinshasa. The
two families made the arrangements, and the two young people had no choice.
His family paid $800, two goats, a complete set of clothes for her father, two
pieces of super-wax material worth $150 for her mother, a big cooking pot and
a big bowl, a ten kg sack of salt, and four chickens. Her father sent her to her
husband; for about two years he tried to educate his wife. But she began to
have children very soon, and, being busy with them and housekeeping, she
could not learn as quickly as her husband wanted. So he started to beat her
and treat her like a disobedient child. In eighteen years of marriage she had
eight children and suffered his continued disapproval and threats; sometimes
he deprived her of food. He also took a second wife to suit himself.

If it takes a village to raise a child, it also takes a community to be a woman.
No African girl's life is separate from the women around her. Every African
woman's experience is interwoven in the family and community. We define
ourselves by our families. We also define ourselves by the women who live
beside us, who trudge with us down to the stream to bring back water, who
help us or call on us for help, who share our Bible study or choir—the women
we see at the market or talk with on the street, who buy our doughnuts or
come to visit us in a time of grief.

Women are the support and strength of most communities and most
churches in Congo, yet they have usually had to struggle to have their own

worth recognized. Traditionally, the primary value of women has been their ability to bear children and feed and care for the family, and women have also accepted this. They have normally had little to no control over their own destinies, marriage being one of the key points in which their futures have been decided for them. Now, however, while never rejecting the importance of this domestic sphere, at least some Congolese women have imagined and sought to engage the church and their society in other, sometimes less conventional, ways. There are women who understand that girls have a right to choose, yet there are still parents who continue the old way, and that is why we go on fighting. Whether within the tradition or in modern society, girls and women encounter many kinds of disrespect and violence in the course of their daily lives—yet they have made remarkable contributions, including "nudging along" change.

Before continuing with my own story line, I want to introduce you to the lives and courage of some of my sisters.

Family Systems in Congo

There are three family structures in Africa: matriarchal, matrilineal, and patriarchal. In Congo there are very few matriarchal groups, in which women hold the leadership. There are significantly more matrilineal ones, in which descent is reckoned through the mother but control is still in male hands, those of her brother. In this case, a man cares for his sister's children, not his own; his biological children are the responsibility of his wife's family. The patriarchal system, in which men are the authority and women leave their families of origin to live in their husband's family, is by far the most common. Thus, although there are different ways of identifying lineage, control remains in the hands of men in the great majority of families and communities. Patriarchal Judeo-Christian traditions have reinforced the existing cultural bias.

WOMEN, TRADITION, THE FAMILY, AND MARRIAGE

Marriage was traditionally arranged by the two families, often without consulting the couple-to-be. Girls would normally be married between twelve and fourteen years old, but sometimes parents would arrange a marriage when the girl was a baby. Today there are more and more young people who refuse these arrangements, sometimes successfully, often not, and this causes a great deal of conflict.

In a traditional marriage the dowry is very important; the payment of money and goods is not seen as buying a wife but is given to her family as a sign of appreciation for rearing her. Wealthy diamond merchants, who are often polygamists, may regard the dowry as a purchase price, but 80 percent of the population sees it as a sign of love. Children are wealth so the dowry is also understood as repaying the girl's family for the loss of the children she will bear since in patriarchal contexts they belong to her husband's family. A girl's dowry goes to her family; sometimes it may be passed on intact as the dowry for a brother or cousin's wife, as was the intention of Maman Mado's uncle in the following story (as told by herself in 2015). Traditional dowry gifts in the Kasai were heavy copper crosses or goats, but today cash also is given and the kinds of objects have greatly increased. In fact, there is currently a huge inflation in dowries. The girl's family may demand money (in Kinshasa, $500-$2,000) and oil, salt, milk, and peanuts, pots and pans, TV and radio, and more, plus a long list of clothing for the parents. Traditionally, the girl was supposed to be a virgin at marriage, and the groom would bring an extra goat to give her mother for his virgin bride. Today, there are many different circumstances that compromise this ideal: drugs, the demand by the fiancé or boyfriend for relations before marriage, and especially poverty—poor girls will finance their educations by becoming the girlfriend of an older well-off married man.

Property in Marriage

In traditional society, if a couple divorces, their property might be divided according to the parties who brought it into the marriage, to be reclaimed by the original family in certain circumstances. Western colonial systems based on the idea of a nuclear family gave all ownership to the father, with the understanding that his wife and children would inherit. That has often come to be (mis)interpreted to mean a man's family takes everything, leaving the widow nothing—more destitute than in the past.

MADO: I am called Ngombe Mukala Mado. I was born in 1960 in the Kasai in a family of eleven children, five boys and six girls. I was the oldest of the girls. I did primary school through the sixth year. My father's older brother would receive my dowry so he wanted me to marry young. He began to send men to marry me, but each time I hid in the garden. So my father told my uncle, "You see, she is still very young to marry; be patient for a while. After some years we will marry her off." That is how I was able to continue my studies and finish secondary school in East Kasai at the Lycée Mobutu, run by Catholic Sisters of Charity from Canada.

In 1974 a new governor was appointed for our province. He began visiting all the villages, including ours. The officials welcomed him; we girls sang for him, and our director gave me a bouquet of flowers to present to him. That afternoon the call came for me to go to the director's office. I found her with the mayor, who said, "It was you who gave the governor the flowers? We have decided that since he will be spending the night here we must find him a young virgin with clean hands." I said, "What?!" He did not back off. I looked at the director to defend me, but she said nothing. The mayor said, "You will be the guest of honor. I will do the introduction myself, and you can have whatever you ask." You can imagine how astonished I was. He said, "Go back and study until 7 p.m., and when you come into the dining room they will come to get you."

I had a very good friend named Margarite, who was several years older. During the afternoon break I found her and explained why they had called me to the office. "What am I going to do?" She said, "Wait, I have an idea. My grandparents live in town; when the day students leave, we will go out with them and go to my grandparents." I said, "Merci beaucoup." At 7 p.m. I hurried to the door of Margarite's classroom, and we left with day students. The next day, when we came back to school, everyone wanted to know where we had been. The director asked, "Where were you?" I said, "We spent the night outside the school." She said, "You talked with the governor (agreed to be with him)." I said, "No, it was not I. It was you who talked with the governor. I am a little girl; I was afraid. That is why I hid." After that, the director was mean to me, but since there were other teachers who liked me, I was able to complete my exams and move up year by year to finish. But to use girls like objects . . . that is violence.

I graduated with the state diploma, but I did not have a chance to go to university because our family did not see any use in it. So I was obliged to marry. My husband and I lived in Kinshasa. After five years of marriage, my husband died in an accident. He was the chief flight attendant of an airplane, and it blew up. I did not even have his body—they just told me he was dead. It was really a shock for me. Then there was the funeral. Then my in-laws told me to sign the release so that they could take my husband's bank accounts. I refused. They said, "She refused; we must make her suffer. This woman is educated; let's take her diploma and her marriage certificate." But when they were conspiring to do this, one of my brothers found out and he came to tell me. He asked, "Where is your diploma?" I told him. He wanted the key to the house, but my in-laws had taken it. A neighbor had a key, and my brother got it and took my diploma and marriage certificate. When my brothers-in-law came, they searched the whole house. They pillaged and cleaned it out but could not find my documents. My children were all that I had left. There were three of them, and I was expecting a fourth.

A month after the funeral my older brother in Mbuji Mayi sent me a ticket to come back to the Kasai. I got to the airport with my children, but all my in-laws followed me there because they wanted to take my children away. The airport authorities questioned me, and I said, "No, I did not steal the children; they are my own children. Their father is dead, and there is no way to support them here so I am returning home." They let me go. But my in-laws in Kinshasa informed their relatives in Kasai, and when I arrived they came to find me. They wanted me to marry one of my husband's brothers; there were about eight. The men lined up in front of me and said, "Choose." I looked at them but did not answer. They said, "You haven't chosen one? Are you stubborn?" When I refused, one of my brothers-in-law took me to court. When we got there, the judge said, "Your husband is there. You were angry, weren't you, and went to your family? But now your husband is asking for you. Why don't you return home?" I said, "My husband is asking for me? Were you with him?" The judge said, "Your husband is here." That worried me: What did he mean? What had he seen? I said to myself, "My husband is dead. Maybe it is a ghost, or he has transformed himself?"

The judge pointed to my brother-in-law, "There he is." I said, "No, that man is not my husband." The judge was surprised, "But who is he?" I said, "Ask him. My husband was not named Louis." My brother-in-law said, "Her husband was my little brother. But the day he wanted to marry I was the one who paid the dowry. Now since her husband is dead, the woman reverts to me." The judge said, "That is a problem. If you want her to come back with you as your wife, talk with her. If she accepts you, fine. But if she refuses, the state can't force her." My brother-in-law said, "No, it was my dowry. Since I paid the dowry, she must come back to me. If she does not, I will call down killing thunder on her!" (That is a form of magic.) The judge tried to reason with my brother-in-law. "Monsieur, if you provide the money and buy trousers for your brother, whose trousers are they?" My brother-in-law said, "My brother's trousers. But the cases are not the same." The judge said, "It is the same." He was very clear.

So my brother-in-law said, "We must make her suffer. How can we steal her children?" They kidnapped my children—they were little kids. Whenever I tried to see them, my in-laws stopped me and shut the children in the house. Overwhelmed by all this, I went back to my family. I gave birth to my baby boy. A year and a half later he became sick with measles, but we did not know how to treat the disease and he died.

Then I decided to return to Kinshasa and plunged into business, but that did not last. I went to work in a center for street children for several years. Then I got more specialized training: one course was how to teach prevention of sexually transmitted diseases and HIV/AIDS, one was how to help children catch up with their grade level, and one was to work with children in difficult situations. That is how I came to this nonprofit that Maman Monique leads, where I work with orphans, unmarried mothers, people who have been abandoned—because I was left a young widow. My children: my in-laws did not educate my daughter but married her off by force at age fourteen. She had two sons and then her husband died. She was still young so they made her marry again, but this time it did not work out. She had three children, but it ended in divorce. Then she came to me with five little children, and I am working to support all the family.

MAMAN MESU: A PIONEER IN THE PRESBYTERIAN CHURCH

Maman Mesu was born at Luebo in West Kasai about 1924. She grew up there and was able to go to the Presbyterian primary school. She also learned from the missionary women as they organized work with women. She married very young and at first could not have children. When they did come, a number died of polio in a widespread epidemic. One daughter, Micheline Kamba, survived, but both of her legs were affected, and she could only walk with crutches—she could not even stand alone. People with disabilities were usually disregarded, and it was extremely difficult for them to go to school at all. But Maman Mesu was determined. She gave her daughter the confidence that she could go to school just like anyone else, and she fought to enable her daughter to study. Micheline did primary school, then secondary, then university. She even completed a doctorate in theology in South Africa with a scholarship from the World Council of Churches. She married—again, something that was not common for a person with a disability—and teaches now at the Protestant University of Congo.

But that is getting ahead of the story. To understand Maman Mesu's story, you must understand the history of the Presbyterian church in Kinshasa. Leopoldville/Kinshasa, the capital of Congo, has always been a magnet for people from other parts of the country. Over the years, people from the Kasai had migrated to the capital, and many of them were Presbyterians. In the ecumenical spirit of the Protestant missions, they could and did worship with the Baptists, who were the main denomination in the area. Eventually, when a large number of Presbyterians had come to Kinshasa, both Congolese and American missionary leaders agreed that it was time to establish their own denomination, and the local Baptists supported this. The Presbyterian Church of Kinshasa (CPK) was officially incorporated in 1960, and Pastor Tshimungu Mayela Joseph became the general secretary.

Presbyterian Churches and the Church of Christ in Congo

In the 1950s American Presbyterians in the Kasai had been increasingly sharing leadership responsibilities with Congolese Christians, and in 1960 they recognized the autonomy of the Congolese Presbyterian churches. There were two, the original center in the Kasai and a second in Kinshasa. The main reason was practical—it was simply too difficult to operate a highly participatory church government when the communities were separated by a significant geographic distance with very poor means of transportation. For the next decade, church and mission worked together; educational and medical programs required continued international support in both finances and personnel. By 1970 the mission had turned over its property to the church.

The Protestant missions had long worked together as the Congo Protestant Council and in the newly independent country this was reorganized as the Church of Christ in Congo (CCC). At the national level the CCC has a bishop, who has often been on very good terms with Mobutu, or later his successor. Each denomination in this federated church is called a community—Baptist, Methodist, Presbyterian, Disciples of Christ, Mennonite, and others—and each retains its own internal organization and self-government.   (continued)

These denominations usually have partnership ties with the overseas churches from which the first missionaries came. The Congolese determine what specific needs they have, whether of finances or personnel and propose these to the partners. For example, schools and hospitals cannot be maintained as before without financial support, and sometimes specialized personnel are needed. A third area where funds have been important is development work, such as the kind of projects that became a hallmark of Maman Monique's ministries. A decline in the national social services, especially since the 1980s, has led to "increased reliance on church-supported institutions. Moreover, by the 1990s and into the early 2000s, many schools, hospitals, and entire mission stations [have been] run entirely by Congolese staff, which sought heroically in some cases to cope with lack of funds and the needs of a population suffering increasing economic hardship."[1]

Among those who helped organize the CPK were Tatu Kamba with his wife, Maman Mesu. He was a well-educated elder from Luebo, who became a pastor, and she was elected to lead the women's work. They were an exceptional couple. Tatu Kamba was very helpful to his wife; he was well organized, and he was happy to teach her and accompany her in her work—which was a very good thing because Maman Mesu really began to change things. This was a period when women did not even have the right to speak; a woman chosen to lead the women had to take orders from the male leaders of the church. Women could not initiate anything.

But Maman Mesu stood up and got things going. She began by organizing classes to teach women about health issues, housekeeping, and other domestic matters. Then she saw that women needed a center where they could hold their activities and learn new things. After the parish of Matete moved to worship in a new building, Maman Mesu persuaded the CPK to let her use the old one for her Women's Center. The building was simply a large hall, with open spaces for windows and a dirt floor. There was no protective fence around the property, and it had become a kind of trash dump for people

---

[1]Emizet François Kisangani and F. Scott Bobb, *Historical Dictionary of the Democratic Republic of the Congo*, 3rd ed. African Historical Dictionaries 112 (Lanham, MD: Scarecrow, 2010), "Missionaries," 361.

passing by. The women got to work to clean it up and began to add some rooms behind the hall where participants from a distance could sleep when there was a workshop. But the church authorities saw this as an opportunity. They began to rent out the rooms to their relatives and friends and let a carpenter set up shop in the front courtyard. Consequently, the women did not really control the property, though they used the main hall.

Maman Mesu started literacy classes. She realized that it was hard for women to be leaders in the church because they did not have enough education. So she asked for a Sunday when women would preach in the church, and the collection that day would go to finance their activities. The church leaders—pastors, elders, deacons (all male)—refused. They said, "The women want to take men's places; they want to become men!" But Maman Mesu was not discouraged. She took the matter to the president of the church. "I am not going to tire of doing this until you give me satisfaction. Even if you chase me away, I will spend the night outside your door. I will keep coming back."

Finally, the men accepted that women could preach one Sunday per year—but many men did not want to come to church that day. Maman Mesu continued her work and encouraged the other women: "You have to speak"—it was a way to claim the rights of women. One time the men organized a special offering for one of their own projects on the women's Sunday. Led by Maman Mesu, the women informed the authorities that if they carried through on this extra offering, the women would all go and hold their worship in the stadium—and the church would not get any of their offerings. The authorities backed down and said, "No more special offerings on the women's day." They also ordered all the male ministers to be present that day as an example to the rest of the men.

That was not the end of it. Maman Mesu wrote to the ruling body of the church about women's ordination, demanding that women be allowed to be elders and deacons. The synod said she wanted to create a women's revolution and called her all kinds of names. But she did not give up. She fought, she negotiated, and finally the church agreed to ordain women elders and deacons. This was possible because Maman Mesu had won over some of the men, starting with her husband, and because she convinced the wives of some other pastors to ask for the same thing. Finally, after four years of struggle, the men accepted, and women elders and deacons were ordained. When they were elected, she gathered the women elders and deacons to teach them: "You must not go the meetings and just sit quietly watching, accepting everything. When they say, 'Who is for?' 'Who is against?' raise your hand. You must speak, give your arguments. If you see something that is not right, raise your hand and say, 'No, that is not good.'"

However, Maman Mesu did not stop there. She said, "We want women in the CPK to be able to study theology." First she had to raise the consciousness of women so that they would want to study theology. Then they had to have places to serve. When Maman Nzeba had finished her theological degree, the men refused to ordain her, but Maman Mesu went to talk to the authorities of the national church (CCC) and the denomination (CPK), and Pastor Nzeba was ordained. After that, Maman Mesu went on to help more women who had been admitted to seminaries seek to become pastors. So now we have women pastors because of this remarkable woman.

There were a number of experiences that helped Maman Mesu do what she did. One was that in the course of her work directing the CPK women's department she was able to travel outside Congo. When she saw what women in other countries were doing, she asked, "Why can't we do the same?" Another reason Maman Mesu developed her ideas and independence was that she was part of the National Federation of Protestant Women from its foundation in 1963. Working with other women in different and wider contexts gave Maman Mesu new ideas.

THE NATIONAL FEDERATION OF PROTESTANT WOMEN

The woman who started the National Federation of Protestant Women was called Marie Mathie. She got an education because her parents worked with the Belgians. She studied nursing and went to work in President Mobutu's hospital and served as one of the nurses who traveled with him. On one of these occasions she was in Nigeria and saw how the women there were organized, and how they not only worshiped together but also addressed the problems of women.

So Maman Marie Mathie brought the ideas back to Congo. She got women together and explained what she had learned. The women agreed and set out to raise the consciousness of other women. Church leaders heard about this and said, "That woman is a prostitute. She is ruining the other women." But Maman Marie was not discouraged. She said, "Let's continue to meet to pray and to identify women's problems and seek solutions."

One idea was to make a kind of uniform by printing the Federation's dress wrap as a means of evangelization. The motto on the material was "A Christian Woman Is a Light," shown with a small kerosene lantern (the typical lamp). It was printed in the major languages: Lingala, Tshiluba, Swahili, Kikongo, and French (and later English). Maman Marie and Maman Ngoyi <u>Kanyinda</u> took the project to President Mobutu. They made an occasion of it, with a women's choir, and he was very pleased to see Congolese women showing such intelligent initiative. (He probably wanted to show off his country's success to other African leaders.) So President Mobutu provided some money, and the wraps were printed. All the women loved these wraps and bought them. (However, men objected to what was written and insisted that they also were Christians. After that, the motto was changed to: "A Christian Is a Light.") The wrap was so popular that it was pirated. The Federation produced them in a Congolese company and sold each for twenty-five dollars, but some merchants had cheaper copies made in China and sold them for fifteen dollars. So the Federation took the merchants to court and won. They had to pay a very large fine and an annual fee, which the Federation has used for repairs of its center. There was also the challenge of printing the wraps more cheaply so that the Federation's product would be competitive.

"Wraps" and African Dress

Traditional dress for Congolese women is composed of several large pieces of material that are used as skirts and wrapped around the body in various ways; the outer piece is often used to carry a baby tied to the woman's back. Usually these wrapped skirts are worn with a simple blouse of the same material (no collar, short sleeves). The influence of Western styles has led to some changes. City women often make the same African-print material into long dresses like the ones Maman Monique is wearing in the photos in this book. The basis is still a piece of cloth about four to six meters long that is usually called a "wrap"; the "super wax" print is the finest quality and most expensive. Dowries often include two pieces of material for the bride's mother so that she can choose her own dress style.

The National Federation of Protestant Women includes women of all Protestant denominations, as a visible sign of Christian unity. I became actively involved in 1995 and in 1998 was elected national secretary, as I will explain later. Today there are branches of the Federation in all the provinces of Congo. When the war broke out in the east in 1996, it was thanks to this women's organization that we knew what was going on there, and it is as part of the Federation that I visited there. The majority of the people in churches are women, and mobilizing them in the Federation has made the church more widely known.

The first presidents of the Federation wanted to create a center where women could hold retreats and training courses of various kinds. They organized a collection among the women, and President Mobutu also contributed, to buy a large property near Kinshasa for a retreat center. Local groups of the Federation meet one day a year, and at intervals there is a national congress. The congresses began in 1967 and are now held every five or six years, during which there are elections for the executive officers. There are 200 (sometimes there have been as many as 250) women at the congress; we meet in Kinshasa for about four days. The executive committee of president, vice president, and secretary, and their assistants, meet every year or every two years to receive and act on reports from all the provinces. They also visit the provinces to do various kinds of training.

At the beginning of the 1990s, during the Decade of Churches in Solidarity with Women, the Federation wanted to raise the visibility and influence of women in the church by setting criteria for leadership in the Department of Women and Families that each CCC community (denomination) has. "We need young women with a good education who are able to express themselves in French, and who are involved in the work of the church, who can travel alone." Mamu Mesu understood the reasoning because of her own experience. Coming from the Kasai, she spoke Tshiluba, and she had learned Lingala in Kinshasa, but she did not know French. Girls in her generation simply did not have that opportunity. When she traveled on church business, a translator had to accompany her, and she recognized that this was a handicap for the work. Many of the women leaders at the time did not want to be replaced by younger women, but Mamu Mesu returned to her community and got to work to implement the Federation's recommendations. She gathered the women of the different levels of the church, she went to talk with the leaders of the church, she began a poll to find a successor—and in many places my name came up.

My New Role in
Church Leadership

In my local congregation and presbytery I saw many poor women so I began teaching them income-generating activities. I worked with all the women leaders of the congregations. Each parish would send two or three women for the training in knitting, crocheting, raising chickens, making doughnuts. They came one day a week; later we went to twice a week because so many women were interested. The project grew; more women came. Women who had known nothing began to knit or crochet baby booties; they began to sell things like doughnuts and accumulate a little money. This was the only presbytery in the CPK that had a visible women's activity.

At first we met in a center in the parish of Lokoro. When we were forced to leave the center, I told the women, "We must not be discouraged. We can sit on the veranda of the church." At the Lokoro congregation we moved the benches out onto the veranda, but the leaders closed the church and would not let us use the benches. We had no place. I said, "We can spread cloth on the grass under the tree and work there." When Maman Mesu heard about that, she said, "The Women's Center belongs to the women. Come and work here."

I grew up in the Presbyterian church in the Kasai, and when I moved to Kinshasa I became active there. It was central to my life and my family's life. We participated in many ways besides Sunday worship: in choirs and prayer groups, helping at times of death and loss, being involved on a daily basis. That is why I was so determined that we would always live close enough to walk to church. Over the years more and more of my time was devoted to serving the church in specific offices. That introduced me to new challenges in a patriarchal world.

My primary activities have been serving as an elder in my congregation and working with women at all levels: parish, presbytery, denomination, national church. Beginning in 1982 I held various offices: secretary of the women's group at the local or presbytery level, president of the women's committee in the Presbytery of Matete. That is where I began creating income-generating activities for women. When Maman Mesu heard that we had no place to meet, she opened the Women's Center for us. At that point people were living in the center, but Maman Mesu found us a room. I asked her if we could raise chickens there, and she agreed. Then we needed someone to care for them. There was a woman in my congregation who was completely alone and destitute. She could care for chickens at the center and also have a home. Maman Mesu welcomed her. So we made cages and bought chicken food—and we had lots of chickens. That is how, when Maman Mesu began to look for a woman to direct the denomination's Department of Women and Families, it was only in the Presbytery of Matete that she found a woman already engaged in the work.

ASSOCIATE DIRECTOR OF THE DEPARTMENT AND
WORK WITH MAMAN MESU, 1995–2000

Maman Mesu talked with the older women in each presbytery about who could direct the women, and everyone gave my name. So she came to talk with me. At that time I was doing my business with my sewing atelier, and traveling to buy and import goods to sell. She said, "Maman Misenga [we spoke Tshiluba so she always used my Tshiluba name], are you ready to stop traveling for your business and do the church's work?" I said, "If it is God's will, I will do it." She said that we should pray.

At the time, Maman Mesu was nearly seventy and was planning to retire. But two weeks before the election for her younger and more highly educated successor, male church leaders began to say to her, "You must stay for now. If you leave, the new one is young and she will not pay attention to you older women." Maman Mesu came to see me. She said, "The president and the church treasurer have said that it is better for me to stay. They think it will not be good for the church and there will be problems. Would you agree to work with me as a second director?" (She said that, not "assistant director," which would have been the normal title.) I said, "I repeat again, Maman, if it is God's will, I cannot refuse." But I asked her a question, "Is the church a place of conflicts so that there will be problems? I did not expect that women would argue about the position." She said, "Oh, there are many wives of the church's leaders who would like to have it. To keep the peace, would you agree to work with me?" I said, "If it is God's will, I cannot refuse. Let's continue to pray."

Education, Gender, and Power

Part of the background of this conflict with the leaders' wives is the character of the educational system in Congo, with primary school in local Bantu languages and secondary or higher in French, and part is gender discrimination. In Maman Mesu's generation, it was an achievement for girls to complete primary. In Maman Monique's, it was an achievement to complete secondary, and a much rarer accomplishment to complete university. The wives of the church leaders were mostly of Maman Mesu's generation and, like her, could not function independently in French. Boys had more opportunity for education than girls so the pastors of Maman Mesu's generation knew French and usually had attended a secondary school. They got some pastoral training but not a regular seminary or university-level degree. A young woman like Maman Monique with a university education was obviously a threat to the older women and, as would become apparent over time, to the older pastors.

Elections were held, and I was elected as Maman Mesu's assistant, but this did not please everyone. The authorities decided there should be a new committee of women who would oversee the women's work. These were mostly the wives of the church leaders; the president was Maman Lusamba, the wife of Pastor Tshimungu (the head of the denomination). They created this structure in order to keep the authorities' wives in power, which I saw as an injustice because they did not meet the Federation's criteria to be the director. I accepted the position of associate director because many people wanted me, and Maman Mesu liked me very much. She had spent a long time without anyone to help her. We consulted regularly at the end of the day, but she left almost all the responsibility for directing the department to me.

However, lots of people were jealous of my work. They saw that the American partners liked me very much because of how I worked. I would make a proposal, and when there was a little money I would do the project. I used the money responsibly to complete the project, and the partners were attracted to that so they began to support the work. The CPK women's committee of church leaders' wives began to say to Maman Mesu, "You see, you don't count anymore; it is only Maman Misenga." They wanted to turn her against me, and at one point they succeeded. She was angry with me and went to Pastor Tshimungu to accuse me of doing things without her permission.

At that time Pastor Tshimungu was my strong advocate. He nominated me to attend church gatherings and workshops to represent the CPK. He defended me to Maman Mesu: "You should be happy that God has given you Maman Misenga. Everywhere we go in international reunions she contributes very well, and she also lives a moral life. Everyone congratulates me, 'You have found a young woman who works very well.'" Later, I talked privately with Maman Mesu, and she said, "No, Misenga, go on with the work. You must not rely on those women in the committee." We were back on very good terms, and we worked together well.

ACTIVITIES AT THE WOMEN'S CENTER OF THE CPK DEPARTMENT OF WOMEN AND FAMILIES

The Women's Center was not in good condition when I arrived. First, it was necessary to make the carpenter remove his shop and to get the people living in the center to move. That took about two months. Then it had to be enclosed. In the village it is common to have a little fence around one's compound, but in a big city, especially Kinshasa, this must be made of concrete blocks. In 1995 I was able to enclose the center. I had been given $5,000, and I was almost able to complete the work. I only needed $2,000 more. Doug Welch, the PC(USA) field representative and liaison, said, "They gave me a proposal for $15,000 to build the wall, and you did it for $7,000." I also put down floors and furnished the center. Later, after I became director in 2000, I added other buildings: classrooms and small rooms along the outer wall where we could sell our sewing school products. One means was a grant from the German embassy. I applied and received the money and began building. The church authorities were upset that the funds had not passed through the church, but I explained that I had applied on behalf of the Women's Center and so it came directly to me. Just to be safe, I hurried the project along. I asked Tatu Mukuna to go and buy the cement and other materials and bring all of it back before the church leaders could insist on our sharing the grant.

When I began work at the department, it was supposed to be training women in various things, but I did not find any organized program. There was not even a written plan. The only documentation was in the minutes of the CPK Synod when the center was established, which I found among Maman Mesu's papers after she died. She had done the kinds of training that the women missionaries had taught her, especially how to prevent or care for infections such as diarrhea (teaching about germs and hygiene). She worked with the church leaders and partners, but there was no sustained teaching activity at the center, and it was not equipped: no dishes or glasses, no chairs. We began to do training sessions for the women in the big central hall, and I got the necessary equipment.

We had already begun raising chickens, and later, when I was director, I added other animals. We began with two or three female rabbits and one male, and soon we had a hundred. Often I sold them to have money for the work; sometimes we used them for food at the center. Eventually, we also had ducks and even pigs. I bought seven ducks—and they multiplied: hundreds of ducks for sale. Our secretary, a young girl named Fifi Muya, was also a student in agronomy, and she became our vet. While we helped her continue her studies, Maman Antoinette became secretary, though Fifi continued to care for our animals. Because of her experience with us, she later got a good position in a Belgian organization that works in agronomy.

In Congo, in the village everyone can have space to make a field, but in the big cities there is not enough room. In 1996, Inge Sthreshley, one of our American church partners, began to do workshops on "house gardens." If a woman can find a corner of her property to plant something, she can contribute to feeding her family a good diet. I began a house garden at the center. Later, I organized a farm outside the city to grow things to eat and to sell. We could help poor women find a way to survive. With support from our partners, we gave the poorest women cassava from our fields, which they could make into a popular food and sell. The women still talk about that to this day.

Cassava—"Food"

The basic food in most parts of Congo (and beyond) comes from a root crop called cassava, which is so central to the diet that the name for this dish and the word for food may be identical—as in Tshiluba. After a considerable process of cleaning and curing, the cassava tubers are pounded into flour and prepared in various ways, as a kind of thick dough or sticky paste. Usually this "bread" is eaten with a dish made from the same plant's leaves, cooked in palm oil for a sauce. If some meat it available, it will be cooked in the sauce. In rural areas, subsistence farming provides cassava and corn; in urban areas, these must be bought. Cassava is almost pure starch; it contains no protein, so a diet of cassava is one reason for malnutrition. Beginning in the mid-twentieth century there have been intensive efforts to teach mothers the value of adding corn or soy flour to the cassava when they prepare food for their families.

Nutrition was another big project. I began my involvement with nutrition in my congregation about 1996. Walking home one day I saw a little boy about five years old who was clearly in bad health. I asked him where he lived, and he showed me. It was close to a little river, and the floor of the house was wet. His parents were also in bad health. I talked with them, "Your child is very thin." They said, "We don't have any work; we have nothing." They had sent the child to beg. I said, "Okay." I began to feed the family regularly. But when I went to their home, I saw another family, and I saw many children. So I said, "We could do something in our congregation." I invited the young women together. "We can each make a donation, buy corn and soy flour, make a recipe. There are many malnourished children, but if we all contribute, we can help them get well." The women accepted. However, it was one thing to agree to work, another to get the money.

We began to prepare the food and feed the children. Many children came! We could not feed all; we must take only the poorest—some children had had nothing to eat for two or three days. I took my pots and pans from home to the church. I gave money to buy flour. Then I said, "Since I am working at the center, it would be good to have a committee at church to look after this project." So I organized this work, we got together a committee, and nutrition became an established activity in the CPK. At first, things went well, but then there were conflicts so I decided that I had to create the nutrition program at the center. I got a woman who had nowhere to live to prepare the food for the children, and this job gave her a home. I went to visit one of the women whose congregation had begun a nutrition program—and when I saw the children, I cried. Every time I see malnourished children it hurts me so much. These children's hands shook when they tried to hold the cups of food—they did not have any plates. I had to do something.

On a visit to the United States in 2001, when I was in the Presbytery of East Virginia, PC(USA), I told them about the nutrition needs, and they asked me to write a grant proposal. Back in Congo I began doing the local part. I identified the congregations where the need was greatest and met with the CPK nutrition committee to raise consciousness about the problem. I asked the women to continue to make their contributions. Then I wrote the grant for $12,000, to buy chairs, refrigerators, pots, large covered water containers, plates, glasses, forks, corn, soy, and sugar. (The chairs were for the center; in the churches they could use benches.) The PC(USA) gave us the money. I called together the women who had begun nutrition work in their congregations and gave them equipment. I showed them how to mix the corn and soy flour to provide a healthy basic food. Everything was going well. We also planted moringa trees at the center. Moringa leaves are full of protein, and we used it at the center, putting crushed leaves in the children's soup. I organized training sessions to teach the women how to use the moringa, and when our trees grew enough we would cut off branches for the women to take and root near their houses.

We were feeding the children, but if children don't go to school, what will become of them tomorrow? In Congo education is not free, and many parents can't pay the fees, or buy uniforms and supplies. (In 2020 free primary education was announced, though there are still many fees.) If parents can't pay, the teachers can't teach because they also have to live. Also, many children are orphans, either lacking fathers, who usually have the only paying jobs, or lacking both parents.

So after we began the nutrition program I wanted to educate the orphans. First, I tried to raise consciousness: the church must help children have the abundant life that Jesus Christ promised us (John 10:10). Also, we wanted to address the gender issue: girls are marginalized so the majority of the children we serve are girls, although we also help boys. I invited the women to meet, and we planned how to equip the children because we needed money for supplies as well as tuition. We worked to find things to sell to raise money for the school fees. Maybe you look at the handbags you have seen and ask yourself, "Can we make bags like these? We don't have this kind of material, but we could make cloth sacks." You begin to interest people, "This sack is good to carry your telephone so you won't lose it. It doesn't cost anything, just 200 francs (20 cents)." So we could take little pieces of cloth and make small phone bags, and the people liked them and began to buy. That creativity is how we live.

POLITICS AND MONEY

When I was elected assistant director of the Department of Women and Families in 1995, I asked the women if they had a bank account, and they said no. But in fact we did have an account where the partners in the United States sent money for the Women's Center at Matete. The day we had our meeting and collected our offerings, the president's wife would bring $100 as the PC(USA) contribution. They had sent much more, but the president used it for other things, and his wife supported that.

When we did the workshops on the house gardens, Inge Sthreshley told me she would send us money for the project, but first she needed to know how much we already had. When I said that we did not have an account, she said, "Yes, you do," and showed me the place where the center's account was in the CPK budget. "You see the account. They should let you administer it, and that way we can send you money for the work regularly." So I went to talk with the president, but only his wife was at home. Since she was a member of the committee for the women's work, I explained—and she began to yell at me, "You have come to destroy the church! You—with your ideas. What money? What account? You are saying whatever comes into your head!" I said, "Maman, pardon. I did not come here to fight with you. I came to see Pastor. Please. . . ." She talked and talked and talked. When her husband came, she started talking before I could say anything. He asked, "What is going on?" I explained what Inge had said.

Pastor said, "Yes, you have an account." His wife was undone. He said, "It was Maman Mesu who gave me the right to administer the account." She was the director; I was assistant. I said, "Now she wants us to handle it ourselves. How much is there in the account? Here is the list of accounts." When the president saw the book, he said, "White people . . . ! But why did they give this to you and not to me?" I did not have any answer. I just looked at him—his exclamation astonished me. He said, "Did they tell you there was money in the account?" I said, "No, Inge asked how much there was. She says the American partners regularly put money into it." He looked at me as if I had knifed him because he saw that the secret was out. He said, "Okay. If you want to handle it, you can." I said, "Okay. Thank you. Goodbye." The next day Tatu Mukuna drove me to see Inge (he helped me a lot, driving me to places). I explained to her what had happened, and I said, "But one thing is necessary for us to administer the account; Pastor Tshimungu must repeat what he said, in your presence." Inge was at the point of going to the United States on leave. She said, "Okay. I am supposed to see Pastor Tshimungu tomorrow at 4:00 p.m." I said, "I will be there at 4:10 p.m. I will call you, and I will talk to him in your presence so you can confirm it." And we did that.

But things were still difficult. I wrote grant proposals to fund projects. When the American partners accepted a grant, they sent me a letter to tell me the amount of money. I would take the letter to the president to ask for the money. The church finance administrator helped me by telling me when money arrived in the account so it was no longer possible to misappropriate the women's money. These experiences taught me a general lesson about managing a communal project. I learned that accountability is necessary and that a leader needs the wisdom to recognize her limits. She may say, "I have weaknesses in these areas. I must get people who have abilities in those fields so that the administration goes well." You are the leader. You have an eye on everything, but you do not work alone. There must be different roles in order to have accountability.

It must be said that I was never paid a salary, and the way the church runs its business does not favor the integrity or health of the personnel. At the graduation of the Higher Institute of Pastoral Theology of our church, Pastor Tshimungu told those who were finishing, "Do not expect that the church will give you something, but go yourselves and try to start little congregations." I said to him, "But those people, they have nothing, how are they going to begin? You create departments, graduate ministers, but you do not pay them.

The proverb says, 'You don't put the goat with the cassava leaves because the goat will eat them.' I mobilize funds myself, and the money comes to the church. You give me that money (which I have raised) for the women's work, but you do not pay me. So you are inviting theft, lies, and all that. When I raise money, give me 10 percent so that this may constitute a salary." I wrote to the General Assembly, and the assembly said, "She is right. She works a lot; you should give her 10 percent of what she raises." But in fact, that never happened.

POWER IN THE CHURCH

It was I who directed the work, but it was Maman Mesu who represented us at the General Assembly and to the executive committee. Jeff Boyd, another American partner, raised the question at the assembly, "But it is Maman Monique who works. Why does she not have a voice?" In response, the church leaders preferred to change the structure to have two committees of women, on the understanding that the pastors' wives or daughters would lead Bible studies and the Department of Women and Families would manage practical matters. The president did not want me to direct the women; his intent was to place his wife at the head by putting the Christian education committee over the practical one. He saw that I was awakening the women's spirits, and he would not have the same power over them.

Maman Mesu died only a few weeks before the elections for the director of the Department of Women and Families in 2000. She had wanted to inaugurate the renovated center before her death and chose July 22, 2000, for the celebration. It was as if she had a presentiment of dying—we buried her on that day. I asked that we bring her body to the center for the inauguration. I was doing almost everything at the center, but Pastor Tshimungu handed the keys to his wife. The people made a great outcry: "No, it is Maman Monique who takes care of the center." They reacted violently, almost knocking over Maman Mesu's coffin.

After her funeral we organized elections. The president pressured the women into accepting two committees—on a trial basis, they thought—but they insisted on electing me as director. The women proposed Maman Annie Ntumba for my assistant. I did not know her, but I had seen her; so I met and talked with her. She was young and well educated, and I could work well with her. She was good at some things, and I worked with her and taught her others.

However, the other women's committee headed by the president's wife made things difficult.

Before her death, Maman Mesu told me, "It is not easy. You are very intelligent. You work very well. I know that you will do better than I, but I know how much they are going to fight you. Even the women will fight you because of your work. The church leaders see the women's work as a way to get money. When there is money for our work, they take it for other things. Now when you rise up, as I know you will—you are a fighter!—even the leaders of the church will oppose you. But you will hold firm." All that happened to me, but I did hold firm by God's grace.

Learning and Working in Contexts of Violence

In 1997 refugees fleeing war came across the Congo River from Brazzaville. We brought aid to their camp, but distributing it was a problem. The refugees did not want us to give the supplies to the administrators: "They steal lots; they only give us a little." Maman Mesu did not know how to manage the situation, and she pointed to me. God gave me the intelligence.

I asked the refugees to choose some representatives, and then I talked with that small group: "What is your problem?" They said, "When food is donated, the administrators here steal it. Give us what you brought; we will distribute it to everyone here ourselves." I asked them, "But these people did welcome you?" They said, "Yes." I said, "They gave you a place to stay?" "Yes." I said, "Good. I will ask you a question. Are you parents?" "Yes, we are parents." I said, "If you saw someone come into your house, take the food, give it your children—while you were there—how would you react?" They said, "Yes, yes, Madame, but . . . There is . . . They don't act right . . ." I said, "Answer my question." "Okay, but . . ." I said, "They are here as your parents; they welcomed you. We have come with food. We must go home now because it is too late to distribute it today, but you may count everything. Tomorrow we will come back for the distribution. We brought the food and will give it to your parents, who welcomed you. But you have the list, and if they take anything—God will see to them!"

We advised the people in authority there. "These people have been displaced, they are unhappy now, they have lost everything. If you take what is donated for them, you will have a curse on your house. Do not take the things. We must give them to these people; we should be sorry for them." They said, "They suspect us, but we have not taken their food. They just say that." I said,

"No, there is no smoke without fire. We are leaving the food, but they have made a list. Tomorrow choose some people from among them, and then you and they can do the distribution jointly. There will be peace."

As a child I had grown up through the civil war in Congo. Then in 1965 General Mobutu took over in a military coup so our lives continued under a dictator. It was very dangerous to speak against him, but people helped each other to survive. In the 1990s in the context of my church responsibilities I became involved in responding to the turbulence and fighting, the struggles of displaced and destitute persons in neighboring countries. And then war came to Congo again in 1996, and rape and violence have spread everywhere.

BANGUI

While I was assistant director of the Department of Women and Families of our denomination, I began to attend various training workshops to be better able to teach the women. These seminars were sponsored by international church organizations like the All Africa Conference of Churches (AACC) or the World Council of Churches (WCC). My first experience was with a workshop sponsored by the AACC. This is a fellowship of Protestant, Orthodox, and indigenous churches, with the vision of "Churches in Africa Together for Life, Peace, Justice and Dignity." The headquarters are in Nairobi.

The workshop in 1996 was held in Bangui, the capital of the Central African Republic, and would take two weeks. When we got to Bangui, we were lodged in the Catholic church's Center of Charity. Mrs. Christine Onyango from Kenya, who was the head of the women's department for the AACC, organized the program, and it was well done. The WCC also sent the head of their women's department, a South African named Mrs. Tembi. We were twenty-four women in all, from Togo, Cameroon, Madagascar, Rwanda, Central African Republic, Congo-Brazzaville, and Congo-Kinshasa, plus several from Equatorial Guinea and Kenya who did not speak French but could understand it.

Everything went well until the last day. We were packed and ready to go. But there was political unrest in the Central African Republic, and we received word that militia had closed the airport; not long after that we heard gunfire. It was war, and we were surrounded. We were praying. Mrs. Tembi found a way to call Geneva, and the WCC began to seek ways to get us out. The AACC was the workshop sponsor, and Mrs. Christine contacted them. They could not do anything, but Mrs. Christine was angry with Mrs. Tembi for taking the initiative away from her. Mrs. Tembi also contacted President Nelson Mandela in South Africa. The WCC contacted France, which had a military base near Bangui. Mandela contacted the United States, which also had a base there. The French were going to evacuate us by helicopter, but it became too dangerous to land so they looked for another solution. But this was taking time. . . .

We were shut in the Center of Charity for a week. In the morning we prayed, and at night we slept on the floor while there was gunfire and war all around us. It was terrible. "What can we do?" "We are going to die here!" "They are going to rape us!" Women were crying, and there was discord because of all the tension. Then I had an idea. One of the participants was Dr. Rose Zoé Obianga, vice president of the AACC and professor of linguistics at the University of Cameroon. Toward the end of the week, at morning prayers Dr. Rose Zoé said, "Am I your mother? You are adults!" and began to speak roughly to the women who seemed to expect her to save them. I looked at her and I thought, "But we are praying. How can she talk like that?" The women were angry. But we were also in a difficult situation. And Mrs. Tembi and Mrs. Christine were in conflict. I said to myself, "How can God answer our prayers when there is no agreement?"

That night I went to Dr. Rose Zoé's room. She welcomed me. I said, "I like you very much because I see that you are an intelligent woman and that you have arrived at the high position of vice president of the AACC. That does honor to women. I have always appreciated you. But I was sorry to see you angry and treating the women in such a way—it was not good. We were praying, and many women were angry. How can God answer us? It would be good to ask the women's pardon for what you said." Dr. Rose Zoé was surprised—and grateful. I then told her a second problem. "It would be good to help Mrs. Tembi and Mrs. Christine reconcile because God cannot answer our prayers if we are divided. Mrs. Tembi has the ability to contact the outside, and it is thanks to her that they are now making an effort to evacuate us. Mrs. Christine must understand and accept that because they are collaborators. But Mrs. Tembi has a lot more contacts. Why is Mrs. Christine angry? The problem is to get us out of here." God truly helped me to say these things. Dr. Rose Zoé said, "Merci beaucoup, Maman Monique."

The next morning when we began our prayers Dr. Rose Zoé said, "Please, I have something to say. I have seen something that I never saw before in my life. There is a woman here who has helped me in a way I have never experienced. I ask your pardon. I hurt you yesterday with what I said. But she had the courage to come and tell me that I had not done right. It is true; what I did was wrong, and I ask your pardon." Everyone was quiet. Then she said, "We are here, we are praying, but Christine and Tembi are not in accord. How will God hear us? It is this woman who had the revelation, who came to talk with me. Christine and Tembi, you must reconcile. Christine, you should accept Tembi's efforts. Tembi, pardon Christine because she did not understand our danger." Mrs. Christine asked pardon of Mrs. Tembi, they were reconciled, and we prayed. We took our time.

Then word came: "The French have arrived; they are going to evacuate you now." Everyone was amazed—it happened right after our prayers. "But no talking. They will come to call you. You can keep your suitcases for now. If it is okay to take the suitcases, you can, but if they say no, you must leave them." We were still praying. When we went out, we found six combat tanks. We found French soldiers in full battle dress—there were weapons everywhere. Women started to cry to see the soldiers and all the sophisticated weaponry. They began to load us into the two tanks in the middle, with two others ahead and two behind, men watching from the turrets for an attack. It was very dangerous.

We arrived at the French base safely and got out of the tanks. There were lots of local refugees from the fighting. While the French were seeking a way to evacuate us from Bangui, they invited us to go to the mess tent to get something to eat. But Mrs. Tembi . . . she is a brave woman. She heard that the American base was not far away, and off she went. We did not find out for an hour or two until she came back with American soldiers. They said, "Let's go." We left the French base—on foot—to go to the American one. It was only our group of workshop women, not the other refugees. An hour later a military vehicle came to take us to the cargo plane. It had no seats. We sat on the floor with seat belts. It was very noisy. Women cried; everyone was afraid. So they evacuated us to Cameroon. The day after the French tanks rescued us, the militia overran the Center of Charity where we had been. God had saved us. We spent the night in Yaoundé at a hotel. The next day they took us to Douala by bus, and there we waited for days to get tickets to go home, but finally I got back to Congo.

My family had been having a difficult time. I had been gone nearly a month: two weeks of workshop, a week under siege in Bangui, almost another week in Cameroon. I got home to discover that my children had not been in school because there had been no money to pay the fees for the third trimester. Tatu Mukuna did not have any money. My daughters Nelly and Nana had continued to make baby sheets and take them to the merchants in town as I usually did so they could buy food, but there was not enough to pay for school. Tatu Mukuna said, "The children can wait until next year to go back to school." I said, "No, no, no. They can't lose a year." I had some new saucepans in the house, glasses, plates, lots of things (which I had bought as a kind of insurance); I sold them. I also had three sewing machines; I sold two to pay for the children's school, and they completed the year. And I began to sew and sell. Later I was able to buy other machines.

REFUGEES FROM CONGO-BRAZZAVILLE

Problems of war were always present then. The year after Bangui, there was conflict in Congo-Brazzaville just across the river from us. President Sassou had properly left power after another president, Lissouba, won the election, but then the French armed Sassou to chase Lissouba out because he was selling oil to the Americans. Sassou got control, and there was war in Brazza in 1997, and people fled to Kinshasa.

We had to do something for the refugees. First, I talked to the church-women, and we made contributions and bought flour and cartons of fish; we took them clothes because they had brought nothing. There were pregnant women who gave birth without even any sterile maternity pads, without any baby clothes. I had made baby layettes to sell so I gave them to the refugees. When an American partner heard what we had done, he was very touched and told me to write a grant proposal. I did, and the American Presbyterian women sent $5,000. All eyes were on that money. I went to the refugee camp myself to see the needs. Since I had done business in Brazza, I recognized some of the people. Seeing the poverty was pitiful. I made the tour alone. I went everywhere to see, to ask questions; I took notes. Then I told the churchwomen what was needed. We bought one hundred pieces of cloth because there were women who only had one wrap. We bought plastic shoes (the usual footwear) for barefoot people. We bought maternity pads, baby clothes, children's clothes. We bought cassava flour, boxes of soap, and milk. We did all kinds of things with that money.

But then there was the distribution. That was a problem of trust between the refugees and camp administrators. I described the conflict at the beginning of this chapter. We resolved it by letting the refugees count the donations and participate in the distribution, but we also insisted that they accept the administrators' role as the "parents" of the camp. We also put the administrators on the alert to act fairly; they would be answerable to God for any theft. Besides, the refugees knew how much was donated and would expect the full amount.

However, there was another problem. Before we left for the camp the women of our committee had said, "You are giving away everything, we don't have . . ." I said, "Okay." I took a sack of cassava flour, a sack of rice, a box of milk, and I said, "Okay. You can take those." They said, "Give us wraps also." When you are with people you cannot always refuse. I said, "Okay, each of you take one dress wrap." Besides the one hundred pieces we had bought, the president's wife came with twenty-four tie-dyed wraps she had made and asked us to buy them. I said, "Those are more expensive than the ones we bought." But since she is the wife of the head of the church, I accepted. But I said to a woman who made baby booties that we would buy hers, and I also got layettes that I made. Then I said, "Put the ten wraps there." (There were ten women.) They said, "And also shoes . . ." I said, "What? No! Put your things to one side, we will divide them when we return." But while we were loading, one woman took a box of milk and a sack of rice and hid them under the benches. I did not know. We left for the camp.

When we returned from the refugee camp, the women began to divide the things; they brought out the milk and rice from under the benches. When I saw that I exclaimed, "Never, never, never. That must not be done. You know that we have taken some things from the donations. Normally we would not do that because the refugees are suffering, but there is suffering everywhere. Since you have worked, you also ought to have something. But you may not have that rice or milk. No, no, no. There are refugees in the city; we will call them to get these things." And we did. That is how we worked to help the refugees. Displaced persons and great suffering are always the consequence of war—the wars of the politicians for power. In Africa there was colonization and that was very bad, but now Africans are killing each other for power.

VIOLENCE, ESPECIALLY AGAINST WOMEN

The Rwandan genocide in 1994 was utterly horrible. It also had immediate and enduring consequences for eastern Congo. In war, girls and women suffer particularly. We did not have rape in our country before, but since 1991 it is everywhere. Especially when there were soldiers everywhere, they raped many girls and women—even children of five years. There is now violence everywhere, but the situation in the east is the worst. Maman Jeanne Banyere, a leader in the National Federation of Protestant Women, has been at Goma since 1997. In the war that year she saw lots of girls whose parents had been killed, and she began a Center for the Protection of Children. When she came to Kinshasa in July 1998 for the Federation's congress, she brought photos and reports, and we collected money, clothes, and other goods to send with her. Three other times since then the Federation has asked the United Nations to transport our collection of food, clothes, and medicines.

Conflicts in the African Great Lakes Region

The part of the Great Rift Valley called the African Great Lakes, a geographic region with its own identity, was partitioned by the European "scramble for Africa."[1] The colonial maps cut through tribal-ethnic groups so "national" borders did not at first mean much. Primarily ethnic Tutsis from Rwanda (called "Banyarwanda" in North Kivu, "Banyamulenge" in South Kivu) had been settling in eastern "Congo" since the beginning of these nations' existence. The fact that Belgium not only ruled Congo but also administered Rwanda-(Bu)Rundi under the League of Nations, and then under the United Nations, contributed to open borders. There were some tensions because these "Rwandans" were very successful and thus resented by the local populace. Beginning in the late 1960s, President Mobutu's program of nationalization led to cross-border raids, which were of course returned, so tensions between Congo and its eastern neighbors increased and unrest simmered for years.   (continued)

---

[1]See Emizet François Kisangani and F. Scott Bobb, "Introduction," in *Historical Dictionary of Democratic Republic of the Congo*, 3rd ed. African Historical Dictionaries 112 (Lanham, MD: Scarecrow, 2010), lxxvii-lxxxiv, esp. s.vv. "Kabila, "Alliance of Democratic Forces for the Liberation of Congo," "Banyarwanda," "Banyamulenge."

But then came the Rwandan genocide. When the Tutsis regained control of the country, more than a million Rwandan Hutus fled to Congo as refugees. From there a number of them launched an effort to take back Rwanda, contributing to further unrest in the region. Laurent Kabila, a former supporter of Lumumba from Katanga who had gotten Chinese military training, was a leader of the resistance to Mobutu. He was based in the mountains of eastern Congo. As the situation became increasingly tense and violent, Kabila and others formed a party called the Alliance of Democratic Forces for the Liberation of Congo (AFDL) on October 18, 1996. It was composed largely of Congolese and Rwandan Tutsis and was reportedly backed by Rwanda, Burundi, Uganda, and Angola.

Kabila and the AFDL were first focused on the Hutus in Congo but then turned to oust Mobutu. Their forces moved swiftly through eastern and south-central Congo. In nine months of fighting they reached Kinshasa. Mobutu's troops were weak, and he was distracted by cancer. On May 16, 1997, he left Kinshasa, and the next day Kabila and the AFDL took it without a battle. The new regime set about undoing Mobutu-era changes: Zaire was Congo again, the currency was the franc, and the national anthem and flag of the early 1960s were reestablished.

There were serious problems however. The fighting in eastern Congo had forced many Rwandan Hutu refugees to return home, but many stayed and were massacred, apparently by Rwandan Tutsi soldiers. Eastern Congo was cut off from communication with other parts of the country, and UN investigators were prevented from doing their job. Fighting among various armed groups of all four nationalities (Congolese, Rwandan, Ugandan, Burundian) continued year after year. The presence of foreigners was also a political problem because Kabila had many in his government. When he dismissed them, in August 1997, a rebellion broke out in western Congo so Kabila brought in more foreign troops from Zimbabwe, Angola, and Namibia to put it down. Many parts of the country were torn by this conflict, which would continue until 2003. In the east, mostly in the Kivu, there is a kind of guerrilla struggle to this day.

But what is terrible is that the situation is not getting better. In that region of Congo, there are minerals—coltan, gold, etc.—and Ugandans and Rwandans come looking for profits, especially since coltan is so valuable for cell phones and other new technology. They kill; they may burn a whole village. They rape—even old women, even little girls. When it is young girls, many get pregnant. In the east, rape is a weapon of war that they are using to destroy the lives of women. One story serves as example. A woman agreed to be raped to save her husband's life. The militia wanted to kill him, but she said, "No, please leave him alive. You can rape me." When the soldiers had left, her husband said, "You can't be my wife anymore because you have been raped." She had to leave—she had nothing. He also rejected their children and refused to support them.

New Responsibilities in the National and International Church

WOMEN GO TO CHURCH TO PRAY, but they remain poor. A woman may go to spend three days at church without leaving food at home for her children. How can she survive? How will the children eat? Women's poverty continues because of their ignorance, their acceptance of the idea that they can do nothing about it. We have to show them that manna no longer falls from the sky (Exodus 16:13-36). We pray, but we also work.

When we teach the women, we start with the Bible and try to help them apply it to their own lives.

At a workshop in Bas-Congo sponsored by the National Federation of Protestant Women, our president had taken the theme of Mary Magdalene weeping in the garden (John 20:1-18). After Jesus rose from the dead, she went to the tomb to mourn. She met Jesus, but she did not recognize him. She thought he was the gardener. The tears filled her eyes so that she couldn't see Jesus, but he was there and he sent her to tell the disciples. After the president's sermon it was my turn to do the practical part of the presentation. I did not go to give lessons but to lead the women themselves to talk and to understand that they are the first actors in changing their own lives. I used the biblical theme to show the women, "Look. You see the teaching is clear. So you have everything; Jesus is there. He has already given everything, but you are still moaning, 'He has not given us . . .' 'We don't do this . . .'"

As we talked, I asked questions, "Why is that not done?" "What was the difficulty with that?" Sometimes the women did not have any answer so I offered advice. For example, about farming: the women make tiny gardens

(1 x 4 meters) and try to get enough harvest to sell and pay for food, medical needs, everything—it is impossible. They are following what their parents did, and yet there is lots of land around them that is not being farmed. So my responsibility was to tell them, "You have land, the land is fertile, land is wealth. I think it is the first thing that God gave to people. When you see the things God has given but do not put them to use, it is a great sin. You can't say that sins are only hurting other people, stealing, and so on. Not to use what God has given is truly sin. So when you go to pray, pray that God will give you strength; then go work. When you work, you will have food." When I said that, the women really liked it because I had told them the truth.

Teaching is one of my most important tasks, in many different contexts. I have always been eager to learn and to share that knowledge, and I have been able to continue to learn and teach through ecumenical church groups at the national and international level. In Congo the key organization has been the National Federation of Protestant Women. At the international level there are three: the All Africa Conference of Churches, the World Alliance (Communion) of Reformed Churches, and the World Council of Churches.

THE WORLD ALLIANCE OF REFORMED CHURCHES

I first came to know of the Alliance when I was invited to attend its 23rd General Assembly in Debrecen, Hungary, in 1997. The assembly meets every seven years; this time the theme was "Break the Chains of Injustice." Before each assembly, the planning team sends study materials so that we can prepare. When I read the documents for Debrecen, I understood that the assembly was not just for the delegates but was also intended to encourage the whole church to get involved. That meant I had to know the viewpoint of the members of our church on different injustices in order to represent them, and after I returned I would need to make the assembly known to them.

Before the assembly I began to organize Bible studies on the theme "break the chains of injustice." I led the women to identify injustices and to seek ways to break those chains. We began with things such as which child could go to school: boys are privileged to study; girls must stay home to work and wait for marriage. We looked at the distribution of household tasks: boys can play; girls have chores. Husband and wife both go to the field and work; coming home, the man carries only the hoe, but the woman carries wood to cook

The World Alliance of Reformed Churches

The World Alliance of Reformed Churches (since 2010 expanded as the World Communion of Reformed Churches) is an international fellowship of churches that have roots in a common heritage in the Protestant Reformation. It is often called the Calvinist tradition although this is not exactly accurate. *Reformed* is now the preferred designation. Europeans took their churches with them when they went to other places, such as America, or when they sent missionaries, and in new places they formed many national or regional churches. In the later 1800s, churches in Europe, North America, and Australia that recognized themselves as members of the same general theological family began to form organizations to work together. At first, most were from English-speaking countries, including a Presbyterian group and then a Congregationalist one (their main difference is church polity). By the mid-twentieth century, there were member churches of these organizations across the globe. In 1970, the Presbyterians and Congregationists held their assemblies together in Nairobi and voted to join together as the World Alliance of Reformed Churches. It was made up of 114 churches in 70 countries around the world. Like some other international families of churches, the Alliance established its main headquarters in Geneva, near the WCC.[1]

supper, cassava leaves, and a child or a gourd of water on her back. At home, the man relaxes, but the woman has to make supper and wash dishes, all with the child still on her back. Then she feeds her husband. Sometimes the man demands meat: "You only cook cassava leaves!" Without any money, where is she going to get meat? If he allows his wife to raise chickens, she has to feed the man the eggs, and the children only eat cassava leaves. All those are injustices that women themselves have traditionally supported.

In the church, when a woman gets up to speak or even to preach, it is the women who have maintained that she does not have the right to speak in front of men. When women are preparing to preach, their leader may say,

[1] For a full study, see Odair Pedroso Mateus, *The World Alliance of Reformed Churches and the Modern Ecumenical Movement: A Selected Chronicle* (Geneva: WCC, 2005).

"You cannot prepare the sermon yourself; go see the pastor." "Don't show what you know; it is better to ask the pastor." There are many injustices supported by women themselves. In our country there is a tradition of polygamy. Men take multiple wives, and girls agree to be second or third wives. The first wife may oppress the others and give orders like the man. "Go wash all the clothes." "Go prepare all the food." When the husband buys cloth for his wives, the first wife has first choice. She may give only one piece to the others and keep the rest for herself. Women have also supported the forced marriage of daughters.

As we did the Bible studies, the women tried to identify the injustices they saw and realized that they could break some chains themselves because they have supported them—or even created them. In the family it is the mother who is the first teacher. She creates a distinction between the boys and girls. If both go to school, boys can choose what to study but girls have no choice. So we have done a big work to help women understand that they should regard both boys and girls the same, and there are many of our women now who do that: boys have chores as well as girls; mothers demand that their daughters have a say in their marriage or studies. Now at least 50 percent of women in the cities respect their children's choices. We decided to organize a worship service to pray and confess all that we as women are doing. We recognized that we are at fault. There were about 460 women the first day; the next week, about 650; the third week about 850.

After the assembly I brought back the insights from our analysis there. We had found many more injustices: economic injustices; social injustices, even in the church; sexual or gender injustices. At the assembly we were taught a system for examining everything we were doing, identifying the injustices, and beginning to make changes. We were encouraged also to teach this to others. I really liked the Alliance's way of working and all its vision for justice. At that point I understood, as I had never done before, that there is also ecological justice. We see the trees, we see the environment, but we do not realize it is useful for life; that is something I learned there. I began to lead the women to understand and care for the environment, to appreciate the importance of trees and fruits. At the assembly I also got many documents that I could use to teach when I got home.

SECRETARY OF THE NATIONAL FEDERATION
OF PROTESTANT WOMEN

In 1998 I was elected secretary of the National Federation of Protestant Women, and I have been reelected several times, so I continue to serve the ecumenical women's movement in Congo. As secretary I participated in meetings and took part in delegations that went to various provinces of Congo to do training workshops. The Department of Women and Families of the Church of Christ in Congo (CCC) provided the funding, and either the director, Pastor Nzeba, or her representative was one in the delegation. There are several leaders for a workshop: the president of the Federation, myself as secretary, plus one woman from the Federation leadership in the province where the training is being held. The composition of the group depends on the work to be done; each leader has her own responsibilities. Often a workshop takes four days; if it is a long distance away, we need a week. When we went to Bas-Congo (which is not too far from Kinshasa), it was three or four days; we would arrive and then wait. The women coming from the distant villages could not get there until the leaders of the workshop arrived because feeding and housing them while they waited to begin would be a burden on the local hosts.

In Bas-Congo we planned to stay three or four days, but the women wanted us to remain much longer in order to teach them well. It is hard to educate large groups, so there are some things it is better to teach the leaders, who can organize workshops to train congregational leaders. However, when you offer a workshop, so many women come that all you can do is raise consciousness and launch the message. For example, at our nonprofit FEBA, the day we gather for monthly worship we raise consciousness and give a message that the women can easily remember. But when it is a matter of teaching, we gather them in smaller groups.

In 2000 I went with Pastor Nzeba to the Kasai to do a training on income-generating activities. I asked myself why the women of the Kasai are poor. When they come to the congress of the Federation, all the women are asked to contribute. The other provinces do it, but it is always difficult for the Kasai. When I taught them, I said, "If you ask each woman in the church to give 100 francs (10 cents), if you have a thousand women you will have enough money. They can always find 10 cents." What is astonishing about the poverty is that there is so much opportunity in the Kasai. Pastor Nzeba and I grew up there; we know that. It is different from the big cities. In the Kasai, people can make farms, raise animals. I wanted to show the women of the Kasai that it is possible to get out of poverty by making use of the fertile soil. We also needed to teach them about nutrition. When we were children, we ate plantain doughnuts. Why don't they make them? Plantains are available; people buy the doughnuts. If they make them well, everything clean (sterile), they can sell these to feed the people and to get some income.

In the 2005 workshop in Bas-Congo that I described at the beginning of this chapter, we were raising consciousness about how women can make some changes for themselves. These might include matters of hygiene, new ways to imagine old activities, or even new products. "When there is filth around your houses, that brings sickness; then, even if you have money, the illness will eat it up and so you will remain poor." After we talked about the tiny gardens, I pointed out, "There are merchants who come here from other provinces to make farms in Bas-Congo because the land is so good, but you are here. You can get one of the fields of the women's committee of your church, organize yourselves, and show the women what they have to gain in farming the field. Then you will have money, and the women will have food." There is also another resource at hand because in Bas-Congo there are many kinds of fruit: oranges, bananas, grapefruit, mangos. A lot just rots, but the women also pick the mangos while they are green, before they are ready. I showed them, "With a mango tree you can live and send your children to school. You have to wait for the mangos to ripen; then you can make jam and sell it. You don't have to go to the shop and buy jam; you can make it with overripe mangos."

That is the kind of thing I did a lot in the Federation, including in Kinshasa in the urban churches. Sometimes people wait for money from outside, but we also show them the things other women are doing, for example making a *ristourne*, or *likelembe* in Lingala. Say there are ten women in the group, each puts in five dollars and gives it to one woman who now can buy dishes for her family. The next month, the ten do the same thing again; eventually, each one has dishes. Women can sell peanuts, charcoal; with fifty dollars a woman can buy a sack of charcoal and begin to sell it. There are women who live by doing that. Some women and orphans are completely destitute, but there are also wealthy women, wives of successful merchants, of politicians. They can make a small sacrifice to help a poor woman with fifty dollars or to pay school fees for an orphan. The women with means can say, "We will each contribute five dollars.

Then we will have fifty dollars, and we can give it to a poor woman. She can buy charcoal and sell it and take care of her children." "We can pay for one child at school and help him live." We are able to finance small activities ourselves if we have the will and if we understand. Everyone needs education, consciousness-raising. So we must raise the consciousness of these wealthy women as well as the poor ones. We can do that in the church, in the Federation, in FEBA.

THE DECADE OF CHURCHES IN SOLIDARITY WITH WOMEN AND THE WORLD COUNCIL OF CHURCHES

In the 1980s international church leaders had begun to realize that there were not many women in decision-making roles, in the church or elsewhere, and their voices were not heard. This is a kind of injustice, and it makes women much poorer and more vulnerable. So in 1988 the World Council of Churches (WCC) launched a Decade of Churches in Solidarity with Women. They asked the member churches to be in solidarity with women, to promote women by education, literacy, training, and support for income-generating activities and other workshops. Dr. Mercy Oduyoye wrote the study that guided the initiative,

World Council of Churches

The World Council of Churches (WCC) was founded in 1948 as an organization to help the churches seek unity and work together. It was based on a longer history, particularly from the eighteenth- and nineteenth-century missionary Protestant movement and the twentieth-century gradual convergence toward dialogue and cooperation of different families of Christian faith. The WCC is not a church itself. To be a member, a church must "confess the Lord Jesus Christ as God and Saviour." At first the WCC was mostly made up of Protestants; since 1961 Orthodox churches have joined, and more emphasis has been put on the Trinity. The Roman Catholic Church is not a member, but it participates in some activities, e.g., the Faith and Order Commission on theological issues. The three divisions of the WCC handle (1) relations among the churches, (2) study of ecumenism and the effort to advance it, and (3) practical aid among the churches and for refugees.[2]

---

[2]For the long view, see Ruth Rouse and Stephen Charles Neill, eds., *A History of the Ecumenical Movement*, vol. 1, *1517–1948*, 3rd ed. (Geneva: WCC, 2004); and Harold C. Fey, ed., *A History of the Ecumenical Movement*, vol. 2, *1948–1968* (Eugene, OR: WCC, 2004).

Who Will Roll the Stone Away? (1990). Thirty Congolese women attended the
first decade gathering in Lomé, Togo, in 1988; its theme was "Rise and Shine!"

Over the next ten years, groups around the world wrestled with the challenges. They sadly recognized that it was women in solidarity with women and
not the churches in solidarity with women. Ordination to the ministry is one
measure of how women are granted power or prominence. Up to that point,
many churches did not ordain women, or if they did, they did not give them
access to positions of responsibility. For example, in my Presbyterian Church
of Kinshasa, they say women are very liberated, but until just a year or so ago
there were no women in the committees that direct the church. We have about
160 congregations, but there are only maybe four or five women who are secretaries of their consistories (congregational governing bodies). No woman
was an executive secretary of a presbytery or synod until 2019, when Pastor
(Maman) Nzeba was finally elected in her presbytery. That is where all decisions are made. Women only go as delegates—the president of the women's
committee of the presbytery—one voice among twenty or thirty. There is a
negative perception of gender. When I say that, the church authorities mis-
understand. When we talk about resisting that form of injustice, they think
women will become uncontrollable and lack respect for the authorities and
will be over their husbands. So there is always a great deal to do to help the
leaders understand.

In our parliament, women are only about 10 percent of the deputies. In the
senate there are a handful of women among 100 or 120. Women are marginalized at all levels. Happily, there are people who understand this and fight
against it. But it is mostly the women who raise their voices. They push the
men (ones who have already understood the injustice) into the dance to lead
many people to grasp that women have the same rights as men, that men and
women can work together, that women can contribute. The idea that women
must always be submissive and do not have the same rights as men—that has
been a great disadvantage to Congolese women.

In December 1998, at the end of the Decade of Churches in Solidarity with
Women, there was a festival in Harare, Zimbabwe, to make an accounting.
There were about thirty Congolese women delegates; some had been at Lomé,
but others (like myself) had not. At Harare we heard many women's stories.
We realized that there were women who had suffered violence in their own

homes, in their work places, in the church. Consequently, these women were closed in on themselves—and that creates a severe spiritual poverty. Women explained the different ways they are blocked from justice: lack of the right to choose in work or marriage, lack of respect as equal human beings, lack of control of their own bodies or earnings, lack of education, frustration at every level. All that makes them much poorer. There is poverty of some kind in almost every home in Africa, and in other countries around the world. Together we decided that we must fight against poverty, against injustice. We decided that allowing poverty is a sin; God did not create us to be poor. Women must work, but women must also be able to relax, which they cannot do if they have an unending struggle simply to survive.

After the women's festival, I remained in Harare to participate in the General Assembly of the WCC as a delegate of my church. At the assembly I was elected to the Central Committee of the WCC. The opportunity to serve on this committee was a good experience and gave me the chance to participate and contribute to the international church in a number of ways that I will describe later.

PART THREE

Flourishing

I came that they may have life, and have it abundantly.

John 10:10

Consciousness-Raising

The Founding of Woman, Cradle of Abundance / FEBA

SINGING AND DRUMMING start the gathering, and Maman Mianda dances as the monthly meeting begins. Ululating voices carry the exultant sound of praise to God. A member of the congregation prays spontaneously, passionately, and all say "Amen." There is more singing. Then Maman Mianda reads the Scripture, and I begin to preach on Mary and Martha (Luke 10:38-42). What Mary chose was essential: listening to Jesus, staying close to him, having the gospel transform her life. But Martha's work was necessary also: the hungry must be fed, and children and widows must be cared for; there are many tasks to do to serve God's people. We must cling to Jesus for our hope and joy and abundant life, and we must also use our gifts to serve God faithfully and share life abundant with others. After the teaching, each person comes forward with singing and drumming to bring her "least coin" to contribute to the ministry of helping other women.

Worship and fellowship overflowing into education and action: this perspective of wholeness characterizes our nonprofit. Woman, Cradle of Abundance / Femme, Berceau de l'Abondance (FEBA for short), began as a movement, an ecumenical women's movement. We would come together to pray and hear inspiring lectures on different issues to educate women; it was a kind of consciousness-raising. But the women brought their practical problems, and that revealed other needs. So we transformed our organization into a nonprofit to seek means to support the women in their poverty of all kinds. At first we focused on practical forms of work that would complement what our church programs were already doing. When we began the second phase of FEBA in 2010, we expanded to meet other unmet needs.

Meeting with women from around the world in Harare, seeing how other African women organized nonprofits, gave those of us from the D. R. Congo a new vision. Each of us was already active in her own way and through her church, but we realized that we could do much more if we had an independent organization. And so, despite resistance, we set about creating one.

THE FOUNDING AND PURPOSES OF FEBA

On January 19, 1999, we established the nonprofit FEBA. We were six women delegates to the Harare festival who came from denominations around Kinshasa: Maman Anekumba Agnes, Methodist; Maman Mfulu Pauline, Baptist; Maman Ndidila Jacqueline, Kimbanguist; Maman Kapinga Marie-Jeanne, Church of Christ Light of the Holy Spirit in Congo; and myself, Presbyterian. The sixth woman was Maman Baila of the Salvation Army, but she did not continue with us. The Kimbanguists and Church of Christ Light of the Holy Spirit are African Independent Churches.

For our theme text we chose Jesus' words in John 10:10, "I have come to give life, life abundant" (author's paraphrase). The primary goal we set was to raise consciousness and teach women that they are human beings created in the image of God. Other specific objectives included identifying the causes of poverty, teaching women their human rights, establishing places for listening to and counseling victims of violence and providing them with help to deal with their trauma, setting up literacy classes, teaching girls and women income-generating activities, and providing small loans to help them start their little businesses.

As noted above, FEBA began as a movement, an ecumenical women's movement, a gathering of any women who were interested. Soon more were coming to our meeting than to all the other women's activities. So we had to address the perception that we were competing with church organizations, not just denominational but also national. I quickly explained that FEBA and the National Federation of Protestant Women have different purposes and different types of participants. The principal goal of the Federation is the unity of all Protestant women. The chief goal of FEBA is to fight against poverty, injustice, and violence, those kinds of things. The second difference is the participants: the Federation is only Protestant women, but FEBA is ecumenical; there are Catholics, women from independent churches, from churches of the awakening (Pentecostal), and Protestants.

African Instituted or Independent Churches

African Instituted or Independent Churches (AIC) are churches founded and controlled by Africans.[1] Although they vary among themselves, AICs are often characterized by emphasis on the Holy Spirit and strongly emotional worship, prophetic or apostolic leadership, attention to traditional African fears of witchcraft, and incorporation of African culture. The largest and best known AIC in Congo is the Church of Jesus Christ Through the Prophet Simon Kimbangu, which will be discussed in chapter twelve. Most AICs have been established by Africans who were converted in church communities established by Western missionaries but who rejected the paternalism of the white leadership and its untraditional spirituality.

It may be useful to give a few examples of the conflicting spiritualities. The Roman Catholic concept of celibacy is foreign to most African cultures, in which adults who never had been married were virtually unknown. Protestants have usually been suspicious of many indigenous arts; most Protestants banned drumming because it was the traditional way of invoking the spirits. Both Catholics and Protestants have strongly opposed polygamy. Today, mission-founded Protestant churches are independent and often have reclaimed aspects of African culture, such as drums in worship, so some of the markers distinguishing AICs are less prominent.

To set up FEBA as a nonprofit, the six founders had to organize a committee to direct it. We met several times. Instead of voting we said, "We are all Christians, and we know each other well. We should proceed by considering each person's gifts." The other women chose me as president because I was already directing so many of the activities that were our goals. "We cannot have another president; she knows the work, she has the ability." (I was not actually present at the meeting when they decided this.) Maman Pauline Mfulu was elected executive secretary; Maman Marie-Jeanne Kapinga, administrative secretary; Maman Agnes Anekumba, treasurer; and Maman Baila, associate treasurer. We went to see the leaders of our six churches, and three

---

[1] See John S. Pobee, "African Instituted (Independent) Churches," in *Dictionary of the Ecumenical Movement*, rev. ed. (Geneva: WCC; Grand Rapids: Eerdmans, 2002).

supported us: Pastor Kayuwa, the father of Marie-Jeanne and principal bishop of the Church of Christ Light of the Holy Spirit in Congo; the bishop of the United Methodist church (Maman Agnes's community); and Pastor Tshimungu of the Presbyterian Church of Kinshasa (my denomination).

FEBA is founded on the understanding that Jesus' mission to bring life abundant means working together to help women and girls believe that they are made in the image of God and have all the rights and responsibilities of beloved children of God. It is a community that works to empower women to live fully. Each one brings her own gifts so it is important for as many voices to be heard as possible, and especially the voices of the founders.

Founders of FEBA

Maman Agnes Anekumba Umadjela (interview 2011).

AGNES: I was born in 1945 at Katako-Kombe, in the Sankuru region of East Kasai (see fig. 1.2). My parents were Shungu Albert and Okako Marie. They had six children, three boys and three girls; I was the youngest daughter. Our language was Kitetela; later I learned Lingala and Swahili. (I gave this interview in Lingala, and Maman Monique translated into French for Elsie.) I did not learn French; in my childhood, it was very rare for rural girls to go on to secondary school.

After I finished the six years of primary, I studied midwifery, 1959–1961, and worked for a year at Wembo Nyama in the region where I grew up. On August 19, 1962, I married Umadjela Luyambe Nicholas. In 1972 I began to practice as a midwife again. We moved to Kinshasa, and I found a place at the General Hospital of Kinshasa where I worked until I retired in October 1987. We had eight children: two boys and six girls. One boy died young, but all the rest grew up, and all of them are educated. Two married daughters live in Kinshasa, and the others are in Europe or America. [Note: In 2013, two years after this interview, I went to live with my children overseas.]

My family is Methodist, and I grew up in the Methodist church. Now it is the United Methodist Church, a community of the Church of Christ in Congo. I worship in a Lingala-speaking congregation, and I have been very much involved in the women's work but also in the larger national church, including becoming a member of the General Council of the Methodist Church. In that capacity I also traveled to Kenya and Harare to represent my church.

One thing I did both in my church and for FEBA was to counsel young couples. I said to them, "When you marry, if you have conflicts in your home, do not take them to your parents because you will create bad feelings. Try to resolve your problems with your husband because if you go to your mother and say, 'See what he did, see how he mistreats me,' your parents will hate your husband." My husband also advised young husbands, "You must love your wife; when you love someone, you can't hit her. If you beat your wife, you will make her bitter. You must take care of her because she is your rib. As the Bible says, God took one of Adam's ribs to create Eve (Genesis 2:21-24), and that is to show that the wife is the rib of the husband." Often the young couples who followed our advice have had model families.

Marie-Jeanne Kapinga Kayuwa (interview 2011).

MARIE-JEANNE: *My life and family.* I am called Kapinga Marie-Jeanne. My parents are Kayuwa Tshibumbu Moise and Katshima Marie. I was born in 1952 at Bibanga, East Kasai. I am the oldest of three; I have two younger brothers.

I must start with my father's story. He was born at Bibanga, the son of a Presbyterian pastor, Kayuwa Samuel, and his wife, Kapinga Elisabeth. My father did not lead a good life; there was drink, and there were women. Then when his mother died he was converted; I was about ten at the time. It was a pastor of the Church of Christ Light of the Holy Spirit in Congo who converted him; this man had a vision that my father would become a great pastor, and that came true. At first my father was a pastor, and then he became the patriarch. The church headquarters are at Mbuji Mayi (East Kasai), but there are congregations in all the provinces (although the ones in the east, in Kivu, were scattered because of the war there). It is a big church with lots of congregations and members; it also has its own schools and health centers.

I did my primary and secondary school at Mbuji Mayi. After I got my state diploma in 1969, I went to Belgium to do a course in administration, which I completed in 1973. Then I began work in the Zaire (Congo) embassy in Brussels and married a Congolese man named Kabuika Jean. After three years, the embassy ran out of money and furloughed us all. They gave me a little severance pay, but I had no work and the severance was not enough to live on. I said to myself, "I must invest." So I began a small business, importing European things into Congo. I would buy cloth, blouses, and perfume, etc., and bring them to Kinshasa or sometimes Mbuji Mayi. There I had women who sold them for me in the market. Meanwhile, I had had two children.

In the third year of my business, my husband got involved in a way that shattered my success. Just before my fourth trip back to Congo, my mother-in-law died. My husband proposed to use my ticket to attend his mother's funeral and deliver my goods to my aunt. But when he got to Kinshasa, he did not give the merchandise to my aunt. He met an old fiancée who had married another man; she was divorced. So my husband went to live with her on the profits of my merchandise. They used it all up. He did not even have enough left to buy a return ticket so he went to live with his oldest brother. And I stayed in Brussels for three years. He wrote me all kinds of stories, but one of his brothers wrote to tell me that they were lies. Meanwhile, I had no money. I looked high and low for the means to support my children, pay rent, and reimburse the bank for the loans I had taken out to buy merchandise. I worked, I paid the debt, and I took care of my children for three years. When the debt was cleared, my father sent me a ticket to return to Congo. There I found my husband with nothing. When I visited my parents in Mbuji Mayi, I told them, "I don't want this guy any more. Look at what he did to me." But people in the family and church opposed a divorce. So I accepted to take my husband back.

We went back to Kinshasa, and my father gave me a house where I still live. I worked to support us. We looked for work for my husband. I went to see friends, and I talked with my father. He said, "There is work, but your husband refused. We found him a job as a principal, but he demanded, 'How much will they pay me?'" Jobs were available—but he did not want to work. He always asked, "How much does it pay?" My father suggested a job as an adviser to a government minister, but my husband refused. "I can't work with politicians. I don't want to do their business." So . . .

Finally in 1991 I said, "We have been married twenty years. What am I doing with this guy?" I called him politely and said, "This is the anniversary of our marriage. I give you forty-eight hours to give me an account of what you have done in our marriage." After two days he said: "You want to be disagreeable?" I said, "I do not want to be disagreeable. Think back over what you have done these twenty years. You have done nothing. I have worked; I have reared our children. You have only gotten me pregnant—five children. That is all you have done in this marriage. We don't have a living room, we don't have a bed—only a mattress on the floor. You do not give me any money; you say, 'At the end of the month.' But at the end of the month there is nothing. I am through with you. You must leave my house." He said, "No, no."

He thought that because I am a pastor's daughter I could not break up the marriage or the church would think badly of my father. However, I wrote a letter to the church about the twenty years of my marriage with copies to my family, to my husband, and to his family. My husband said to the pastor, "No. There is nothing to what she says. The important thing in marriage is love. The material—what is that? My wife is seeking material things, but I put importance on love." The pastor called us together with our families and church leaders of the congregation. My husband repeated the same words. The families said, "It is the wife who must decide." I said, "I don't want this marriage. But I will give him conditions; if he accepts them, we will stay in the marriage. If not, he has to leave." I gave three conditions: (1) He had to convert and believe in Jesus Christ because I saw by his behavior that he was in another world. He never allowed us to say the name Jesus; if we said, "Let's pray," he was stiff and defiant. Maybe he believed in other spirits. (2) He had to find a job. (3) He had to find a house for us and our children instead of living in my father's house. Otherwise it was over.

He did not accept my conditions. I got his things and took them to his brother's house. After spending two days outside my door, he left. I stayed with the children, and I supported and educated them; all have studied and succeeded. I worked as an administrative secretary at the National Assembly of Congo.

Church and women and the beginning of FEBA. I am a pastor in my church and director of the Department of Women and Families. We have weekly women's meetings on Wednesdays, and I counsel the women about how to live with their husbands and children. I do projects with the women, teaching them how to become self-supporting, how to buy merchandise and sell it, so they won't be lazy. I give the example of myself: I was alone to care for my children— that is the work that women do.

I also represent the women at meetings and travel to conferences, to training workshops of the WCC and the AACC. I went to the meetings for the Decade of Churches in Solidarity with Women, starting with the first one at Lomé in 1988. The whole world was there—we were so many people! We brought back what we had learned. In our church we have women pastors in charge of congregations, and we have deaconesses; we take part in all the big meetings of our church. Women are not marginalized; I participate in all the meetings at all levels, without any problem. Nevertheless, men do not accept this easily, though my father, the patriarch, supports us.

We went to Harare in December 1998 for a big assembly to evaluate the Decade of Churches in Solidarity with Women. What have the churches done for women? What have women done in the churches? We met many women from many churches. When we were exchanging experiences, each country was supposed to say what their churches or women had done. Those of us from Congo realized that we did not have anything consistent to say; we could not report, "We are doing this and this and this." That opened our eyes, and we saw that other women organized nonprofits in their countries; they had ways to defend themselves. We said to ourselves, "When we return home, we must try to do something." Maman Monique, since she is always very ardent and courageous, said, "We should meet and talk about what we have learned in Harare and what we can do here in Congo." Then we gathered in Kinshasa around a table to reflect about how to bring women together—and we did it.

OTHER FOUNDERS, DESCRIBED BY MAMAN MONIQUE

Maman Pauline Mfulu, our Baptist founder, was married and had two children. The second one weighed about twelve pounds at birth, and Maman Pauline almost died. The doctor told her she could not have any more children. Then her husband abandoned and divorced her, and went to Gabon where he re-married. That was before the Harare festival. She was left alone in Kinshasa with her two children. After the festival, she became national secretary of the Baptist women. Later, when she was working with us in FEBA, her ex-husband came from Gabon. He wanted her back, but she had learned some things in our nonprofit and she refused him. However, when he returned to Gabon, he took their daughter.

(Comment: There are people who come to FEBA because they think of it as a way to financial security, and Maman Pauline was one of these. When nonprofits were being created in Congo, many got their funding from international organizations, and they paid salaries to the Congolese involved. Naturally that has led many Congolese to regard roles in nonprofits as jobs rather than ministries. It is true that it is difficult for a nonprofit to work if it does not have money to pay salaries and working out a balance between commitment to a ministry and doing a job can be very challenging. In FEBA, the women who work with me cannot do so unless they have a salary to live on, so I have to do everything I can to pay them. But these women also carry on when the money may be late, they put their hearts into the people we serve, they do not expect their families to get something more or better than others do. In the United States people can do volunteer work with no pay, but in Congo it is very difficult. I am working as a volunteer; I do this because I love the work, and I accepted the sacrifice of not having a salary. I work to support my family because I have learned how to organize in order to survive. That is not given to all women.)

The final two women in our group were involved only briefly. One was Jacqueline Ndidila, a Kimbanguist. She stayed in FEBA for two years; then she left and went to London. She was a good woman, but she had trouble with her church. When church leaders decide they would rather see someone else in your place, you may decide you must leave. The final member of our organizing group was a woman of the Salvation Army, the president of the women. After the first meeting she sent another woman to represent the Salvation Army, but soon both of these women moved away from Congo. For our meetings we rotated among the different churches, and we continued to include the Salvation Army congregation in our meetings, but there was no more engagement by their leaders.

THE PROBLEM OF POVERTY

The chief problem we identified at Harare was poverty. We decided that tolerating poverty is a sin, and we must fight against it as the foundation of most of women's problems. So it was necessary to identify the various kinds of poverty in order to help women and girls find the abundant life promised by Jesus Christ (John 10:10).

One kind of poverty is mental, the poverty of not even knowing one is poor. Women are afraid to speak. They have a terrible inferiority complex; they accept their situation without knowing anything else is possible. Such a woman thinks that if she complains about her husband, she is sinning. She has never learned to read or write or reflect. She has to ask her husband for permission for everything. She has a child every year; she is always pregnant. She suffers and accepts it. He abuses her, and one day he may kill her. There are lots of battered women here.

Many health problems come from ignorance—another kind of poverty. People do not realize how serious a threat filth is: it leads to diarrhea, typhoid fever, and more. Women set out the bread or fish or chicken or doughnuts or whatever they are selling in the open, along the road, and passing cars spray dust on it, flies light on it. They set up a table at the market to display their products, but meanwhile they also clean the cassava leaves for their dinner and throw the waste under their table. When I see members of FEBA doing that I say, "You sit there with all kinds of filth around you. You breathe it, and your neighbors breathe it; that spreads illness. If someone eats what you sell without cooking it, he eats sickness." A similar problem is allowing water to stand around the house; then there are mosquitos. So we help them identify these dangers.

Of course there is also material poverty. There are times when I have talked with the other founders of FEBA because they did not understand that we are leading women out of poverty. I said, "You are poor yourselves, we are poor, the whole world has its poverty. But there are different levels. There are the very poor who are completely destitute. You can at least find food for your families, but there are others who have nothing at all: for example, widows with no children or relatives, who have lost everything, who have no one to defend them." By world standards I am poor, but I am very much aware of the different levels of poverty. For example, in Congo sometimes people said that I spoiled my children because I fed them three times a day when often others only eat once or twice a day. There are women in the city who cannot get running water (in the village they usually still have to carry it from a stream), families who eat once or at most twice a day. In Kinshasa a family of six or seven persons may live on less than five dollars a day; they may have tea made of hot water with a little sugar and a bit of bread at 11:00 a.m. (no breakfast)— that counts as a meal. In the evening they have a little cassava, maybe a bit of salted fish with a bit of vegetable. But that is not enough to live on; many people are dying. Others are worse off; they may eat only once every other day.

So we must help women identify different types of poverty and recognize that they do not have to accept everything that is done to them. If they can imagine having the right to something different, they can begin to understand their poverty and look for ways to a better life. FEBA is there to help them see their situation and envision and work for change, a way out of spiritual, mental, and physical poverty.

11

THE KEY TO EMPOWERMENT IS EDUCATING WOMEN

FROM PERSONAL EXPERIENCE I know how important education is, and one of the things we as women can do for each other is to share what we learn. Maman Antoinette is one of my oldest colleagues. She uses her medical training to help educate girls and women. Listen to this story she tells.

> ANTOINETTE: We often hear from young women whose husbands and in-laws complain when they bear girls. The wife has a baby, and the husband asks, "Boy or girl?" They tell him, "Girl." He does not even go to see his wife. So I tell the women, "You can politely tell your husband or in-laws: 'At the creation the Lord made us women with XX eggs (instead of saying chromosomes) and you men with XY eggs. When you give an X, I have a girl; when you give a Y, I have a boy. So you, my husband, are responsible for the sex of the baby.' Say this very politely, and if your husband is not happy, he can go to talk with the doctor." It is good for men to learn this because they always blame the women for having girls, which traumatizes the wife and daughters.

The chief way to respond to poverty is by education. Sometimes we must first extend our own understanding, and then we can better teach others. Because I was director of the Department of Women and Families in our Presbyterian church and a member of the WCC Central Committee, I had the opportunity to attend conferences and workshops. I saw how others organized themselves, and I learned a lot. Women in other countries were much more advanced. When they talked about what they were doing, I took notes and tried to recreate those efforts at home, in the department and in FEBA.

LEADERSHIP AND HUMAN RIGHTS

One of the international church organizations that contributed to my education was the All Africa Conference of Churches (AACC). In February 2001, the AACC organized a month-long workshop on leadership in Kumba, Cameroon, for women of its French-speaking member churches. There were many of us, from eight countries. In the church it is thought that a woman should always be silent and obey. Sometimes if she becomes a leader, she oppresses others, she acts like a man: "You have to obey, you have to do this." This workshop showed us that we needed to teach women human rights and their own rights. If they accept discrimination or a position of inferiority as normal, they practice this.

One aspect of a woman's rights that we emphasize is encouraging her to claim just consideration for her own health and well-being. We want to change the mentality that says a woman must satisfy her husband in everything. For example, there is a tradition that women should put the powder of some trees in their vaginas to make sex better, but doing this can cause illness: cancer, infections, blood loss. We help women learn how to recognize that this kind of tradition is not law and they can refuse it. To teach the women about the dangers of such practices, we invite a doctor. Another common example is a man who lives with other women and gets HIV/AIDS; he comes to his wife who is not infected and demands sex. If she says, "Go have the AIDS test," he answers, "You don't have the right to say that. Because you are my wife, you have to accept sex with me whenever I say." Through FEBA we have helped women understand that they can say no. Many have the wisdom and courage to protect themselves like that. We also have women lawyers who defend women's causes. In FEBA we have played a big role, especially in education, so that women can take charge of their own lives.

I also participated in a training session sponsored by the AACC and led by CORAT Africa (Christian Organizations Research and Advisory Trust), which does workshops on capacity building for leaders. They taught us: "If you never identify the women's needs, you will not know how to plan activities. If everything you do is planned at the top and comes down to the base, it will not work. If the people at the bottom are involved, things will work." Before deciding each thing, we should have a meeting of all the women and identify needs and resources and how we can resolve the problem and who should do it. What I learned drove me always to seek to form and train the women, taking into account first their ideas.

Educating, forming women covers a vast area. It is not like primary school or secondary or university. There are different problems that you have to work through, and that takes time.

PRACTICAL EDUCATION

There are different kinds of training. Some we can do ourselves; for others we have to invite specialists. At the department, I called together the women leaders of each congregation to try to identify needs and then to plan activities to respond. In FEBA we first gather the women, and they bring their problems. When we listen to the women, we ask them questions to try to understand the source of their difficulties. Sometimes we help them share their experiences. For example, a woman's garden is not producing. When she explains, we ask other women to tell how they have succeeded with their gardens. Sometimes we can organize a lecture or other training, according to their needs.

We also use different media for teaching because we know that words are not sufficient. Sometimes we act out little theater pieces, the way we learned Bible stories with traditional proverbs as children. People remember that. One play we have done has this theme: A person who does not work cannot get on in life. The piece presents four women; one listens to and counsels the other three. The wise counselor has a garden and raises chickens, ducks, etc. The women who come to her are a widow, the wife of an administrator who earns fifty dollars a month, and a woman who expects to get what she needs by her sexuality. The widow was left alone with her children; her in-laws took everything in the house. She hoped for help from her brothers-in-law who had lived with her family while her husband was alive, but they have done nothing for her. The administrator's wife has wasted her husband's salary and doesn't have anything to feed her children. The third woman has had many men but is now left pregnant, with four kids.

The wise neighbor invites the three to sit down. She gives them something to eat but then teaches them that they must work: "You should organize yourselves. Don't you have a little piece of land where you can make a garden? You can eat some produce and sell some." The administrator's wife says, "We rent our home and don't have a place." The wise neighbor says, "I have enough space; I can give you a part. If you work and combine that money with what your husband earns, you will have enough for a good life. He will pay the rent, and you can pay the school fees. You can also get the children to do little jobs, such as selling telephone cards or sacks of water." To the woman prostituting herself, she says, "This is your fault; now you have experience. You must stop this life. Go to the health clinic and learn about family planning. The way you are living, you are going to get some disease and won't be able to raise your children." The widow's situation is more difficult, but her experience presents an opportunity to discuss advice for others in planning for the future. "If you have work, when your husband dies you can support your children. There is no one who is going to take care of us, so we have to be organized, prepared, so that if something happens we can face the situation."

After the play we ask the audience what they have learned. One girl said, "This play taught me that we must fight against poverty. These women were poor. They went to their neighbor who supports herself with her manual labor. So I learned we must work so that we will have means to survive." Another girl said, "The play touched me because I myself have two children with a man who is not my husband, and I see that I can't go on living that way. Now that I have come here (to FEBA) and am learning to sew, I will sew and earn my living and I will never go back to that situation." A third girl said, "This showed me that there are women who sit with their arms folded, waiting for everything from their husbands. If he does not earn anything, the children go hungry. If illness comes, the children may die. This teaches us to work; we women must work to have the means to help us support our families." We want to lead women to understand that they must take charge of their lives, resolve their own difficulties, and not depend on the head of the family. We try to teach them to think, "What is my problem? What do I have, and how do I use that?"

We also educate women to work in groups. In the village, five women might work together to weed and harvest their fields. When I gave this example, many village women in Bas-Congo or Bandundu followed my advice and said, "It is good now that we can work together." To transfer this idea to the city, I said, "When you work in a group, each person brings her different gift. There are various things to do in selling. One person is good at finding materials, another at producing, another at attracting customers; they work together." We show women that together they can succeed.

Economic Literacy and Microfinance

When I began to lead other women on income-generating projects, I already had experience because I had worked in business for a long time. Still, I continued to learn in order to teach better. The first major conference was the one sponsored by the AACC at Bangui in 1996 (which ended in our being trapped in a war zone and evacuated by French and US soldiers, as described in chap. 8). The purpose was to educate women in financial literacy and administration. International partners were sending money to African churches for particular projects; the money came to the leaders who were, of course, men. A project would be defined and the budget set, but the money often was not used for the stated purpose. So it was decided to develop women leaders, and maybe they would be able to do better than the men. It was also clear that women needed to learn how to handle finances for their own families. Many parts of Africa have moved from a barter economy to a money economy in only a couple of generations, but training in economic administration has lagged behind. Women traditionally receive less education than men. What they get does not include any instruction in money matters, but women need to know how to plan and manage money. This workshop is where I learned how to distinguish between desires (things that you can do without) and needs (things you must have or take into account). The participants were to teach other women, especially how to make family budgets; even with a small income, if you make a budget you can manage better.

In 2003, I went to a workshop in Cameroon where we learned how a woman can direct an enterprise, and we visited businesses created by women. I also made the acquaintance of a woman from Business Women's Network in the United States. That is how I began to go to the United States for FEBA; the network invited me in 2003, 2004, and 2005. They showed how women could lead companies, starting small and building up to large ones. I learned some important lessons in ways to think about business. When you do something, you must first be passionate about it and know that this is the source of your success; you must not underestimate what you have. In Congo people often say, "I only have a little money; that won't do anything." But what I have can change my life. When you love what you do and give yourself to it, you study different strategies to make what you have productive. A second lesson was that you must improve the quality of the products you make. When the quality is better, you can sell anywhere.

It is very important to help women comprehend economic reality. When women are trained how to manage their little businesses, they know what they can do, what their goals are, how to attain them. First, they have to identify their own gifts, not just follow what others are doing. They also must learn how to identify quality in what they produce. Another factor is distinguishing between doing business and finding food for themselves. A woman sells bottles of water and uses her profits to buy food for her family. Then she cannot buy more bottles of water, but the need for food is still there. She must first determine what her family's needs are, what she must do to meet those needs, and whether she will still have profits to continue her business.

Before providing microloans we have to teach the women. They must understand what is involved, how to plan to reimburse the money, and the need for discipline to guard the capital instead of spending it even on things that seem necessary. They must also choose their projects with knowledge of what a particular project requires. Usually, for a microloan women must work in groups of five to help and support each other; they themselves choose the members of the group because they must have confidence in each other. There is a president to see that the money is reimbursed, a treasurer to handle it. We give a group $500 together; they choose their project or projects. When they have done the project, the president must be able to tell us what they have done and how the project has helped them.

There are difficulties that are not of a woman's own making. For example, a woman gets a microloan of $100; she buys oil, sugar, and flour to make doughnuts and should get $50 profit. She has to feed her family from the profits, guard her capital, and keep $10 to repay the loan. But when she returns to buy supplies, the cost of materials has gone up to $125; she still has to eat so she must borrow more to continue her business. The key thing is that I always ask the women to explain what has happened so that they understand the source of the problem. I also tell them not to borrow in order to pay back the microloan. What I won't allow is for a woman to get a loan and not work, or spend the money for something else. She must buy merchandise for her business.

Sexuality and HIV/AIDS

The HIV/AIDS epidemic has become a terrible problem in Congo, as elsewhere in Africa. It has been spread in various ways. In the wars beginning in

1996 there were lots of soldiers from different countries in Congo, and they raped lots of girls. Those infected by rape passed on the disease. Men who have the disease give it to their wives. Widows are traditionally forced to sleep with a brother-in-law, and if a widow got AIDS from her husband she may pass it on, or her brother-in-law may give it to her. There are men who make it their express purpose to infect girls or women, paying them money and keeping records of their prowess. Plus, there is extreme poverty; girls or women may have to sleep with a vendor to buy what they need, or with an employer to get a job, or with a professor in order to pass. Rich men take many wives or girl-friends. Because we have identified the problems, we have begun to raise people's consciousness.

But how to respond to HIV/AIDS . . . I was the coordinator of the AIDS program for my church, and I went to lots of conferences and workshops. At FEBA we had a project for consciousness-raising. We also trained women to recognize signs of the illness so they could encourage people to be tested, and then accompany them as they lived with it. Besides medicines, people living with AIDS must have nourishing food and cannot do heavy work, so they need special care. Many also have children, and that adds another level of challenge.

In Congo I organized seminars or workshops on HIV/AIDS. It was not easy because in our country it is taboo to speak of sex in the church. There are other ways to be infected, but sex is the most common, so we must talk about sex or we are contributing to the spread of AIDS. When we talk about sex, people are shocked. One day I was teaching women; my mother was present, and the women said, "Maman Monique . . . Her mother is here, but she is talking of sex! That is not allowed." I said, "No, in teaching there is no law which says that if your mother is present you cannot talk about something." They said, "We are your mothers; you are our daughter. You can't talk about sex." I said, "Okay. You are the grandmothers of many girls. If you accept that they will practice sex secretly, you can continue to tell me to be quiet; but if you want to help them, please, we must speak openly about sex." The pastors did not like this either, but finally in 2005 they began to acknowledge the re-ality of the problem, and that marked the point when our church really began to face up to HIV/AIDS (see fig. 11.1).

One important means to address the epidemic and its effects was the creation of Bible studies. Among other things, the studies helped to fight stigmatization, a very serious problem for those living with AIDS because it makes them lose hope. Most of them do not want other people to know their condition, but some are willing to speak in order to inform others. I invited these individuals to the Bible studies. When we study the Bible, we try to help people talk about what they learn. We ask questions: "What did you hear? What does that mean? Have you ever seen that in your life? Do you know a similar situation in our society?" They begin to understand, and that helps them apply God's word to their lives. This is true for many things, but especially for HIV/AIDS.

Stories of Women Living with HIV/AIDS. Maman Odette Kalanga is a remarkable woman. When Kasaians were chased out of Katanga, her husband could not find work in Kasai so he came to Kinshasa. Here he drove a taxi. Eventually he caught AIDS from a friend's widow; he and she were both treated. When his wife came to Kinshasa with the children, he passed on the disease without telling her. A member of FEBA who had been trained to see the signs of AIDS recognized them in Maman Odette and brought her to me. We prayed, and I asked about her life. She told me her husband was ill, maybe with tuberculosis. I asked if she was willing to be tested. "You do not need to be afraid. If you have the virus, you can take the treatment and it won't continue to develop." First, she had to ask her husband. He said, "If that woman (Monique) takes you for testing, I will have her arrested." When Maman

Figure 11.1. Maman Monique (R) teaching a seminar on HIV/AIDS to pastors. Kinshasa, 2005. The woman on the front row is the president of the women in one of the presbyteries.

Odette told me, I knew her husband was already infected and I said, "I am taking you; let him have me arrested." Finally, she accepted.

It took three tries before she was willing to be tested or hear the results, but we did not give up. When Maman Odette learned she was infected, she fainted. Then she wanted to kill her husband. I talked with her. "If you kill your husband, you will be imprisoned or killed and your children will be left destitute." I told her we would help her with the medicines and food and support. I also wanted to help her work through the anger and sense of betrayal. "You are a Christian." "Yes." "You love Jesus." "Yes." "If you love Jesus, you must forgive; Christians forgive." "Oh, no! My husband . . ." We prayed. I prayed the Lord's Prayer, where Jesus says to forgive as we are forgiven. Finally, she agreed not to kill her husband. She even told him that he should be tested also because she wanted to help him. He cried and asked his wife's forgiveness. Eventually he died, but she is still living. We have helped her with a microloan and the education of her children.

Orphans. There are many destitute children, many orphans, in the streets. Parents die of poverty—of hunger, of AIDS or other illnesses, of accidents. Working with people living with HIV/AIDS led me to begin taking in orphans. Usually we helped them stay in families (their relatives or others willing to care for them), but occasionally we brought them to live in the Women's Center. Here I will give two stories. A family of five children was left when their parents died of AIDS. The oldest was a boy too old to go to formal school (children who do not start school by the time they are twelve cannot attend); he found a job as a porter and sold plastic sacks. The next was a girl who chose to make her life by prostitution. The third, another boy, was intelligent, and we paid for his schooling and helped him get a little job taking care of a telephone booth so he could contribute to his expenses. The fourth returned to his parents' village. The youngest, Ygette, was fourteen. She was living with a cousin who mistreated her so she asked to come to the department. Her oldest brother agreed, and she became the first child to live in the center. The second child who came to live in the center was Bob. His family was very poor. He had been able to go to school up to the fifth year of secondary, but the final year is more expensive, and he could not continue. We agreed to pay his school fees so he could finish, but his home was a distance from the school so he needed to live in the center to attend.

All of the work we do at FEBA is a gathering of different women's talents together. At the beginning of this chapter I introduced one of my colleagues who has been particularly in charge of medical issues, working with HIV/ AIDS, teaching good health practices, and more. Let's hear Antoinette Muleka Tshisuaka tell her own story now.

ANTOINETTE: I was born at Kananga, West Kasai, in 1947. My parents were Mukanya Benoit and Musau Marie. We were twelve children, eight girls and four boys. For secondary school I went to Muena Ditu and Bibanga (see fig. 1.2). I began my nursing studies at the Christian Medical Institute of Kasai at Tshikaji, near Kananga. After my marriage I finished my education at the Institute of Medical Studies in Kinshasa. When I was eighteen my family arranged a marriage with Dr. Tshisuaka Kanda Samuel. It was his second marriage; he already had thirteen children. Unhappily, I never had any living children though I suffered many miscarriages. When I came to Kinshasa, I became acquainted with Maman Mesu, and we got on well. She encouraged us younger women and helped us in our work in the church. It is thanks to her that I went to Lusaka, Zambia, in 1974, for a conference organized by the AACC.

By training, I am a nurse. In Kananga I worked with people with mental problems. In Kinshasa around 1984 I began working at the General Hospital at Mayemba, in the blood bank headed by my husband. I really loved my work; I was there until 1991 when my husband died. After his death, things were terrible for me; I lost my home and everything. Maman Monique came and found me and brought me to the Department of Women and Families to be secretary, and I lived there until she was forced out. Of course I became involved with FEBA.

In my work at the blood bank there were many mothers with very anemic children. Helping them gave me the desire to work for others, especially the children with sickle cell anemia. We took blood to see the level of the macrocytes; if it was very low, we did a transfusion. Before that, we had to check to be sure the blood we were giving was compatible with the child's. When I saw these children, I was filled with pity for them. There were some who were malformed. They had multiple crises and transfusions. I am very grateful to God that I was never infected while I was at the hospital because we did the transfusions without gloves, and the blood flowed over our hands. Later, we were obliged to wear gloves—maybe it was when we heard about HIV/AIDS.

We also educated the children's mothers. "You have other children. Before they marry, you must test to see if your child and the fiancé are both carriers. If both are clear, your children will not have the disease. If one is a carrier and the other not, your children will be either clear or carriers. But if both carry the disease, your children may be clear, or carriers, or actually suffer from sickle cell." These children impoverish their families. Every time the child has a crisis, they must go to the hospital, do a transfusion, care for the child. That is expensive; without that, the child dies. One of my husband's cousins refused to be tested before his marriage; he said, "I love this girl." But it turned out that both he and his wife were carriers; four of their five children had sickle cell. They were always at the hospital until all four had died. The husband died, and the wife was left with one child. That is why when I talk with girls in FEBA I counsel them that before marriage, they should do a voluntary blood test. Sometimes they accept our advice, but we cannot force them. Our job is to repeat, repeat, repeat.

UNEMPLOYED YOUNG GIRLS

When I see young girls or women who have not been to school, who are excluded from society, I always want to surround and support and mentor them to regain their dignity and be valued as others are. Despite all we do to educate parents, they still favor boys. Or families may be too poor to educate any children. And of course there are orphans. Even if girls have been to school, it is still hard to find means to earn a living so many end up in prostitution. In the Department of Women and Families I created training programs for unemployed young girls. It was my initiative; I did not find any such project, but I created it. First, I consulted other women who were concerned about these girls. They said the best way to help the girls support themselves with self-respect was to teach them to sew so that is what we did.

After I went to work at the department, I had continued to sew at home because I had no salary and needed to support my family. Maman Jeannette Adiyo was working with me in my business; she sews very well, and she is also a gifted teacher. She and my daughter Nana Katanda came with me to the center. I brought my own machines from home and wrote a grant proposal to buy more for the center. We also began tie-dyeing. One story of our first graduating class is a lovely memory. Miss Kalala Kambala was the daughter of a widow; she had her state diploma but could not find a way to support her mother and sisters so she came to us. And succeeded wonderfully. After graduation she worked in Congo for a while and then went to Angola, where there was a very good market for her creations. Finally, she moved to France, where she has a large clientele for her couture.

AGRICULTURE AND THE HAND OF GOD

Agriculture is the basis of life and of much of the economy in Congo. We showed the city women how to make box gardens, and we advised the women of Bas-Congo to enlarge their little plots. But it was also necessary to have more space to grow corn, cassava, and beans and other things to feed the children in the nutrition program and other destitute people. To have a farm you have to go a good distance outside Kinshasa to find land you can afford to buy. The department had a farm, but in 2002 FEBA also bought six hectares (about 15 acres) for a farm. Then Mme Kabila, the mother of Congo's national president, settled on the property next to our farm. Her compound was protected by many soldiers. That led to difficulties; the business of soldiers is to rape and steal.

One day we were going to our FEBA farm. Approaching from the main road, our farm was on the far side of Mme Kabila's farm so we had to pass hers to get to ours. The soldiers stopped us, pointing their guns at us. Everyone in our car was afraid. I got out and went up to the soldiers, "What is the problem?" They asked, "Where are you going?" I said, "We have our farm over there." They said, "No! You do not have the right to go past here; you do not have the right to have your farm there." I said, "Okay, but I thought that we were safe because our farm is beside your farm, because the president's mother is our mother, she is us." They looked at each other. Then the president's mother sent one of her women to ask, "What did she say?" When what I had said was repeated to her, she said, "Okay, let them pass." I was afraid, but God gave me the courage to speak and to use words that could touch her heart.

We worked on our farm and harvested what we could, but there was no safety because there were always soldiers around. We had to stop working. We told the neighboring women they could use our farm, but they were only able to do that for a little while before the situation with the soldiers became too difficult for them also.

FEBA IN THE YEARS 2005–2010

When I was reelected as director of the department in 2005, I asked Maman Pauline to share the responsibilities of leading FEBA. I did not think it was good for me to have two major positions. I said to her, "As executive secretary, you will direct our nonprofit and organize activities, and I will work on raising money." There were a number of problems however. Maman Pauline concentrated on the economic benefits of the nonprofit and did not continue the educational and inspirational parts of the ministry. Her vision was the traditional idea that assistance should always go first to those closest—her family, her clan, her denomination—and this meant that she also did not engage the whole of FEBA. There were only two activities that continued (microloans and the HIV/AIDS ministry) because I was doing them also at the department. That is why I took the lead again in 2010.

12

New Roles in the Church, Peacemaking, and Justice

WHEN YOU ARE GOING ABOUT your business, God can open the door to unexpected opportunities to speak and to work for justice. In 2001, as a result of a presentation I had made at a church conference, I received an invitation to visit Sweden. At that time Sweden chaired the European Union, and they invited four Congolese to talk about the situation in Congo. I was asked to talk about humanitarian issues, especially in eastern Congo (primarily the Kivu), which had been cut off from the western part by war for five years. After I spoke, they asked me to repeat it again the next day for a much larger audience, including Congolese who lived in Sweden. The third day they invited me to speak to the Minister of Foreign Affairs.

After hearing about the terrible conditions in the east, the Swedes and the European Union decided to send a boat with food and medicine up the Congo River to the east and to make a special effort to reopen contact so that people in the east could get food. That served to unblock the situation in the east and even brought a little change because UN troops were sent to intervene. This is one example of how, alongside my ministry with women and girls in Congo, beginning in 1999 I became involved in international ecumenical, justice, and peacemaking work, especially through the World Council of Churches and the World Alliance (Communion) of Reformed Churches.

THE CENTRAL COMMITTEE OF THE WORLD COUNCIL OF CHURCHES

At the General Assembly of the WCC in December 1998 I was elected a member of the Central Committee. This group of fifty people representing member churches around the world is elected at the General Assembly for a term of seven years to help direct the WCC between assemblies. The committee meets every twelve or eighteen months for a week, usually in Geneva. In January 2001 we met in Potsdam. It was the beginning of the Decade to Overcome Violence, and I had been asked to make a presentation on "The Market Economy in the D. R. Congo." I served in the Central Committee for seven years and also attended the next General Assembly as an alternate. After the end of my term, the Church of Christ in Congo (CCC) wanted to reelect me to a second term, but my denomination refused and nominated Dr. Micheline Kamba.

While I was on the Central Committee, I was able to make the WCC better known in Congo because often people did not understand the organization and its objectives and the conditions of membership. I said, "You are members. It is the members who sustain the WCC financially, and with their ideas and vision." People think that the WCC is an ecumenical donor organization, but they forget that member churches must contribute in order for the WCC to function. The churches in Congo have a very hard time contributing financially; some never contribute. But when there are General Assemblies, they want to be supported by the WCC to attend. During my term on the Central Committee I visited the Congolese member churches to raise consciousness; sometimes I actually took donations and sent them to Geneva myself.

Another part of my work with the Central Committee was to be the WCC liaison to help Congolese member churches in various ways. Sometimes that meant informing the WCC of special needs in Congo or representing the WCC to assist member churches in resolving their differences. The most sensitive of these discussions involved the Kimbanguist Church's challenge to the fundamental WCC creedal statement, to "confess the Lord Jesus Christ as God and Saviour."

A MISSION AMONG THE KIMBANGUISTS

When I was a member of the Central Committee I went on several missions to the Kimbanguists. The first was in 2000. War was widespread, and when I explained the situation in Congo to the Central Committee, they resolved to make a visit of solidarity with the Christians in Congo. The delegation was made up of the general secretaries of the WCC, the AACC, and others, including four women.

The Church of Jesus Christ on Earth by the Prophet Simon Kimbangu

The Church of Jesus Christ on Earth by the Prophet Simon Kimbangu is an African Instituted (Independent) Church and a member of the WCC. It was founded in the 1950s by followers of Simon Kimbangu, a man from Bas-Congo brought up in the British Baptist church, who was recognized as a prophet by the Bakongo people in 1921. The colonial rulers considered Kimbangu's preaching politically dangerous and exiled him to a distant part of Congo until his death in 1951. His three sons, led by the youngest, Joseph Diangienda Kuntima, established their father's church, which was officially recognized by the government in 1959, and in 1969 it became a member of the WCC.

We went to visit Nkamba, in Bas-Congo, which is the Kimbanguist holy land and the center of their church. They have built an amazing little city there with a very large church. Because Nkamba is sacred land, Kimbanguists remove their shoes; that is not required of others, but our delegation thought that we should remove ours out of solidarity. We met the head of the church, Salomon Dialungana Kiangani, the last surviving son of Kimbangu. He was not in good health, but he received us, along with his son Simon Kimbangu Kiangebeni (the present spiritual head of the church since his father's death). I was the only Congolese in the delegation, and the Kimbanguists were very impressed. "You are very lucky. You will live a long time because you have come to see the spiritual chief. There are sick people who come and wait a whole year for him to receive them. When he touches you, the sickness is gone. When you go to talk with him, ask him to give us peace in Congo." When we spoke with him, I said, "Papa, it is good to do everything possible for there to be peace." I would not pray to him to give peace. Nor, when they invited us to visit the mausoleum of Simon Kimbangu and his son Diangienda, was I willing to kneel and touch the coffin as a sacred thing.

My second major work with the Kimbanguist Church came in about 2003–2004. The Kimbanguist Church was a member of the WCC, but they began to change some teachings. They called their spiritual head Dialungana "Jesus" and began to celebrate Dialungana's birthday on May 25 as Christmas. The other Congolese churches said this broke the WCC confession of Jesus Christ as Lord and Savior, and they contacted me. I explained to representatives in Geneva what had happened, and they organized a delegation to talk with the Kimbanguists. Included were the Congolese Methodist theologian Dr. David Yemba from the WCC Faith and Order Commission and Mr. Hubert van Beck from the WCC office responsible for the relations among the churches. And, because the issue concerned an independent church, the third was the WCC representative of the African Instituted (Independent) Churches.

We organized a theological dialogue in Kinshasa between the Kimbanguist theologians and the theologians of the other Congolese WCC member churches. The Kimbanguists maintained that the date of Christmas was May 25, the birth date of their spiritual head, Dialungana. They continually praised Simon Kimbangu's miracles as evidence of his divine status. The conversation did not seem to advance. I said, "I am not a theologian, but I would like to ask you one question. Elijah did many miracles; there were people who by faith in God touched Elijah's coffin, and they were healed. It was because they had faith in God. We accept that Simon Kimbangu had faith in God and God did these healings; it was not Kimbangu. If you explain things that way, people can understand. These people came from Geneva; the churches here have come together. But you are trying to distract us from the issue. You must speak in concrete terms. Simon Kimbangu was a believer; he had faith. No one is objecting to that claim. But you cannot call him 'Father, Son, Holy Spirit.' We cannot say of Elijah, 'He is the Holy Spirit.'"

Dr. Yemba said, "What you have said is very important, Madame. You must not say that you are not a theologian. You are a theologian because you have shown the issue well." When the Kimbanguists heard that, they whispered among themselves. They said, "Oh, we ask your pardon. You should not trust the 'popular theology' of the church members. They believe in the people they can see. When they hear the things Papa Kimbangu did . . ." Hubert van Beck said to them, "You say 'popular theology,' but you are the ones who support it because it is what you tell your people. But if you say, 'Yes, Kimbangu was inspired by Jesus Christ; he had faith in Jesus Christ, but it was the power of Jesus,' the people will always understand." The Kimbanguists promised to educate their faithful about the true teaching of Jesus Christ as Lord and Savior. Then the delegation went to NKamba to speak with their spiritual head—and discovered that they had removed all the posters on which they had written "Kimbangu" instead of "Jesus."

WORK FOR THE CONGO

While I was a member of the Central Committee, I asked them to organize a round table for the churches in Congo to help them. Help is not always financial; it can be administrative so that things are well structured and the life of the church may correspond to God's vision for it. For the preparatory meeting in Geneva, they invited Bishop Marini, the head of the Church of Christ in Congo; Bishop Onema (Methodist); Pastor Tshimungu (Presbyterian); Pastor Kitikila, who directed the committee of coordination of the Congo member churches of the WCC; and myself. Also invited were all the partners who finance or accompany the Protestant churches in Congo. Among these was VEM / Vereinte Evangelishe Mission / United Evangelical Mission, a German organization that gives both financial and moral support. VEM was represented by Dr. Kakule Molo, a Congolese.

We gathered in Geneva in March 2001 to plan for the round table in Kinshasa in 2002. There were no prepared presentations for this initial meeting; it was to be a discussion. But when we arrived, they asked me to speak the next day about the humanitarian situation in Congo. Since the war that began in 1996, Congo had been divided, east (especially Kivu) from west. There were no boats going up the Congo River to bring food to the east, and the people were suffering very seriously. There were people with no clothes: a family might have one set of clothing, which they had to take turns wearing when they went out of the house; the rest staying naked at home. There was no food; women were being raped—even old women and children. A woman might go out to seek food, maybe into her garden, to her field—sometimes only two hundred meters from her house—and she would be raped. It was terrible! It was thanks to my colleagues in the National Federation of Protestant Women that I could tell about what was happening in Goma and that region. What I said got everyone's attention. Everyone was moved. The people from eastern Congo were surprised that I knew so much about their area.

This speech opened the door for me to speak more widely about the humanitarian crisis because it led to the invitation to Sweden, recounted at the beginning of the chapter. I was very glad to have a little part in moving the international community toward helping eastern Congo. In 2003 I myself visited the area with a delegation from the National Federation of Protestant Women. We went to express our solidarity with the women there. It was dreadful, awful. We cried—we kept on crying. We saw the great destruction. The missiles fell on people, on houses, on everything. We saw many orphans. We found children traumatized by the war; some were in class when a missile dropped on their school. There were forty children in the class, and only three survived. A child looks and sees blood everywhere; he sees all his classmates dead. Children did not want to return to school: "At school they will kill us." It was terrible. We comforted the women about the horrible reality and destruction and encouraged them to go on. We have sent them assistance from time to time through the National Federation of Protestant Women.

A Peace Mission to the Ivory Coast

I also traveled to different places for the WCC. In March 2004 I was in the Ivory Coast. There had been problems and violence there since 1999, but this time the conflict was because the president refused to organize elections. In Geneva we formed a group of fourteen African and French "Women in Solidarity for Peace." (Most were African.) We said, "We must go because we cannot leave those women and their children to die." We were told, "There is no war right now," so we left for the Ivory Coast. Travel was arranged by VEM (United Evangelical Mission).

When we arrived in Abidjan, we were warmly welcomed and went to a service in the Methodist church. They were truly surprised to see that women had come to help them. We met with groups of women of all different religious persuasions to learn their views on peace and what we as women can do for peace in Africa. There were Muslims, Catholics, and other churches. We questioned the Muslim women because there are many Muslims in the Ivory Coast and it is Muslims who are much more active in the war. "You are women who pray. Why can't you plead with your husbands, your brothers, to stop that?" One woman said to us, "The Qur'an does not allow killing. I was a Christian before I married a Muslim. Everything that is said in the Bible is also said in the Qur'an. If you see a Muslim who rises up to kill, or to lie, or to do violence or aggression, ask him: 'Does the Qur'an allow that?' No, no, no. It is the politicians who are killing people." So we understood that we all have the same problems, despite our different doctrines, our different religions. We all come together with regard to the situation before us; we live the same problems. So we are called to work together for peace.

After these general meetings with women we had to see the ministers. We began with the women ministers. They received us; we talked. They said, "The problem is much more at the level of the presidency." An opposition leader had been elected, but collaborators and ministers of the (outgoing) President Gbagbo were supporting him to stay in power forever so they could get rich. Our job was to show the women's situation, to call the ministers to return to a spirit of peace, love, forgiveness, in order to have peace in Ivory Coast. To do this we had to go to the capital Yamoussoukro, where many people had been killed, but when we were ready to leave for Yamoussoukro, the war began again. Our mission was at an end.

But we were blockaded at the hotel. When there was a lull in the fighting, they told us it was better to leave the hotel. I telephoned the airport, and they said there was an Air Africa plane going to Cameroon. We looked out of the hotel, up and down the street to see if it was calm, and then I went out of the hotel to get a taxi to the airport. Along the way we saw how they had killed and burned. I was afraid . . . We got to the airport, and I found other people wanting to fly. Then they announced that there would be no flight because the plane could not land; we should return to town. "What?" I went to see the airport manager. "I telephoned you; you said there was a flight. But here—there is no gunfire—why do you refuse to land the plane?" He said, "Oh, no, Madame. Go back to the hotel; we will see about tomorrow . . ." I said, "I won't leave; you can lock me in your office. I am on an official mission; they know that I came here. The international community will ask you if anything happens to me. I will not budge from here." It was a good thing I did that—I don't know how the idea came to me.

Meanwhile, they had told the hotel that there was no flight, and the women of our peacemaking group communicated with the WCC in Geneva: "We don't know where Monique is." Geneva started telephoning but could not reach me. I think they must have called the airport manager because finally he said, "The plane is landing. You are going." When it got there and people started lining up, they pushed me out of the way, but the Air Africa agents and airport manager said, "This woman is the one who got the plane," and they made sure I could get on.

You see, it is risky . . . the events at Bangui, at Abidjan, in Rwanda (I will tell about that next). It is hard for women when there is war. African presidents want to hold on to power. They kill people. There are exceptions. In Senegal, maybe there are little problems, but when President Leopold Senghor was supposed to leave, he did, and now he can walk freely around Senegal. President Abdoulaye, his successor, also. But these are exceptions. In many workshops where I have done training on conflict resolution, for example the AACC workshop in March 1997, they ask us to do advocacy, to go to see the authorities. But when you do that, the authorities may send people to kill you. We want to work for peace in Africa, but the problem is that the men in power do not want to leave, and they don't accept mediation. Even if they are under pressure from the people, they are the ones with the armies.

Peacemaking Missions in Rwanda

My first visit to Rwanda was in 2002. War between Congo and Rwanda was continuing and causing much suffering. In Congo, people accused the Rwandans, though it was mostly the Interahamwes, the Hutu military force leading the Rwandan genocide, who had taken refuge in eastern Congo after the genocide but were trying to regain control of Rwanda. They are still in Congo today, but they were killing many more at that time. We were part of an ecumenical gathering of churches from Congo and churches from Rwanda to seek peace. The WCC and AACC were involved, but it was particularly the VEM (United Evangelical Mission) that did the most to organize and finance the conference. In our delegation were Bishop Marini, the head of the Church of Christ in Congo; various other pastors; and four of us women. Together we attempted to talk and see how, as the church, we could envisage a solution that might lead to ending the war between our two countries.

We went to Kigali. They showed us the different sites of the genocide. We saw the skulls; we visited the churches where they had killed people. Some Rwandans living in Congo came to explain their experience. We decided that pastors from Rwanda would preach in congregations in Congo, and Congolese pastors would do the same in Rwandan churches. That was to deal with the hatred in the hearts of Congolese toward Rwandans and get back to the way we lived before, when Rwandans were in Congo and Congolese were in Rwanda. There was no problem at that time (before nationalism separated us).

As the church, our task in 2002 was to see if we could begin to lift the reigning climate of hostility that was destabilizing the region.

Border Conflicts

The time when "there was no problem" that Maman Monique refers to was before Congo's independence. When Belgium ruled Congo and administered Rwanda-(Bu)Rundi, borders were permeable. As independent nations, however, there have been conflicts because African heads of state have been determined to maintain control of all their territories. The unrest caused by military action on both sides escalated sharply when the Rwandan genocide brought both refugees and their enemies into Congo in 1994.

My second visit came in 2004 when the international church sponsored a gathering in Rwanda with the title "Never Again Genocide in Africa" to seek solutions of peace. It was not just war in Rwanda and Congo, but almost everywhere. The workshop was funded by the VEM and organized by Dr. Kakule Molo. I was invited because Dr. Kakule remembered me from the meeting in Geneva when I had spoken about the humanitarian situation in Congo. During this workshop we talked together about seeking the causes of genocide. Hutu and Tutsi people were there to explain how the genocide happened because it was not the first time that there had been bloodshed in Rwanda. In 1958–1959 there had been killing, though the latest conflict was much worse. Many Tutsi came to tell us how they had been mistreated. They also showed us a kind of truth and reconciliation process that they called *katshatsha*. Hutu who had killed Tutsi or moderate Hutu would confess and tell the families of the victims where they had buried the bodies. The families could then exhume and rebury their murdered members with honor.

It was shocking to see the genocide memorial. They show it daily if there are visitors: innocent babies killed, innocent people killed. What horrified me was that people had fled to the churches, and they were massacred there. I am Congolese, and they have harmed Congolese, but I cannot accept any such a massacre; it truly made me ill. When I came home, I reported, "What we are suffering, the Rwandans are suffering like us. They are victims of the politics of our countries; it is the politicians who are killing us and dividing us. We don't need to be divided. We should love the Rwandans because they are the victims of a situation that they did not will themselves." Many Rwandans were killed, women as well as men, and yet the women have begun the hard work of rebuilding. I saw many courageous women who work in the fields, who grow beans and other food to bring up their children.

At the conference I also spoke up. They said they wanted to avoid genocide in the future, but they only presented one side of the story. "You say, 'the Hutu did this, the Hutu did this . . .'" I asked, "But did the Tutsi do nothing in return? You say that you were a single people and that the Belgians divided you. But how come you have different names? There are Hutu, and there are Tutsi." They said, "No; in the time of our ancestors the person who had more than ten cows was rich and was called Tutsi; the poor person was called Hutu." I said, "You had already created social classes in your country so it is you who created this situation. If we want to resolve the problem of genocide so that it does not happen again, we must see what we ourselves have done. We must know the negative side of each tribe. That has not been done."

Proper Mourning

In Africa, as in most traditional societies, honoring the dead is a very important religious duty. Families will go into (sometimes great) debt in order to give their relatives a proper casket and funeral and mourning rites. It is common for friends and others to take up a collection for the family of the deceased to help pay for these ceremonies. Communities experience lingering bitterness when people are not able to bury their dead, so recovering the murder victims and burying them properly constitute a significant part of the process of seeking reconciliation.

That day I was asked to lead the evening prayers so I began by first leading the Rwandans to confess and ask pardon because it was they themselves who prepared the genocide. "The problem was privileging one social class. The Tutsi were privileged. They went to school; the Hutu did not. The Tutsi were the minority, but they had the power. The Hutu were the majority, and their means to get power was by force. But if everyone goes to school, they can meet on the same level, and that is a way to avoid bitterness, hatred." They were very happy to hear me. I was very aware, I am still emotionally very aware, of the situation of my Rwandan sisters and brothers. They are my brothers and sisters. It is the war that has divided us because of politicians and their personal interests, but we are one people, we live the same situation.

Also I spoke another time. One of the people present was a Frenchman named Jean Carbonare who had been involved with the International Federation of Human Rights Leagues. Before the genocide Carbonare had made a visit to Rwanda on behalf of the Federation, and he now said, "The churches did nothing. They let the people prepare for genocide and kill." I asked him, "You say that you were sent here by the United Nations to investigate the human rights situation before the genocide. The United Nations have power because they have men, arms, money. They could send people to prevent the genocide. You saw preparations for genocide. What did you do with your report?" He said, "We gave the report to the proper office." I said, "The church has only the word, but you had means to send men, arms, food. You did not do that. It was necessary to act at that moment to stop the genocide. You, the United Nations Commission on Human Rights, you are strong. I think you could have done something, but you did not." I tell you, the whole meeting place was stunned. The man turned red. Everyone saw that.

International Voices Warning of Genocide

In January 1993 Carbonare made a televised report in France about the preparations for genocide in Rwanda, but it was disregarded. He was speaking on behalf of the French organizations working to counter neo-colonialism in Africa through the International Federation of Human Rights Leagues. As is seen here, for Africans this is easily confused with the similar activities of the United Nations.

Now everyone knew who I was and wanted to talk with me. When we left the meeting hall, the members of the Congo delegation from the Kivu took me aside. "They use poison here. Since you have said the truth, they might do you harm." They gave me honey to drink "so if they give you poison it will not hurt you." I was very nervous. . . . When we gathered, the Rwandan pastors asked me to pray, though there were lots of important pastors and church leaders there. It was awful. I prayed—I don't know what I said. Various politicians began trying to persuade me to join in politics, but I did not want to do that. The leader of our delegation, Pastor Afumba from the Protestant University of Congo, heard people saying, "That woman—she is not from the east; she is from Kinshasa. She has courage, she spoke the truth." He realized that I could not remain there so he organized a plan for our delegation to leave very early the next morning. That night I even went to another hotel and barricaded the door with the bed, but I still could not sleep. Then at 4:00 a.m. Pastor Afumba came with the taxi-bus, and we left Rwanda. We got to Goma and then flew to Kinshasa. When we were in the air, I could breathe. "Ah, Rwanda . . . !"

(Later, when we chose the theme "Women as Agents of Peace and Reconciliation" for our Tumekutana meeting, I saw that Rwanda was a good place for women to learn peace and reconciliation, but in 2004 I was very glad to get away.)

POLITICS OF STATE

I was home from Rwanda, but the matter did not stop there. Mr. Carbonare continued to try to engage me in politics the next time I went to a meeting of the WCC. He and a friend met me in Geneva: "Mme Monique, since we were in Rwanda we have realized we should ask pardon. You are brave. In Congo they are killing people and raping women. You must rise up to denounce them. So we have come to talk with you, for you to gather a group of women, one from each province. You will make a tour of Europe in different countries to denounce what is happening in Congo. (German women will pay for the travel, lodging, everything.) You will tell President Chirac, 'You are killing us.'" I looked at Jean Carbonare, and I said, "What will be my security? I am married; I have children. It is better to ask me to do development activities for youth and women so they can take charge of their own lives. I can't do what you say—those are political things. I do not have a political calling. I can't do that."

Carbonare said, "Okay, Mme Monique. It is good to continue to reflect." He said, "In Congo you have only one single man, Mr. Etienne Tshisekedi, who is incorruptible. They have brought him trunks of dollars, and he refused to take them. I will give you a letter; you must go and talk with him." I said, "Okay." He gave me the letter. When I got back to Kinshasa, I told Tatu Mukuna about this, and he said, "Oh, well, we should go." Our son Eddy came with us. It was the end of 2004 or the beginning of 2005. Carbonare had written to Tshisekedi. When we were announced, he stopped what he was doing: "I want to receive this woman." He asked me, "But how is it that I do not know you?" I said, "I am in the church." We talked, and I said, "You have a good vision of nonviolence, but people are always saying that you should take up arms. I always answer them, 'If he takes up arms, he will ruin his vision.'" He said, "Very good! I have always said that. When you take up arms, it is to kill people. Those people who come to fight me—they are Congolese—but if I fight them I will kill them. I cannot do that. I would really like to work with you. It would be very good for you to come join us." I said, "I am in the church with Pastor Tshimungu." (Mr. Tshisekedi and Pastor Tshimungu were neighbors and knew each other.)

So I refused all those things. I believe that the work we do to raise consciousness is better. One day it will bear fruit because, if children grow up with good ideas, good ways, things will change. It is a task that takes time, but it will bear fruit. That is why I continued to seek ways to bring justice through my ministry in the church. (See Maman Monique with Mr. Tshisekedi in fig. 12.1.)

Figure 12.1. Maman Monique's visit to Mr. Etienne Tshisekedi, longtime nonviolent opposition leader. Kinshasa, beginning of 2005. Seated: Etienne Tshisekedi; L-R standing: aide to Tshisekedi, Tatu Mukuna, son Eddy Lukusa, Maman Monique.

Etienne Tshisekedi

Etienne Tshisekedi (1932–2017), the longtime opponent of Mobutu, continued his nonviolent political opposition under the next two presidents. Laurent Kabila, who led the military coalition that ousted Mobutu, ruled from 1997 until he was assassinated in January 2001. His party then quickly installed his young son, Joseph Kabila, who remained in power until the end of 2018. Joseph Kabila's term officially ended in December 2016, but elections were delayed. The death of Etienne Tshisekedi on February 1, 2017, removed the single most trusted political figure in the country and so prolonged the transitional struggle. But at the start of 2019, Tshisekedi's son Félix became the president of Congo in the first peaceful transfer of power since 1960.

THE CHURCH AND THE STRUGGLE FOR JUSTICE

In November 2003 I attended several large meetings that were being held in Cameroon. These were the General Assembly of the AACC; a consultation of African member churches of the World Alliance of Reformed Churches; and a pre-assembly meeting for women. Usually, a church nominates representatives, and the international body pays for transportation. Our church sent the names of some youth and other pastors, but they did not include mine. However, Dr. Setri Nyomi, the general secretary of the WARC, told our president, "If the women's representative is not there, we will not pay for the tickets of your delegates." So I went to this consultation, which led to the creation of the Alliance of Reformed Churches in Africa. In fact, I was elected as the coordinator for the churches in Central Africa. Of course, it is a volunteer job, but it is a work of reflection and accompanying others, and that is a good thing for me. At the meeting we decided to follow the same objectives as the WARC: to fight for justice and life, for economic and ecological justice, and against all the negative things that destroy life. We must truly fight for there to be a sincere partnership between men and women in the work of the Lord in the church.

Since I was there, I was also able to participate in the AACC General Assembly and the women's pre-assembly. At the pre-assembly they talked about the women's organizations that participate in the International Fellowship of the Least Coin. They said that for all of Africa, only FEBA sends its contribution to the international headquarters. They thanked me very much and asked me, "Is there a reason you send the contribution?" I said, "I am there, and I am the president of FEBA." They saw that we are participating despite the poverty in Congo. We are giving from the little that we have so we can help others, and that is a good thing.

International Fellowship of the Least Coin

The International Fellowship of the Least Coin is an organization founded by an Indian woman named Dr. Shanti Solomon in 1956 as a way for women around the world to pray in concert for peace and reconciliation. Inspired by the widow's tiny gift in Luke 21:1-4, Dr. Shanti and her friends agreed that whenever they prayed, they would set aside the least coin of their currency to contribute to ministries by women. All the "least coins" are collected when the women of a fellowship meet for corporate prayer, and the money is used for both local and international projects. Over the decades, the fellowship has spread around the world. FEBA collects the least coin at each monthly meeting; see the description at the beginning of chapter ten.

In 2004 I also participated in the World Alliance's General Assembly in Accra. The theme was "the plenitude of life." I was happy to share in the Bible studies about Naomi and Ruth. We saw many things that spoke about justice, and that was good. We also created the Accra Confession, which says we must always be engaged in fighting for economic justice, ecological justice. We rejected empire: whatever leads to the creation of a wealth gap between the rich and the poor, a gap that leads to destruction. (Even among the poor there are different levels, and gaps are created.) The confession also pledges to refuse any kind of exploitation and to fight for the fullness of life. That was something special for me because our foundation text for FEBA is John 10:10, where Jesus says, "I have come to give life, life abundant" (author's paraphrase).

13

CATALYST FOR NETWORKING WOMEN AND SOME CONSEQUENCES OF SPEAKING OUT

ON ONE OF MY FIRST TIMES in the United States I began to speak in English—somewhat in spite of myself. It was a gathering of women from partner churches of the Presbyterian Church (USA), and I was invited. The other delegates were all from English-speaking countries; I was the only Francophone. I asked my friend Doug Welch to translate for me, but five minutes before the presentation he said, "Monique, you should make do with your English, even if there are mistakes. If I translate for you, people will hear this as if I were telling the story myself, and they won't know that it really comes from you. You should make the effort." I said, "Ah . . . !" But then I began. I said, "Don't pay attention to my mistakes, but please hear the story. I will do my best to be clear." The people applauded. I spoke, I finished, and at the end they showed that they appreciated my courage. Everyone wanted to talk with me. So my advice: "Speak for yourself." I did not know English well (it is my fourth language), but God helped me and I expressed myself. I made an effort. I did not learn English at school like others, but I worked on it myself because knowing English helps with communication.

English was especially important as I began to expand my acquaintance with many African women who did not speak French. One of my special dreams was to build a network of African Presbyterian women for mutual edification and support. At the same time, I was working to strengthen the voices of the women in my own denomination to benefit from this international fellowship and to carry on after I retired.

As I wrote before, I was elected as associate director of the Department of Women and Families in 1995, and then as director in 2000. As director I had more responsibilities, such as representing my church to our partners—which is how I came to speak in English at a meeting in the United States. Over the course of my service as director I continued to develop projects, and I also added more, both at home in Kinshasa and abroad. I reached out across the continent and across the ocean to build new partnerships to help women speak together and to speak out. In the course of being a catalyst, a networker for women's voices, I could not help but step on some men's toes, and that had consequences. . . .

POLITICS IN THE PRESBYTERIAN CHURCH OF KINSHASA

The term of office for the director of the department is five years, and in 2005 new elections were due. There were women who had studied theology because they wanted to direct the department. One tried to use the moderator to get herself elected. People were accusing me of all kinds of things: "She organized workshops on HIV/AIDS." "She took money and did not give it to us." "She did workshops without passing it by Pastor Tshimungu. He asked her, and she said, 'No, I have already given you the report in the executive committee; I cannot come ask you for permission to do a workshop.'" Finally, the moderator came to talk with me.

I said, "Okay. I will begin by answering about the problem with Pastor Tshimungu. He is president of the church and the executive committee. According to the little administrative training that I have, I know that when activities have been planned, when reports have been given to the executive committee, and the committee has accepted the reports, we are sent to do the work. When I do an activity, am I supposed to come ask permission first? No. I have already presented the plan; now I do the work. When I finish, I bring the reports, and you can see if I have done the planned activities or not. If I have not done them, what was the reason? I must explain that to you; I must write it out. But I cannot—before doing a workshop for the women of a presbytery—come and ask permission of the president of the church. That isn't done." When I said that, the moderator said, "Yes, you are right."

I said, "Now for the question about the workshops on HIV/AIDS. I am the coordinator of the AIDS program, recognized by the partners who sponsor it. I wrote the grant, I asked for the money, they sent it. I gathered the coordination committee. I said, 'They have sent the money for the workshops. Here is the proposal, here is the money, here are the activities and the money for each activity.' They said they needed money. I said, 'There is money for transport and necessities so I will give each person an advance of $100, and you will sign to show that you have received it. At the end of the workshop I will give you the other $100, because if I give it to you now you won't come to work.' So I gave it, they signed, and when the workshop was over I gave each one the remaining $100, and they signed. The secretary (the one who accused me) came to me and said, 'The others, they are not working much at all, but we who are working a lot (he meant himself, the treasurer, and me)—we should take more.' I said, 'Why didn't you bring this up when everyone was here?' He said, 'Oh, no, you see . . .' There was a little transportation money left. I said, 'I understand that you come more than the others—you and the treasurer and I. So I can add $100.' I made him sign for it." I told the moderator, "If I had known what this was about, I could have brought you all the documents." The moderator realized that he had been deceived by my accuser.

I said, "For the last question about Maman Astrid Ntumba. These are elections; she only has to pose her candidacy. If the women elect her, I have no problem with it." He said, "Okay." That is how they failed to make me leave in 2005. The elections were organized, and the women said, "No, no, no. We only want our director to continue." So I continued in the work. As I did so, I was also in the process of organizing things to prepare others so there would be women who knew the work to be candidates for the next elections.

Successes at Home and Abroad

During my second term as director I continued the activities we were already doing and developed some others. The sewing school began to sell its products even in the United States. We created a wrap to sell to support the AIDS program, especially orphans. The microcredit project was going very well, with forty-seven little groups of five women each. We supported about 120 children at school plus nine in university. The nutrition program had also grown; we had more than 700 children in our nine centers, supported with the help of our partner the PC(USA). I also bought a vehicle for the department in 2007–2008, thanks to the efforts of Caryl Weinberg, an American Presbyterian colleague.

For my work as director of the department I began to visit our partner church, the PC(USA), where (as noted above) I unexpectedly started making presentations in English. Often these travels were in the context of the Peacemaking Program of the PC(USA). The first was October 2001. This program brings a number of leaders from partner churches each year to spend a month visiting different congregations and organizations of the PC(USA) to talk about situations of conflict and peacemaking in their home countries. These trips gave me a chance to meet other Presbyterian women and to talk with them. It was when I came for the Peacemaking Program in the fall of 2008 that I met Elsie McKee. She invited me to speak at Princeton Theological Seminary, where she teaches; it was very good. Elsie began to support my ministry at the department, helping with the sewing school and the AIDS program. In 2009–2010 I was building rooms to shelter battered women and girls, and Elsie contributed for this project. But before the money arrived, my work with the women of the CPK came to an abrupt end, and the building remained unfinished. Before continuing to explain my plan to strengthen women's voices on the denominational level, it is important to tell about the way God blessed me to give a collective voice to African women across the continent.

TUMEKUTANA

One of my long-term dreams was to get African Presbyterian women together so that we could develop a common vision of our work, share experiences, and identify the challenges we all face. I first talked about this with women in our partner church in 2002. The PC(USA) had sponsored a gathering of the leaders of their African church partners . . . but the leaders were all men. We wanted the same for the women.

The person who most shared my dream of organizing a meeting of Presbyterian women in Africa was Caryl Weinberg, and she has made this her project. First, there was a planning session in Nairobi in November 2006. There were three African women: Mrs. Veronica Muchiri from the Presbyterian Church of East Africa, the Reverend Dr. Bridget Ben-Naimah from the Evangelical Presbyterian Church of Ghana, and myself. There were also three North Americans: the Reverend Debbie Braaksma, who was then working in Sudan; Dr. Amy McAuley; and Caryl. We began by thinking how we could organize, what biblical text would be our theme, what kind of program, what our conditions would be. Since we were in Kenya, Veronica proposed that we call our gathering Tumekutana, which is Swahili for "We have come together." We decided the theme for the conference would be "To Identify the Challenges Which African Women Face."

The first Tumekutana meeting was held September 9–13, 2007, in Nairobi (see fig. 13.1). We invited the directors of the Departments of Women and Families and at least one other woman (a pastor, if possible) from each partner church. There were forty-six delegates from seventeen countries: Cameroon, D. R. Congo, Ethiopia, Ghana, Kenya, Lesotho, Madagascar, Malawi, Mauritius, Mozambique, Niger, Nigeria, Rwanda, South Africa, Sudan, Zambia, and Zimbabwe. (Women from Cameroon could not get visas to come, but they were counted as being among the participants. Women from Guinea never responded to the invitation.) There were also eighteen representatives from the PC(USA) and three speakers from Africa: Dr. Mercy Amba Oduyoye (Ghana), Dr. Agnes Aboum (Kenya), and Dr. Isabel Phiri (Malawi-South Africa). Gathered in Nairobi, we identified challenges, told our stories, cried,

Figure 13.1. Maman Monique and colleagues at the first Tumekutana conference. Nairobi, 2007. L-R: Maman Monique, Mrs. Fati Ibrahim Salifou from Niger, Mrs. Mercy Chintu from Zambia.

laughed, sang, shared, and danced—it was wonderful to see so many together. We had translators, and everything went well. We organized committees to take charge of various activities: prayer, food, reflection time. We also discussed and approved some resolutions, which each woman was to take back to her church. I was elected president.

When the executive committee planned the next Tumekutana gathering, we chose the theme "Women as Agents of Peace and Reconciliation." I proposed Rwanda as the place: "Rwanda has experienced genocide. I have been there; I have seen the situation. It is good to go there to be inspired by seeing how the women of Rwanda have worked, what they have done to deal with their situation. That will give women an example to help their countries. We are not talking about peace only in contrast to war. There is also the lack of peace by the exclusion of women, or by lack of food." Caryl Weinberg was the principal fundraiser; at the first meeting we had not asked the African churches to contribute. This time we decided that each woman who came should bring $200 from her church, to provide money for feeding the conference or some other part of the program.

The gathering took place in Kigali, October 16–20, 2011. There were delegates from eighteen countries, fifty-three African women and ten Americans. Rwandan women came to talk with us, to testify about their situation; we heard their stories. We invited women to speak to us about the role of women and the contribution of women to the search for peace. We also made resolutions to fight against poverty, to address the issue of AIDS, to do advocacy for the problems that oppress women—even advocacy to the political powers— and to fight for the ordination of women and their integration into levels of decision making. These were our ideas; African women decided. I asked that when we make resolutions at a meeting we also follow up. Participants are supposed to bring those resolutions back to the women at home, but then they should show us what the women have done in response. At the meeting we exchange experiences and seek ways to accompany the women in our churches to help them escape the situations that oppress them. My concern is to get the participants to seek practical results from implementing the resolutions.

Reflecting on the meeting, the executive committee decided that in the future we would not have a large number of North Americans, even if they paid their own way. American women had contributed to the financing, but the committee decided that now the African women must come to the point of being able to meet together without always counting on the partners. So for the next gathering in Ghana we set $400 as the contribution from each church; it was to be from the churches, but the women gave the money.

The third reunion of Tumekutana took place in Accra, September 19–25, 2015, and the theme was, "Liberty in Christ: From Slavery to Strength (empowerment)." The theme was based on the text of Jesus healing the woman who had been crippled for eighteen years (Luke 13:10-17). Jesus saw her and healed her; then there were reactions, "Why did you heal this woman?" He answered, "She is also a daughter of Abraham. For eighteen years she has been crippled by illness; we could not leave her like that" (author's paraphrase). Women cannot stay forever in the situation of suffering and difficulty. In the day when Jesus healed this woman, it was a hard time for women; they did not have value. This woman did not even ask for Jesus' help, but he saw her suffering. That is to show women that Jesus has sought us, has loved us, that now we must make efforts ourselves to take charge of our lives to escape from our situations. I really liked that theme. This time I did not attend; my son was very ill. Dr. Bridget from Ghana was elected as president, Mrs. Veronica became treasurer, and the Reverend Dr. Bukwela Hans ("Buki") was elected vice president. Mrs. Jessie Fubara-Manuel continued as secretary.

I had been in Tumekutana from the beginning, but as time went on, this became less feasible because my circumstances had changed. In the first years I was in good health, and I could go to the cyber café so that we could communicate by email. However, when my health became less good it was very difficult to keep up with the necessary communications. We organized conference calls for meetings of the executive committee, but there were days when I had to excuse myself because I was in severe pain. Also, I said to the staff, "I am no longer director of the Department of Women and Families in my church. I cannot continue to be president of Tumekutana because it should be a woman who is directing women in the church." (Just before the second gathering in 2011 I was deposed from my ministry in the department, as I will tell in the next section, and that contributed to my determination, though I also believe that having new leaders is good.)

In September 2018, however, I had the joy of participating in the fourth Tumekutana conference in Johannesburg. It was wonderful to see so many friends again! And to be able to share some of the work of FEBA, because we were asked to produce the special tie-dyed wraps with the logo for Tumekutana 2018. At the gathering, I was surprised and very touched when the women honored me with a special award, a beautiful inscribed plate. This visit to South Africa was bittersweet. There was the joy in seeing so many friends, and also some of my family who live in South Africa. This was followed by the deep sadness of my mother's death. She had been ill for a long time and living in South Africa with my sister. It was a blessing to be able to visit her in those last days of her earthly life.

Gathering together in Tumekutana has fulfilled a special dream of building a network of women across Africa, but in the meanwhile I was still working to help my sisters in the CPK develop their own voices, and that kind of speaking out has a cost.

Raising Consciousness and Strengthening Women's Voices

We are raising women's consciousness to say "no" to things that are not good. Often men are aggressive and try to intimidate women so they won't talk. People think that when you say no you are impolite, disobedient. "It is the head of the church; you must not say no." "It is the pastor; you must not say no." No. No. No. The head of the church should be the model. I respected the president. I greeted him with lots of respect, but when he acted in a way that was not good, I could not accept that. I was director of the Department of Women. I had to defend the rights of women, advocate for them, open their spirits. But how can you defend women's rights if you just accept everything men say to you?

There are many ways to serve in the church; sometimes one of the most important contributions is to stand up to power. Throughout my time as director of the Department of Women and Families there were difficulties when I raised questions that disturbed the authorities. Frequently, it was a matter of money, but at the root was a struggle for power and the fact that I was a woman. Each small conflict added a layer of tension until in 2009–2010 things exploded.

Many national leaders are there for their own interests, for wealth. It is the same with some church leaders. In African countries there are women who have courage and work hard; when they speak the truth, they suffer. I am myself a victim of that. When I stood up against the church president and all his entourage, they said that I was disrespectful. I have already spoken of some conflicts with the church authorities. There were many more. Here I will explain the series of events that led to my departure from the position of director of the Department of Women and Families of the Presbyterian Church of Kinshasa.

THE END OF MY WORK AT THE DEPARTMENT
OF WOMEN AND FAMILIES

In April 2010 I was suspended from my position at the department because I had organized the first women's congress. The women of the CPK had never defined their vision, and there were no bylaws for their organization. I took the problem to the General Assembly in 2009 when I made my director's report, and the assembly agreed that we might organize a congress of women.

Everything was agreed, and letters authorizing the congress were sent to every congregation to invite delegates. The moderator of the church opened the five-day congress on November 29, 2009. Since 2000 the women had had two committees (as the president had insisted so that the pastors' wives would have a position of power), but now the women voted to return to one organization. They also defined certain criteria for being leaders. But, sadly, before these resolutions could be established, the church authorities decided to declare the congress null and void. They said that we had not respected the decisions of the General Assembly. I wrote to them to defend our whole procedure, and I asked them, "What did we not respect? You wrote the letter of invitation; you opened the congress. We followed all the instructions. You did not even wait for the minutes to appear to see if there was something wrong with the women's resolutions." It was just a move to impose on women and maintain their inferior position.

After the congress our partners in the PC(USA) learned that there was a problem. A regular meeting of our church with the PC(USA) was already planned for March 2010. The Reverend Debbie Braaksma, the new executive secretary for contacts with African partners, came with the PC(USA) delegates to the meeting in Kinshasa. She asked to speak with the women; sixty gathered to meet her, and we told her what had happened. She talked with our church authorities to hear what they said. But the church leaders decided that we had gotten them in trouble. Not long after, when we were gathered to prepare for the women's annual preaching day, the head of the church suddenly came. "You have accused us to the partners. Who are the women who spoke to the partners? I want to see them. You did not respect the leaders of our community." And so on. The women were afraid. Maman Antoinette raised her hand, "They told the partners the truth." It only took one person speaking, and the women began to talk. "You annulled our congress; we don't agree with that. We were at the congress; we made the decisions. It was not our director. These were the resolutions of the women; it was we who made them. If there is a woman who did not work on the congress, who did not accept the resolutions that we made, let her stand up." No one did.

After the PC(USA) delegation left, on April 10, 2010, the president suspended me for three months from my position. The authorities evicted the people I had been sheltering at the center so I took them into my home. There were ten: eight women and two little children. There were also other children for whom I had to find a place—and some of the equipment and sewing machines until the center was in a state to care for them.

On May 24, elections were held to choose a new director for the department. The women are supposed to organize their elections themselves, but church leaders tried instead to impose their own choice of candidate. The women refused. The procedure started at 9:00 a.m. and went until 5:00 p.m. The women kept on refusing. Finally, they said, "If you do not want our director Maman Monique, we will choose her assistant because we want to continue with her vision." It was the first time that the women rose up to say, "NO!" Finally, they elected my assistant.

The authorities were not finished with me, however. They said, "We must ask her to return all the property of the church, the car. We can give her another job." (They meant for me to raise money for "the church," but they would spend it.) They invited me to meet with the president, Pastor Tshimungu, and all his staff. I answered their questions; then afterwards I repeated the main points in written form. The key problem was money. I reminded them that I had equipped the Women's Center, using my own sewing machines and pots and pans until I could get funding to buy them for the center. The scholarship aid from partners was very important, but it was not enough. I personally borrowed the money needed to complete the school fees for the children. Through my friend Caryl Weinberg I got the car for my work, and I made sure that it was registered in the church's name, even though it was given specifically for the women's work and I was using it to take those with dis-abilities to church. I had not even received the 10 percent of what I raised that was supposed to be my salary. Yet, all the authorities cared about was getting back the car; they did not even ask about the women and children evicted from the center.

I told them I would not accept any job they could give me. I always said to the authorities, "I am not a do-nothing. I have work in my hands. It is God who hired me here. If you make me leave, God will give me something else to do. You will see me working. I will not be idle." When they made me leave, people came to weep, but I did not cry. "Why are you crying? God will give me an-other work. It was God who hired me; I was there to serve God. God gave me exceptional courage."

After the elections, which the men had manipulated, many women were discouraged about continuing to work in the church, or even continuing to worship there. Indeed, my dismissal was not accepted by them and it was unjust, but we do not want to destroy the life of the church for that. As a Christian, I went on December 28, 2010, to the women's Christmas worship service to raise the consciousness of the women, to ask them to tell others who no longer wanted to work in the church to come back. When the women saw me, they cried out for joy; they demanded that I be welcomed and asked me to speak. I was no longer a part of the leadership. I had come to worship. I said, "The person who makes peace cannot accept destruction. So I invite you to return, to take strength to work, and to energize others who are not here." They asked if they could come to consult with me because they did not have much experience. I said, "Fine. I will always help as much as possible."

PART FOUR

NEW DIRECTIONS

Tabitha-Dorcas "was devoted to good works and acts of charity. At that time she became ill and died. . . . [When Peter] arrived, they took him to the room upstairs. All the widows stood beside him, weeping and showing tunics and other clothing that Dorcas had made while she was with them. Peter put all of them outside, and then he knelt down and prayed. He turned to the body and said, 'Tabitha, get up.' Then she opened her eyes, and seeing Peter, she sat up. He gave her his hand and helped her up. Then calling the saints and widows, he showed her to be alive. This became known throughout Joppa, and many believed in the Lord."

ACTS 9:36-37, 39-42

14

SAD ENDINGS AND
NEW BEGINNINGS

AFTER THE ELECTIONS, Tatu Mukuna and I went to speak to the head of the church, Pastor Tshimungu. Tatu Mukuna was angry: "Why do you hate my wife? You have done everything possible to get rid of her." He cited many examples. I said, "No. Let it go. We did not come for that. Please wait in the car while I talk with Pastor Tshimungu." Tatu Mukuna went to the car, and I said to Pastor Tshimungu, "How are you going to repair the harm you have done to the heart and spirit of my children and my husband? I am strong; I can resist everything. For me this is nothing because for me life will continue. But you have hurt my husband and my children very much. How are you going to correct all that?" Pastor Tshimungu was silent.

In less than a year my world was broken. Being cast out from my position was not all or even the worst. My engagement with the wider church was challenged, and my dear family suffered this upheaval. And then my heart broke when my beloved husband suddenly died. But as we teach the women, nothing can separate us from the love of God in Christ (Romans 8:28-39).

THE AFTERMATH OF MY DEPARTURE

Politics on the Ground. Firing me from my position was not enough for the authorities; they tried to exclude me from every other place too. I was an elder in the church. The church authorities wrote to my congregation to suspend me from this office, accusing me of mishandling church money. I explained what had really happened, and the consistory (session) refused to suspend me. The church authorities also tried to get other church bodies to exclude me, but they failed there, as they had at the congregational level.

First, they wrote a letter to try to have me excluded from the National Federation of Protestant Women when we had the congress in July 2010. The leaders of all the provinces of the Federation gathered without my knowledge and rejected Pastor Tshimungu's letter. "No! Monique is here as a Protestant woman, national secretary of our organization. It is the congress that elected Monique. Her church does not have the right to suspend her here. She has left her position in her church, but she cannot leave her responsibilities at the Federation because it is the congress of Protestant women that elected her." They informed the church's president: "This is not the CPK; this is an ecumenical association. You cannot tell us what to do."

The next context was the international church, at the Assembly of Unification of the Reformed Churches, which took place in Grand Rapids, Michigan, in June 2010. The two families of Reformed churches, the World Alliance of Reformed Churches and the Reformed Ecumenical Council, had decided to unite; they would become the World Communion of Reformed Churches. I had received an invitation from the Alliance, but Pastor Tshimungu suspended it. I said, "I am the Central African coordinator for the Alliance of Reformed Churches in Africa; I will go in that capacity." He said, "Who will pay for your ticket?" I said, "The people who invited me." The Congo system requires a letter of invitation from the international sponsor and a letter of authorization from a local body, so I named FEBA as the local sponsor. I went to the consul and got the visa. The Reverend Debbie Braaksma and her PC(USA) office paid for my ticket and reserved the hotel for me. (What I did not know then was that the money the PC[USA] used was part of what Elsie had sent for my work at the department, before she knew that I was suspended. Elsie had said that the money was for my work so Debbie Braaksma used it to pay for my trip to Grand Rapids to represent the women. It is a small world.)

When I got to Grand Rapids, everyone was surprised—and they welcomed me. At registration I told Doug Chaal: "I came in the capacity of an observer, not as a representative of the CPK." He said, "Nonsense. I am putting you down as a delegate; let them come chop off my head!" Other American partners who had known me in Congo came to welcome me. I said, "I told your colleague that I am not here as a delegate, but he put me down as one." (I knew the church officials who did not want me to attend would be angry.) My friends answered in Tshiluba, "*Bualu buabo.*" ("That's their problem.")

At the assembly they wanted to elect me as a member of the executive committee of the World Communion, but I declined. How could I do that with the situation in my church? But I fought to have Mrs. Veronica Muchiri elected. Her church refused. I was astonished! I worked to convince people to nominate her. When her name was presented at the plenary, some people wanted to nominate a man. I raised my hand. Dr. Setri Nyomi, general secretary of the Alliance, recognized me. I said, "I do not know why people are objecting to what we have decided. We passed a resolution here that we must have 50 percent women, 50 percent men on the executive committee. Why do you refuse Mrs. Veronica's name?" I continued by explaining all the things she had done. People applauded, and that is how she was elected. Then the moderator from our church came to me and asked me to present his name because he saw that I had power to sway people. I told him I had already nominated Pastor Elisee Musemakueli from Rwanda, and I would not substitute another name. The Rwandans have helped me find partners to finance women's activities; they are open, they express themselves publicly. Why should I be their enemy? When we returned to Congo, the church leaders of the CPK criticized me.

But leaving aside politics, the Assembly of Unification was very good. One reason was the choice of Grand Rapids, where we were with the Native Americans. They were present and spoke; they participated with everyone else. Another reason was the unity: Why should Reformed people be divided? It is good to be together and so to show our unity in Jesus Christ. The vision should always be the same: fighting for justice. Also, we women were able to secure a resolution that delegates for meetings or work should be 50 percent women, 50 percent men. I was one of the two people who read the French version of the resolution in the General Assembly. And we got 50 percent women for the executive committee. The World Communion walks with justice, and we must practice this justice in our families, churches, society, country.

Mediation in Congo. The World Communion of Reformed Churches also worked to bring justice to the situation in our church. After I was forced out of my position, the whole issue was referred to the World Communion, and in December 2010 a delegation led by Dr. Setri Nyomi came to talk with all the parties. Pastor Tshimungu was absolute: "She does not want to submit and has not given us the minutes of the congress."

When Dr. Setri and the delegation came to my house, we talked for three hours. They had asked me to include some other women, and there were also the children who had been evicted from the center whom I had at my house. The delegation listened to me, to the women, to the children, to my husband; then they asked what we wanted. Personally, I asked that the congress be recognized and its resolutions accepted. The women wanted the same but also that the elections be held again and I should return as director. The children said they wanted my ministry to be supported because without what I had been doing for them, they had nowhere to live and nothing to eat. When Dr. Setri asked me for the minutes of the congress, I explained that the secretaries were discouraged because their resolutions had already been annulled. He asked me to do the minutes and send him a copy so he could follow up. Each member of the World Communion delegation gave his or her testimony about me; I was very much touched. They discovered that there is a lot of injustice in the church, but the delegates were happy to receive positive testimony about me.

But our church leaders refused to accept the counsel of the mediators. The CPK was sanctioned, and many of the international partners refused to continue in fellowship with this denomination at that time.

New Beginnings in the Church

In the women's work there were still two committees, as Pastor Tshimungu had insisted in 2000. His wife was the head of one; Maman Annie Ntumba was the director of the department, under the supervision of the president's wife. Control of the property was also divided. All projects had been stopped when I left. After a time, Maman Annie started the sewing school again, but there was no nutrition program, no school support for orphans, no welcome to battered women, no AIDS ministry, no animal husbandry, no microcredit. When elections were to be held again in 2016, the women wanted me to return to work in the CPK. They said, "We need you; you must come because nothing is running." I said, "No, I already have other business. I cannot leave what I have begun in order to come back there. I cannot direct two big projects."

I have very much loved my work in the church, more than being a businesswoman, because in the church I was touching the lives of people, and I really liked transforming lives. I have heard the witness of the women:

"Maman Monique opened our spirits." "Maman Monique transformed our lives." Still today women say that. It is why when the church celebrated the Women's Jubilee, the fiftieth anniversary of the Department of Women and Families in 2016, they asked me to speak. I said, "What I am, is thanks to the church." I spoke to Pastor Tshimungu and the authorities: "Thank you, because as head of the church, you agreed to give my name to be a member of the Central Committee, and that experience was very formative for me. We went to many meetings together, and I took advantage of them to learn. But I want to say one thing; even a slave can always defend herself because it is the Jubilee. You must not be so restrictive with the church decisions regarding women's activities. You have formed a person, she has gained knowledge, but now you throw her out and the church loses, and that is not good. Since it is the Jubilee, one must speak the truth."

For the eight years after my exclusion, I remained involved in my local parish and devoted myself to FEBA. In 2016 Pastor Tshimungu died, leaving the denomination in severe debt from misappropriation of church funds. His friends expected to continue to control the CPK, but at the General Assembly in the summer of 2017 some courageous younger ministers, led by the pastor of my own congregation, rose up to object and to insist on new candidates. And the "revolution" succeeded. Over the next year the new president, Pastor Kalonji Isaac, and his colleagues began to make changes. They worked to address the internal issues, including my dismissal, and to rebuild ties with international partners, including the PC(USA).

In 2018 I was warmly invited back into church leadership. It was a surprise, an honor, and also a challenge. The post they offered was "president of projects"—to oversee grants because they knew that the partners would trust me. My condition was that they must accept the resolutions of the women's congress from 2009. I also told them frankly that I had my hands full with FEBA, but that I would work with them as much as I could, informally, to build up the CPK again to follow Jesus more closely.

MY WORK: SUPPORTING MY FAMILY AND LEADING WOMEN

The Department of Women and Families had been the focal point of my working life for fifteen years, and I supported my family by participating in the income-generating projects that I developed for the department. After I left the department, I began my business again to be able to feed my family, and also so that I could continue my ministry for women and girls and orphans through FEBA.

To start business again in 2010, I got a bank loan of $8,500. First I took out a tithe, to pay for school for some children. Then I rented a shop at the Kinshasa market and began business in Brazzaville. The commercial world had changed a great deal since 1995. Dubai had become an important center, but the biggest producer was China. Their merchandise was of good quality and less expensive. Many Chinese were coming to do building projects in Congo so travel to China was cheaper than to Europe, and Congolese merchants were also going to China. To make a profit you have to buy your materials in China yourself because otherwise your competitors who purchase there directly can undersell what you produce. I calculated and decided that when I could get the money, I would go to China. Late in 2010 I began to travel overseas once or twice a year, to Dubai sometimes but more often to China. Sometimes I took commissions for others; sometimes another person would take an order for me, but it had to be someone with a good sense about the market. One Congolese friend has been very helpful, but his store is very upscale so he is less good at identifying what a lower-price-bracket clientele might buy.

Reestablishing FEBA on a firm basis became my main ministry. During the period 2005–2010 it had not functioned well under Maman Pauline; there were no monthly meetings and very limited activities. When we began again, the only other founders involved were Maman Agnes and Maman Marie-Jeanne, but the women who had been my colleagues at the department—Maman Jeannette, Maman Antoinette, and others—followed me to continue to work with me.

But I must reintroduce Elsie. In August 2010 there was a visit that was the beginning of a great partnership which God gave me, to me and my very dear sister Elsie. She came with her husband, John, and one of her sisters, Beth, to visit us at my house (she told you about this in the first chapter). We talked; we had time to share a little about what the church problems meant for my ministry. Elsie, John, and Beth met the women and girls and children whom I had brought home when they were evicted from the center with me; my visitors were very moved by these stories. They saw the church center where I had worked: places where there had been moringa trees, where there had been rabbit hutches—all destroyed. We saw the rooms I was building for battered women, for which Elsie had sent money, incomplete and empty. We saw from outside the rooms where there had been classes (one still marked "English" on the door). We could not enter the big hall or offices. Elsie wanted to help us, but we knew that we must see how the situation evolved with the World Communion's mediation. When that intervention failed to persuade the CPK church leaders to affirm the women's congress, and it was definite that there would be no reconciliation, Elsie set out to find a new avenue to continue her support of my ministry.

The Death of Tatu Mukuna

Then Tatu Mukuna suffered a sudden health crisis and died on January 6, 2011. It broke my heart. At first all I could do was cry. We had lived together so well; I called him "my friend." He accompanied me in many things. When there were problems, he would lend his strength and support. At church many women said that ours was a model marriage. I could ask him to help me; he was very good. He wanted very much to protect me; he did not want me to be sick, or to have problems.

Tatu Mukuna's health had already been somewhat fragile because of his asthma, but I think that he died suddenly because he had had so many shocks. He wanted me to serve God, but the way I had been forced out of my church position was very hard for him, and he blamed it for my hypertension. In fact, the day he died I was ill. It was a bad day. The night before I had seen visions; there was something that was not right. That morning I was crossing Kinshasa on my way to Brazzaville, but my head began to hurt badly. "Lord, what is wrong? I must see a doctor." I walked slowly, carefully, holding my head in my hands, and got back to our parish health center. The doctor took my blood pressure, and it was *very* high. He gave me a prescription and told me to go home and sleep. When Tatu Mukuna came home from his work at church about 1:00 p.m., his cousin told him about my blood pressure. Tatu Mukuna exclaimed, "Eeeh—where did that come from?" He sat waiting for me to wake up. When I got up, he said, "I ate a banana, but I feel stuffed. But you—eat, eat! That way you will feel better." He gave me the water to wash my hands and took some food but ate only one spoonful. I began to eat. He ate a second spoonful. And stopped.

Then he began to gasp, "Maybe it is the asthma." He had an inhaler, but it did not work. I immediately forgot all about my blood pressure. Our son Kanyinda came with the aminophylline. His cousin said, "Maman, find a car—let's get Papa to the hospital quickly." We did not have a car. The church had taken back the one I used for my work, and Tatu Mukuna had sold his because it was beginning to have problems. I said, "I will call a taxi." "No, ask the neighbors." Our son Moise said, "Put him on my back; I will carry him to the car." Kanyinda helped. They all got in the car, and I gave them the money for the hospital.

But he was already dead when they got him to the health center. We did not know it, but the people at the center did. They knew that I had had high blood pressure that morning and feared I would have a stroke if they told me. On my way to the health center I passed by Maman Antoinette's place and told her, and she spread the news at church. We arrived at the clinic. From the way people spoke I sensed that Tatu Mukuna was already dead, and I cried! Moise came to hug me, "Papa is there." "Where?" They pointed to another room. I saw him and touched him . . . it was terrible. They took me out. Moise did not know his father was dead. When he saw me, he burst into tears and fainted. Kanyinda did not want to see me; he was over in a corner crying. He was the one who called everyone: the family members in the United States, his sister in South Africa (who was expecting a baby very soon). It was dreadful.

For me, Tatu Mukuna's death was a terrible shock. Everyone loved him; everyone began crying. The pastor had called just one elder, but all of them had heard. When we got home, we found the place full of people; all the elders were there. Our daughter Judith had wanted to come with us to the hospital, but I told her stay and keep the house. When she heard that her father was dead, she fell down the stairs and almost died.

Tatu Mukuna's death broke my heart.

Not long before his death he had said, "Funerals are expensive. Why spend so much for death? To buy a fine coffin? That is useless." It was like he was already preparing us. But funerals are very important for the living, and Tatu Mukuna's was very well organized. Lots of choirs sang; lots and lots of people came, including some American friends. I am very grateful to the church, to the women of the church for helping us. I remember one of them told me about her child who said, "Eeeh. I see today how it is good to die. He will go directly to heaven."

LIFE AFTER TATU MUKUNA'S DEATH

After his death I could not sleep. One day I saw Tatu Mukuna in a dream. "Ah, you are there! You left on your trip without telling me goodbye." He said, "No, I did not want to make this trip. It was Papa (God) who decided that I would travel." I said, "But why did he want you to leave?"

It is customary for relatives to take the dead person's property. After Tatu Mukuna's death, his family came and took all his things from our house. It was his cousins—all except the young man who is now our pastor and whom I had brought up. He said, "Leave it." But the others did not listen. They took our bed; they came into our room and threw my things on the floor. They took my jewelry and my little cupboard. I said, "No, you have no right to take those things." And they stopped. But they took everything that had been Tatu Mukuna's. Then they said, "Call the children." But there was nothing left, just some old clothes. Eddy took his father's Bible and hymnbook. Kanyinda took a shirt. Mukuna Junior took a pair of shoes. But the cousins had taken everything. They took the pens and markers that I had bought in the United States for the children—everything.

I stayed at home for six months. I could not even go out; I did not have the energy. My husband and I often sat outside together in the evening, but after his death I was always in the house, on the floor. There was no bed, only a thin little mattress. That was the beginning of my back problems: maybe partly humidity but also partly staying immobile for so long. Before, I walked quickly, but afterwards I could not walk well. It was hard for me, and I asked myself, "Why must my life be like this? But it is God's will." At first I cried almost every day; my children were anxious. It was only by prayer that I could return to life.

One thing was very good: I received the love of the community, of many women. Lots of people came to visit me to console me. You know, our ministry is to help people in need. I saw the love of every kind of people, even the church. They suspended me in April 2010, and my husband died in January 2011, and I saw all the women. They collected money for me, and they decided to come to visit me in groups. Each week a group came to pray—it was very good. I have the habit of teaching women who are experiencing these circumstances, but for me it was very difficult. When the women visited, they said, "But you are the one who teaches." I said to myself that I must accept the situation, and I prayed for God to give me the strength. Every day I asked God to help me forget and to begin life again.

Woman, Cradle of Abundance / FEBA Renewed and Flourishing

When American friends asked about my greatest joy in my work, I answered, "When someone is in trouble and when I talk with him or her, if she recovers, if she now has hope to live, if she regains joy and dignity: this is my joy. It goes to my heart. When I can find a woman or a girl who has completely lost hope, and when I can talk with her so that she has hope and thinks that she can change and transform her life—it makes me very happy."

When she has hope, we can work together to find practical ways to make those changes: learning to sew, starting a small business, making a safe home for her children, passing on the hope and help to someone else. We are a community of sharing and supporting and creating. In this chapter you will hear the voices of some of my friends and colleagues and members of FEBA, all of us who work together to live Jesus' promise to bring life abundant (John 10:10).

The Renewed Work of FEBA

The original focus of FEBA had been consciousness-raising and the monthly meetings for inspiration, which led to various types of education and empowerment, particularly around health and sexuality, financial literacy and microcredit. Most of the income-generating projects were organized through my ministry at the church Department of Women and Families. However, my departure from the department meant that almost all of these services were discontinued in our area so the renewed FEBA stepped into the gap to become a miniature, multifaceted social service organization as well as a force for fellowship and education. It was miniature because for the first eight years it had no place except my house, and no outside partner except Elsie and her friends. And yet—it has demonstrated afresh how a determined group of women have been able to inspire each other and build a beacon of hope for many others. An important part of that story is hearing the actual voices of leaders and a few of those whom they have touched. This chapter tells about our work and our community.

In 2010 we began afresh to raise women's consciousness about their identity as human beings created in the image of God with all human rights. We have done this with more than a thousand girls and women. Our monthly meetings are the one time when as many members as possible gather. The singing, Bible reading and preaching, prayers, offering of the least coin, and dance give the women, girls, and orphans an opportunity to express their pain, share their joys, strengthen each other to go on.

Here is perhaps a good place to tell you something about our Bible lessons. The fundamental biblical texts of our work are John 10:10 (Jesus came to give life abundant) and Genesis 1:26-27 (God created male and female in God's image). Once when I was speaking in Princeton I suggested with a twinkle in my eye that when God made the man, he did not really know what he was doing, but the woman was his masterpiece because he had practiced on the man. The audience laughed with me. Naturally, many of the biblical texts we have used are about women who are models for us.

- Deborah (Judges 4), who was a courageous and honest judge.

- Naomi (Ruth 1:1-14), a mother-in-law who freed her daughters-in-law with wise counsel and expressions of her love.

- Ruth (Ruth 3–4), who despite her youth attached herself to her mother-in-law and her God, which brought her the joy of becoming an ancestor of Jesus Christ.

- Hannah (1 Samuel 1:1-19; 2:1-8), who was barren, her heart bruised by the taunts of her rival Peninnah, but she trusted in the Eternal, prayed and promised, and God consoled her.

- Abigail (1 Samuel 25:14-28), who spared David from committing murder and saved her own people by her spirit of listening, her intelligence, and her wisdom.

- The Shunammite woman (2 Kings 4:8-37), whose generosity, spirit of hospitality, faith, and attachment to God's work brought her happiness.

- Esther (Esther 4–6), a woman with a humble soul, a woman of prayer, wisdom, and strong faith in God who saved her people by prayer.

- The woman of Proverbs 31, virtuous, worthy, and wise, who gave her son good counsel, provided for her family by her work, and was appreciated by all the world.

- Elizabeth (Luke 1:5-25), rewarded for her integrity and righteousness, as she and her husband worshiped God with fervor: age does not limit God and nothing is impossible to him.

- Mary (Luke 1:26-38), a young girl, a virgin chosen by God to give birth to our Savior.

- Mary and Martha (Luke 10:38-42; John 11:1-44), each one with her gift, each one confessing her faith and acting on it.

- The Samaritan woman (John 4:1-26), who was saved by speaking the truth, and, thanks to her, the village believed in Jesus Christ.

- Mary of Magdala (John 20:11-18), the first to see Jesus after his resurrection; he saved her, and she remained devoted to him.

- Dorcas-Tabitha (Acts 9:36-43), a generous woman who helped widows, whose coming back to life because of the widows' tears led many people of Joppa to convert.

There are others, like the story of Jezebel (1 Kings 21:5-24), who abused her husband's power to kill innocent Naboth, and God's justice for the oppressed was manifested. Sometimes the good and bad examples are presented together, as in comparing the way that Zelophehad's daughters went about getting their rights (Numbers 27:1-11) and Lot's daughters took matters into their own hands (Genesis 19:30-38).

We also preach on many other texts that might not seem like they apply especially to women, but we are all Christians. Some point to the fact that though we are sinners, Jesus dwells in us and loves us (2 Corinthians 4:5-16; Ephesians 1:3-14), and we are healed by his wounds (Matthew 8:14-17). Some emphasize love: God's for us and our calling to love (Isaiah 43:1-5; Romans 8:28-29; 1 Corinthians 13). Some remind us that we work together with God

(1 Corinthians 3:8-16; Matthew 28:18-20). Some challenge us: Galatians 5:16-25 (the fruits of the Spirit: which is yours?); John 14:27 (Jesus left us his peace; let us always seek to live in peace); Matthew 5:43-48; 25:31-46 (let us love our neighbors and pray for them, and care for the least); Mark 11:24-26 (we are called to forgive); and Isaiah 1:15-18 (flee evil; do good and justice). Our preaching is to inspire and energize our members.

DIRECT ASSISTANCE

FEBA has about 1200 members; anyone is welcome to join, without regard to language, religion, or origin. Sometimes many members are able to come to the monthly gathering. As the economic situation has become more and more difficult, fewer have been able to attend. They are too weak from hunger to walk long distances, and there is no money for a bus.

Regularly—at least ten times a week—we have battered girls or women or other victims of violence who come seeking help. One was a thirteen-year-old orphan. Ephrasie's parents had died of AIDS, which is considered a mystery and curse, so she was accused of killing them by sorcery. Her relatives beat and starved her, and she caught tuberculosis. A cousin finally brought her to me. I took her into my home and got her medical care. Some

---

Sorcery

The words *sorcery* or *witchcraft* sound exotic to Western ears, the kind of thing one reads about in fiction. In order to make this "foreign" concept more comprehensible, it is helpful to place it in the larger context of how material and spiritual are related. In traditional religions, physical health and spiritual well-being are inextricably interrelated. Western medicine has often led to making a significant split between body and mind, health and faith, although more recently it has been recognized that a human being is a whole and what the mind believes has an effect on what the body experiences. In its early years, AIDS was regarded as a curse far beyond the bounds of rural Africa, so it is not surprising that Congolese explained it as sorcery. Human beings strike out at any threat, particularly a mysterious one, so attacks on children—or elderly women or others—as sorcerers are not uncommon.

women said to me, "Maman Monique, this child might infect you." I said, "I cannot leave her to die." We helped her get well. Later, other relatives promised to care for her and send her to school. Just recently I saw her and learned that she has completed secondary school and has her state diploma. Another story is about Kenge, who also was an orphan. Her uncle took care of her until he died, but then his widow told Kenge she must become a barmaid-prostitute to survive. Kenge hated this. She found her way to us, and we enrolled her in the sewing school.

We also visit those who are sick or in trouble, and we accompany those living with HIV/AIDS, as Maman Henriette will explain. Besides practical care, we provide counseling. We help with medical expenses and, in those sad cases when someone dies, with burial. Survival is the first step. We regularly give food to the women of FEBA because many of them are very poor, and others are very elderly (women of the "third age") who are unable to work for a living. Caring for the starving or broken also goes beyond those immediately at hand. We have sent assistance to those in eastern Congo. Then in 2017, when there was the Kamuina Nsapu fighting in the Kasai, we sent clothes and food. We focus on girls and women but also help anyone in a desperate situation who comes to us. Ntambue Patrick, a young refugee from this Kasai war, was trying to survive on his small business until he was attacked by thieves, robbed, stabbed, and left almost dead. We took him in and got medical care for him so he was healed. Now we are helping him prepare to return to secondary school for his final year. Meanwhile, he is serving as a good messenger and assistant for FEBA.

Civil Conflict

Besides the ongoing guerrilla war in the Kivu in eastern Congo, in 2016–2017 there was effectively a small-scale undeclared war in the Kasai, Maman Monique's home province, between a local chief and government forces. It devastated the region, with many villages destroyed, thousands killed, and hundreds of thousands displaced and starving. Some refugees fled to Kinshasa. Recovery in the Kasai has been slow and difficult.

The Story of Maman Henriette, FEBA's "Jane of All Work"

HENRIETTE: I am called Kibadi Nzeyi Henriette. I was born in 1960, in Kinshasa, where my father was living. Before telling my story I need to explain where my parents came from. My father was the son of a slave. My mother's uncle, the hereditary chief of his village, bought people, including a boy and a girl. At that time, instead of adopting children who had no family, people sold or bought them. Men were bought as laborers; parents might sell a child to pay a debt. Also, sometimes there were famines, and families would sell their children to have a bit of money to survive. Although normally a woman's children belong to her husband's family, when a slave had children with a woman of the village, the children belonged to the woman's family, to the village, because the father was not from the village. The slave couple who worked for my mother's uncle had a son who became my father. He was also a slave, but that was not generally known in the village. My mother's uncle sent his own children to school but not this slave boy. Then he decided to make his niece marry the slave. She objected because they had grown up in the same household, "How can I marry my cousin? He is my brother." But her uncle insisted.

My father lived in the village until the age of sixteen, but then he met some friends who said, "You are a slave here; don't stay. Go to Kinshasa." With them he walked the long distance to the city—it took twenty-one days. In Kinshasa they found a white man named Mr. John. My father said, "I don't have parents. I will come work for you." Mr. John said, "No. I will send you to school to learn to be a mechanic." So he became a mechanic. After several years my father called my mother from the village. She came, but she did not want to be here. She stayed some years and had six children (two girls and four boys). I was the oldest. At primary school I was always the first in my class. But my mother went back to the village and told her uncle, "I am divorced." He said, "He is our slave. Since you had children with him, he can never flee but must stay in our clan. Go back to Kinshasa." She refused. Finally, her uncle agreed.

My mother left when I was twelve. My father did not love us anymore, "Since your mother has fled, I don't want you anymore. You are going to suffer. I am alone; I will die alone." We said, "Papa, if you are alone, where did we come from?" He repeated, "I don't have parents, I don't have a village. Your village is there—it is not mine; I don't know mine. I am alone." When he died recently, he left his money to a pastor. But the children of my mother's uncle came to say, "He was our slave, and all his things are ours." They went to court, but we don't know how it will come out.

After my mother left, my father took another wife, a girl my age. My sister and brothers and I were abandoned, and we cried all the time. My father decided he did not have to house us; he would have children with another woman—and in fact he had a lot of them. We had a hard time to live. He did not feed us, or pay for school. With what I earned from selling sugarcane and oranges and mangos on the street I paid school fees for my little sister and myself; my brothers did not go to school. I did not study a lot but was able to go to the Athenée Lumumba for two years of secondary school, and then three years in nursing school to become an assistant nurse. Then I worked at a state hospital at Matonge; they didn't pay much so I decided to do a little business. I did not have much money, but I went to Bas-Congo to buy little articles and brought them back to sell.

Then I married Mr. Bayin Zitanda Ferdinand; we have six sons. My husband has his master's degree, but he accepted me despite the fact that I did not have a lot of schooling. He said, "I must marry this girl. She has many difficulties." I do what I can to help my children. My husband is a teacher, but he does not have enough money to pay school fees for our children so I have to work too. I have done different kinds of training: tie-dyeing, hat-making, jewelry-making. Two sons have not studied much; they are mechanics. The third and fourth went to university, and one did a master's. The youngest is still in school.

Since I have lived such troubles in my life, I wanted to enter FEBA to show other women like myself how to make hats and jewelry. I also did a training on HIV/AIDS, and I work to raise consciousness, take sick people to the hospital, and accompany those living with the disease. We do everything possible for them to have access to medicine. We educate them and their families, in order to avoid stigmatization. Many families abandon a member who has AIDS, but we accompany her and show her Jesus so that she can understand that she is accepted just like others. In addition, I work with our mill; we have had lots of trouble with it. And I help take care of the schoolchildren, to visit schools and pay fees.

ECONOMIC AND EDUCATIONAL EMPOWERMENT
FOR WOMEN AND GIRLS

Microsavings. Besides transformed consciousness and assistance with immediate survival, women and girls need practical means to become self-supporting. FEBA has begun a microsavings program that is open to all its members though it is particularly important for older women. We do not have enough money for more than a few groups of microloans, but with microsavings each woman can put aside a little bit. Eventually she might have enough to start a small business, or to deal with an emergency (an illness, a funeral, etc.). After the monthly meeting women bring their small earnings—sometimes only 500 Congo francs (about 50 cents). The leaders of FEBA note the amount in each woman's little blue booklet: the beginnings of a tiny nest egg. When we gather, members in need also receive some assistance. In the last few years, with the new farm, FEBA has been able to help the poorest women with flour or other produce (see fig. 15.1).

Sewing School. For destitute young girls we opened classes of literacy, sewing, life skills, and Bible studies to help them orient their lives by the light of Christ. Our program has the goal of educating the young women to be able to create their own careers so they will be useful members of society. FEBA's main activity on a daily basis has been the sewing school, and at first it was all outdoors in the courtyard around my house. The sewing machines and materials lived in my storeroom and were taken out for class. Naturally, this was not possible when it rained, and the seasonal rains have become stronger and more destructive each year. In 2013 we decided to cover part of the courtyard to be able to sew in bad weather, and Elsie found the money. Still, there was room for only about half of the fifty students; they had to come in shifts. There

Figure 15.1. Gathering after a FEBA monthly meeting for practical exchanges. Kinshasa, 2015. Maman Monique offering counsel after a monthly meeting while her colleagues register the microsavings and distribute the gift of vitamins brought by Elsie.

were never enough machines even for the ones present, so progress was slow. Besides teaching them to sew well, we encourage imagination. We help the students notice and think. "You see an attractive dress or blouse and say to yourself, 'If I took off that ruffle, added long sleeves, changed the neck, did this, did that. . . . ' When you modify a style, and a person buys and wears what you have created, someone who sees it will say, 'Oh, who made that?' And you get a new customer."

Maman Jeannette, the head of the sewing school, tells her story and explains about the school and its organization.

JEANNETTE: My name is Adiyo Jeannette. I was born in Kinshasa in 1964, the oldest of ten children. I studied at the Lycée Bisangni, and from there I went to Molende, where I finished my secondary school education. I had done six years of sewing classes, and that gave me the training that has enabled me to continue to today. I did not have the chance to go to university. I began my work at home, in order to have the money to bring up my little sister. I married, but I had many operations and never had any children. When I was twenty-four, my father died; then my mother died in childbirth, leaving me to bring up my baby sister. She always called me Maman. She grew up and married and has two children, but I am now supporting the orphaned children of some other sisters.

I came to work with Maman Monique in her workshop at her home about 2000. At school they taught us how to make a skirt, a blouse, dresses. Maman Monique needed someone who could make baby layettes so I learned new things. We began to make handbags, tablecloths, pillows, and other articles that we sell now. After Maman Monique was named director of the department, she said, "Let's bring the shop to the department, and then we can enlarge the work." When they made us leave there, we came back here to Maman Monique's house and opened the FEBA sewing school. I had begun with Maman Monique; I could not leave her and go somewhere else. So I am teaching the girls until they succeed and receive their certificates.

Many children who come here have experienced terrible things, and they don't have much confidence. We take unwed mothers who have no work. We also have young married women. There are some who have been to school but don't know anything at all about sewing, and we show them how to earn a living. We have many girls who have never been to school; for them we must begin with teaching reading and writing. (We enroll the poorest girls because they are the ones who have nowhere else to go; those who are better off can afford another school.) For all the students, there is education in life skills; we want them to be able to leave behind where they were and know how to improve their circumstances.

It is FEBA that provides the equipment. We ask the students to bring scissors, measuring tape, pins, and booklets for writing, but all the rest we supply. We have to have cloth and machines for them to practice. Often the machines are not good; they break easily. (The treadle ones are better than the manual but also twice as expensive so most are manual.) The first step is hand sewing; next they learn how to guide the sewing machine needle to follow the lines I trace on paper. Then I check to see if a girl is ready to go on, if she understands or not. That way I can put them in groups according to their levels. If they are slow, we don't send them away, but it takes them longer.

When they have completed the basic training, they do an internship. We do not send our students elsewhere as used to be the practice. We tried that and found that they were not well mentored. During the internship the student makes twelve articles for herself: dress, shirt, trousers, *dashiki*, suit, etc. First, she finds the picture of a style she would like, and we work out a plan for the article she has seen pictured. Another student takes the measurements— "Don't move!" Then she starts on the cloth; she applies what she has understood from the picture to what she is creating. If that fits, she cuts the material. We guide her in each step.

There is a government office charged with testing and validating vocational education. If representatives of this office examine students and conclude that their work is acceptable, the students qualify for a state certificate. The examination used to take two days. The sewing school must pay a fee for each candidate, and we also have to buy the students' materials. When the day of the exam arrives, we prepare the girls for it: they are afraid. The jury is there. There is a poster with pictures of styles. I number each one and write the number on a bit of paper and

Sewing Students' Preparation

For a young woman who has done secondary school, the sewing program should take about six months, plus the internship. For one who has a good primary school education (competent literacy skills), it should take nine or ten, plus internship. For one who is illiterate, the basic course is a year or a little more, then internship. Because the students must come in shifts, the actual time required may be nearly double this. In the new Women's Center, where the sewing school moved in July 2018, there is more space, but equipment is still limited.

put the papers in a box. The student comes and chooses a number from the box. Then she looks to see what picture it is; she has two days to make the garment. (We only watch; she cannot ask for any advice or help.) Members of the jury question the students on general knowledge and particularly on their understanding of sewing and the care of their machine. At the end of two days, the jury takes what the students have made, finished or not, and grades the articles and the students' responses to questions. Our students regularly come out at the top of the exams. Finally, we have the graduation, and each student receives her certificate from the state and a manual machine from our partners.

Sewing School Certification

Sewing and other "vocational-technical" programs are under the state Ministry of Social Work. In 2018 that system underwent some changes. They discontinued the individualized system of arranging with a school for a jury on the spot when the sewing candidates were ready, which Maman Jeannette described in her interview. The new standardized examinations are held once a year in a central location for four days, with two days for literacy and general education and two for the sewing practical.

Knowledge is vital, but a personal sewing machine is also critical. For a young woman to create a business, she must have the tools so we resolved to give each graduate a machine. (Electricity is not available in the village, and expensive and unreliable in the city, so manual machines are necessary.) One young graduate was living in a tent because her family had no home. She was afraid that the machine would be ruined by rain so we offered to house her precious new machine, and the grateful young woman came to sew at FEBA until she had a solid roof over her head. As the story of Jeannette Boyata shows, others, even if they can't afford a personal shop, can set up business in their homes, earn a living, and serve the neighborhood. The first year, 2012, we celebrated the graduation of twelve young women, and by the end of 2020 ninety-six had completed their course with the prized state certificate. One of those students, Boyata Jeannette, tells her story.

BOYATA: My name is Boyata Jeannette (interview in Lingala in August 2015; translated to French by Maman Antoinette). I was born in Kinshasa in 1978. I am the wife of a soldier, and we live in Camp Kabila. I am very happy to sew.

When my husband was passing by Maman Monique's house, he saw the poster for FEBA, which said they were seeking people who wanted to learn to sew. He talked with me about it, saying, "You like to sew; you are the mother of three children (whom we must educate)." It was my husband who urged me to come. I enrolled in 2013, and now I sew very well. He came the day of graduation and saw me in my beautiful dress; he was very happy when he saw the machine: "That was a dream, and now the dream has come true!" A machine is something extraordinary in the house. When someone sees how I sew and asks where I learned, I say, "At Maman Monique's." I have brought many young girls to this sewing school.

Since the salary of a soldier is not much, I thank God that I can now sew and contribute to our household. If someone comes with a broken zipper, I can repair it and earn 5000 francs. Or if the pants are too big, I can adjust them and earn 5000 francs. I can earn 20,000 Congo francs and pay the school fees for my children, two in secondary and one in primary. (We only have three because we practice family planning as FEBA teaches.) My husband and I have decided that our daughter will learn to sew. My husband told her, "Your mother learned to sew; in time she will grow old. You must replace your mother, and so you should learn to sew and that will help us." I don't have much money; I cannot open a shop for myself and my daughter. But, despite that, now we do not lack food. I thank the Lord for this machine, and I appreciate Maman Monique very much—she has done so much for us.

It is practically impossible to fight against poverty and injustice if you are not educated. As Maman Jeannette noted, many sewing students are virtually illiterate. They need to master reading and writing and basic math in order to succeed at any trade. Maman Mianda has been the main literacy teacher for FEBA.

MIANDA: I am called Mianda Kashala Ernestine. I was born in 1951 at Kasansa in West Kasai. My father died when I was four months old. He left my mother, my five-year-old sister, and me, and we were adopted and brought up by his brother. I grew up without knowing that my biological father was dead until another uncle came and mocked me for being ignorant. That hurt me very much, especially when everyone in the family began to cry because they were reminded of my father's death.

For secondary school I went to the Lycée Mobutu at Muena Ditu for several years, but then there was no more money to pay the fees and I could not complete my education. I married in 1969; my first son was born in 1970—he is now a pastor in the Presbyterian Church of Kinshasa. My husband and I had eight children; we wanted to educate them. Among them are four who completed secondary school and got their state diplomas and four who went on to higher education. My husband died in 2004; the youngest child was in primary school, and I had to work to see that all of them finished school. In December 2014 the youngest graduated from university in architecture, and he is an engineer now. Now I have ten grandchildren (boys and girls).

When we left the Kasai to move to Kinshasa, we lived in Maluku, 80 km (about 50 miles) from the city. In Muena Ditu I had attended church, but I was not involved in the women's activities—didn't even know about them. But when we came here to Kinshasa I fell into the hands of Maman Mesu. At the time they were opening the congregation at Maluku. In less than three months the women of the congregation proposed me as president of the women. I said, "How can I direct the women when I have never participated in a single meeting where I came from?" But Maman Mesu encouraged me, gave me advice, and said, "It is the Lord who has chosen you." So I accepted the responsibility, but I could not speak Lingala (the local language); I spoke Tshiluba and French. That same day I got out my money and bought a Bible in Lingala. So, with Bibles in all three languages I could read in the Tshiluba and French and at least understand what it was about as I learned Lingala. That was the way I worked all the time we were at Maluku. We successfully started that congregation: we paid for the property, built the church building, organized the consistory. Our work was done so we moved to Kinshasa and I continued in the women's work.

With regard to a job: I had the opportunity to go back to school to study to be a kindergarten teacher. I did extremely well—I was first in the class in 1976. After three years I stopped teaching because life was a little difficult. This job did not pay much, and my husband was not paid regularly at his job so I wanted to do some business to help our finances. I made a little money and paid for the property where we now live; the Lord always helped us. Also in 2002 I did a course offered by the Baptist Church of Kinshasa to become a literacy teacher. Then, because of what I had experienced in my own childhood, I wanted to help other children. There are children whose families have no means to educate or bring them up, who abandon caring for them. There are even people who send away their own children. So we have gathered them at FEBA, and I am here to teach them.

The story of Makongolo Dina shows the confidence a young woman gains from knowing that she is able to read and write, and is on the way to personal and economic self-sufficiency.

DINA: I am called Makongolo Dina (interview in Lingala in August 2015; translated to French by Maman Antoinette). I was born in 1988, the third of six children. My father died when we were young. We did not go to school, except my oldest brother, who paid his own way. My older sister is married. My next younger sister lives in Goma with our maternal aunt and helps her sell things, but she does not go to school. The two youngest, who are with our mother, do not go to school. One of my sisters told me that there was a nonprofit here where you could study sewing. I wanted to do that. I came and talked with Maman Monique, and she accepted me. When I came, I could not read or write, but now I have learned to read and write, and I am learning to sew. There were many things I did not know, but now I am learning and advancing. I understand sewing now, and I am making clothes for a five-year-old child.

I am a Muslim and worship there. My maternal uncle and my cousin took me there, but my parents are Christians. When I am here, I pray to Jesus with other girls. I am not married, but I have two children, a boy of six who is in first grade and a girl of eight who is in third. After my father died, I had lots of problems. There were times when I did not have anything to eat for three days, and nothing to wear. That is how I got acquainted with a policeman. Policemen are not well paid; he gets $40 or $50 a month. So he does not have enough money to rent a house for his family, but he supports his two children. Every two or three days he brings 3000 or 4000 Congo francs (less than $5) to buy food. Sometimes he gives me 10,000 Congo francs to buy clothes for the children. At the end of the month when he receives his salary, he pays the school fees for his children.

I like to sew because in the future that will allow me to support myself. If I have my work, I will not wander here and there, or prostitute myself to have a little money. I will be able to take charge of my life myself.

EDUCATING CHILDREN

We also began another service, that is, paying school fees. Education is the key to getting out of poverty. At this time there were many children who did not go to school so we paid fees for seventy and helped in various ways for others, up to 164 when the economy was doing better. Most of those we enroll are orphans; others come from very, very poor families. We only take two per family so that we can give some assistance to more families. The sewing school can help with uniforms, but coming up with funds to cover school fees is very difficult. Some of us, usually Maman Henriette and Maman Antoinette, visit each school to ask them about ways to organize paying by installment or even getting a discount. Some schools are helpful; others expel students when we cannot pay.

We still provide uniforms and school supplies for as many as possible, but because of financial limitations we have had to discontinue paying school fees regularly until we have another source of funding. However, each year we have still helped about ten secondary school students to finish the sixth (final) year and take their state examinations. We are happy to say that up to now (October 2020) we have supported seventy-seven young graduates, both girls and boys, to gain their coveted diplomas. Papy and Daniel share their stories.

PAPY: I am called Mayimona Santu Papy (translated from Lingala to French by Ngalamulume Mbombo Théophile 2015, probably because Papy was uncomfortable speaking to us directly about his experience). I was born in Kinshasa in 1991. Our family was at Tshikapa in the Kasai because my father sold diamonds (see fig. 1.2). In the war in 1997, Rwandan soldiers kidnapped my mother; we thought she was dead. Many years later someone told me that she was at Mbuji Mayi. We became refugees in the war, fleeing in a boat to Kinshasa; I was seven and my brother was ten. Then my father traveled to another city and was gone seven years. He left us with relatives who mistreated us a lot; there was no money even for food so we had problems to go to school. A friend of mine in primary school went to see Maman Monique, and she telephoned the school for him. He called me to say there was a woman at his church who could help me.

Maman Monique supported my studies; when I need something I go to see her. To earn a bit of money for food, I worked as a motorcycle taxi driver. One of my friends asked to use the cycle to do errands for another person so he could earn a bit of money for food . . . and the cycle was stolen. I talked with the owner, "I will find another motorcycle to do taxi service and repay you bit by bit." But she refused. She sent soldiers to put me in prison. I suffered a lot there; I called Maman Monique, but she was in the United States then. When she got back, she telephoned me to ask me to bear it while she worked to get me free. During this time members of FEBA brought me food (because prisoners are often not fed). To get me out they had to pay a lot and also replace the motorcycle. Thanks to Maman Monique and her friends in the United States, she found the money. Because of the bad conditions in the prison I was not in good health when I got out, and they took me to the hospital. But I forced myself to do my state exams and succeeded; I got my diploma.

Refugees, Minerals, and War

The Kasai's special wealth is industrial diamonds, centered in East Kasai. The provincial capital, Mbuji Mayi, is usually considered the diamond capital, but Tshikapa in West Kasai is also an important center for diamonds. The war to overthrow Mobutu began in the Kivu in 1996 before spreading south and west in 1997, the point at which Daniel's family fled from the armies.

DANIEL: I am called Mpinguyabu Daniel. (Interview given in French by himself.) I was born in 2002. I came here with my grandmother, who is a member of FEBA. We are seven children. I have an older sister and a twin sister; the others are younger. With the help of FEBA my older sister and I go to school. She is in the second year of secondary; I have finished primary school. The others don't go to school. I like math and want to learn to teach. At our house we have a blackboard which belonged to my grandfather; I use that to show my sisters and brothers what I have studied, and I helped my twin sister learn to read.

A NEW HOME FOR FEBA!

From 2010 until 2018, my home was the headquarters for all FEBA's activities. A Women's Center was our dream. In 2013 we decided to begin seeking funding. Thanks to our friend Elsie McKee, who is our representative in the United States, and her friends who joined her in fundraising, the money was found. There were concerts—I was able to attend one—and friends contributed from their personal funds. Thanks to their gifts, today we have FEBA's center, where the sewing school students study in good conditions and the women can gather for workshops. There we have a good place to counsel battered women and space to house a few sewing students who live too far away to come to class regularly. We call this a Center of Justice, of Love, of Peace, because women now have a place where they can learn, where they can express themselves. They will come to know their rights, they will have work, and that is a very good thing.

Sometimes I have been asked if we have men who work with us, and I say, "Yes, indeed." From the beginning my husband, Tatu Mukuna, has supported me in all kinds of ways, often serving as my transportation even when it was frightening, as when we faced the soldiers at Mme Kabila's farm. Our son Eddy also has been a great help, especially with the new Women's Center. He lived on the property while the center was being built to keep an eye on the construction and continues to serve as a kind of resident guardian. He personally paid for FEBA's beautiful big sign on the front of the center. Eddy maintains good relations with all the neighbors so that they also will care about the center and accept the people who come and go there. My son Kanyinda has helped with various computer matters. Ngalamulume Mbombo Théophile, a young lawyer who grew up with my children, has assisted us with some legal matters, such as helping get Papy out of prison. Ntambue Pierre, another lawyer, has been very active in helping FEBA with all its government registrations, and it is thanks to him that our incorporation as a local nonprofit has been confirmed at the national level. A relative of Tatu Mukuna, Mukendi Augustin, has been a constant support to FEBA with building up the farm. When I go to inspect and teach best practices, he always comes with me and contributes skills such as constructing rabbit hutches. My son Moise also helps me in oversight of the farm project because travel back and forth several hours each way on bad roads is hard on my bad back. Lufuluabo Fortunat, a bright young man whom we supported through school, and Ntambue Patrick, whom I mentioned above, have been very helpful in the day-to-day maintenance of the center or trips to the farm or other practical errands. Many things in Congo have to be "done by hand," and my women colleagues are always busy, so we are very grateful for the good will and generous engagement of these (mostly young) men.

SHARING OUR MINISTRY IN NORTH AMERICA AND THE JOY OF A NEW FARM

In 2013 I began to visit churches in the United States, sponsored by Elsie and the new little nonprofit that she and her friends established that year. (She will tell more about it later.) Then in 2014 I gave my first lecture at Princeton Theological Seminary, where Elsie teaches. I was invited to talk about "womanhood in Africa," about the place of women in society, about the challenges that they face, how they see themselves in society and in the family, where they traditionally must do exactly what their fathers or husbands say. I also talked about the impact of this wrong view of women on the life of young girls and the impact of having a large family of girls (because boys are preferred).

I took the occasion to speak about my own life and experience of being born to Christian parents, and especially to a father who was wholly Christian, who loved us, educated us, who made us know that we are human beings created in the image of God with all rights, beneficiaries of all the promises of life. My father did something extraordinary. He defied the tradition and customs, he sent us to school, he allowed us to choose our own husbands, he did not let us be treated roughly, he taught us practical skills, income-generating activities. He always said that he did not want us to become slaves (through poverty). He taught us to be autonomous as people and in economic matters, how to be independent. We thank him from the bottom of our hearts!

At Princeton in 2014 I also had the opportunity to present all the activities we do to advance women and girls. In the following years I was repeatedly invited to Princeton to talk about women in Africa, with special events in 2016, 2018, and 2019. I could make the situation of women known to theologians, to those who will become pastors in congregations and in other professions: they are able to share our vision of social transformation, our message that both women and men are human beings made in the image of God. That knowledge will help them to break human injustice. I also spoke in church congregations and in schools, where I showed the situation of our children in both eastern and western Congo. The problems are especially bad in the east, where war continues and dehumanizes women, young girls, even little girls by rape. In 2019 I was invited by the Peacemaking Program of the PC(USA) to talk about women in the CPK and my ministry.

In 2017, in response to our appeal, some North American friends at First Presbyterian Church of Evanston enabled us to buy a new farm. We grow cassava, corn, beans, and vegetables. The farm gives us food, helping us feed the hungriest and poorest of our members. It also provides income by the sale of its products, so it supports our ministry. In 2019 small animal husbandry was added, and a market garden was started to provide more cash crops. In 2020 we began planting citrus and moringa trees, eucalyptus and oil palms, though it will be some years before they bear fruit. We also arranged to be registered with the Ministry of Agriculture as a nonprofit farm so that we will be invited to workshops and perhaps get discounts for seeds. The farm enables us to bring employment to the neighboring village. We are trying to introduce more knowledge of best agricultural practices and hope to help this community prosper too. The chief's daughter is also enrolled in our sewing school.

MINISTRY DURING COVID-19

In 2019 the renewed and flourishing FEBA was planning a series of new projects. One was a culinary school, as an alternative career; sewing is not for everyone. Another was starting an orphanage. A member of FEBA who was also a graduate of the sewing school, Maman Bethye, died in 2018, and her two small children had nowhere safe to live. We worked to help them get to distant relatives, but it would have been better if we could have kept them in a familiar place. Then came Covid-19, and all plans had to be set aside.

Congo managed the pandemic admirably, with fewer than six hundred deaths by the end of 2020, most of these in Kinshasa because that is the focal point for people coming into the country. Managing the pandemic has had its own price though: everyone stayed home as ordered and then began to starve or be forced out onto the street for not paying rent. The great majority of women live by the informal economy: if you don't work, you don't eat. Many became ill; many died of minor illnesses complicated by malnutrition.

The work of FEBA shifted gears. The primary task during the lockdown was to feed our members. This meant the new farm became central to the mission; fields were added and chickens and rabbits carefully tended. (Proper precautions were observed, but in rural areas well away from Kinshasa it was possible to carry on some activities.) In the city the women could not meet for comfort or encouragement; the sewing students were sent home. Only a few of the community (staff and a few volunteers), wearing masks and maintaining social distance, came to the center to work on producing thousands of masks. We made 25,000 for one order from a medical nonprofit. The months dragged on . . . until finally in August 2020 some restrictions began to be lifted and students preparing for final exams were allowed to return to school.

Then it was time to pick up our work again, but of course we could not go back to the old ways. No culinary school, no orphanage yet. The nine young women who were almost finished with their sewing program came back to prepare for their state examinations—and, despite the long Covid interruption, they all passed with flying colors. The other students are returning as permitted. We are continuing to build up the farm because we know that food is an essential ministry. The main new thing that we have begun is an intensive microfinance effort. Since 2010 we have had a very small microloan project, but now it has become our priority because so many of our members, who were supporting their families with their small businesses, have lost all they had. Thanks to some generous American friends, by the end of September 2020 about sixty women were able to participate in this new program, and there will be more as funds allow (including money reimbursed by the first sixty). Each woman must attend a one-day refresher workshop on microfinancing and then receive $100. Let me introduce you to one of these courageous women.

Maman Mascabi's husband had abandoned her and her five daughters because she did not bear him a son. She still managed to feed her children and pay rent with her little business selling plastic sandals. Then came Covid. As ordered, Maman Mascabi stayed home—until she was evicted. Landlords were supposed to grant three months' grace, but the shutdown lasted six months. Maman Mascabi and her daughters had nowhere to go. A church gave them shelter for a week; then they were on their own.

They camped on the riverbank, using plastic bags for cover, with nothing to eat and no clean water to drink. Then Maman Mascabi contacted me, and I arranged for the family to stay with another member of FEBA for a week. When Maman Mascabi found a place to rent, FEBA provided $50 (one-half a month's rent) and invited her to join the microfinance group. She eagerly began her little business again and has already begun to repay the loan, at the rate of $12.25 every two weeks.

Despite pandemics and political and economic challenges, despite the heartbreak of illnesses and deaths, FEBA is still cradling abundance, empowering girls and women, one at a time, to gain confidence in their own value, to deal with poverty and build lives of joy and dignity for themselves and their families and their communities.

ᴀFTERWORD

Partners for FEBA

ELSIE TSHIMUNYI McKEE

ONE TITLE FOR THIS CHAPTER could have been: How to start a nonprofit almost by accident. But it was really by God's grace and amazing providence, and God's motivating many generous people to see the wonderful work that Maman Monique and other women are doing in Congo. I explain our little nonprofit by saying that our sisters in Congo are doing everything "on a shoestring" and usually giving away half the shoestring, so we are privileged to look for ways to provide some more shoestrings.

THE BEGINNING OF NORTH AMERICAN PARTNERSHIPS

After it became clear that leaders of the Presbyterian Church of Kinshasa had refused the mediation of the World Communion of Reformed Churches, I decided that some other way must be found to support Maman Monique's ministry. We started by exploring a partnership with the nonprofit Rivers of the World (ROW, now Mission: Hope) so that North American friends would have a structured channel for tax-deductible contributions to FEBA. The founder and director of the Congo branch of ROW was Jimmy Shafe, a friend of mine from schooldays in Congo. In early 2011, I initiated contact between Maman Monique and Jimmy, and FEBA was accepted as an affiliate of ROW.

My job was fundraising. I began to talk with family and friends, with people at my church, with colleagues and pastors who had been my students at Princeton Theological Seminary. On September 26, 2012, I was invited by PTS graduate Will Shirley to speak about Congo at the Presbyterian Church of Titusville, New Jersey. Shari Oosting, another recent PTS graduate, was present. She said that this African women's project was exactly what she had been looking for: a way to get involved in global work with/for women and girls. We set a meeting and. . . .

That was the beginning of the new nonprofit FEBA, Inc., doing business as Woman, Cradle of Abundance, Inc. As Shari said, it would be easier to raise money for our sisters in Congo if we had a separate identity. The tie with ROW was very helpful, but we wanted a distinctive presence for Woman, Cradle of Abundance. With the help of Shari's lawyer relatives, Jeanne and Eric Martin, our brainchild was incorporated and launched as a registered 501(c)3 non-profit under the name FEBA, Inc., in February 2013. (Having the same name for Maman Monique's work in Kinshasa and ours is the United States has been confusing. For all who are thinking of starting a nonprofit, I recommend avoiding this. For most communications we quickly changed to the English "Woman, Cradle of Abundance.") The board was made up of a group of friends: Shari Oosting; Sandra Larson, pastor and PTS graduate; Gordon Govens, lawyer and second-career doctoral student at PTS; Lisa Robinson, women's studies professor and second-career student at PTS; and Karen Oleri, web designer. Karen and her fiancé, Christo Claassens, a friend from Witherspoon Street Presbyterian Church (my home congregation), made the website. Over the years, there were some changes, mostly owing to members moving away from Princeton: Sandra in December 2013, Lisa in 2015, Karen in 2017. New members were added: Cheryl Ciaranca, Anna de Groot Preston, Beverley Williams, John McGlaughlin, Alicia Jay White, Susan Lidstone, Anjali Dhay-agude, and Patricia Stewart. But that is getting ahead of the story.[1]

Visits Between the United States and Congo

After my visit to Congo in August 2010, I had remained in fairly close contact with Maman Monique. My own academic research focus is the sixteenth century, but I had long wanted to see the women of Africa brought to life for my students. Encouraged by what I had been learning from Maman Monique, I decided this was the time to do a class on Women in African Christianity. A PTS-supported research trip in June 2011 allowed me to interview three

---

[1]See womancradleofabundance.org for additional stories, photos, and videos about FEBA and Woman, Cradle of Abundance.

founders and other women. My visit coincided with one by Jimmy Shafe and some other mutual friends; because of the partnership with ROW, Jimmy wanted to get to know Maman Monique and the women personally.

So on June 16, 2011, we all went to visit FEBA, and it was wonderful. The women had kindly agreed to move the date of their monthly meeting so that I could attend, in the church building of Maman Monique's congregation. Transportation being what it is, the American visitors were late. But the women kept right on waiting and singing, and they welcomed us with open arms. It was a marvelous service, with many, many women, a number of children, and some men. Three of FEBA's founders were there: Maman Monique, Maman Agnes, and Maman Marie-Jeanne; the music was led by Maman Mianda. Afterwards, we were invited to Maman Monique's home to see the sewing school and share a delicious meal. What a day!

Shortly after Woman, Cradle of Abundance, was officially established, Monique made her first visit to the United States sponsored by this sister non-profit. As she has told in the previous chapter, this was followed by a number of visits to Princeton. In 2014 she met and connected with middle school students of Cheryl Ciaranca, which was the beginning of the "youth appeal" for Woman, Cradle of Abundance. In 2015 I made another research visit to FEBA in Kinshasa to gather more interviews for this book. It was a gift to be able to talk with Maman Monique's current colleagues, with students and graduates of the sewing school and children supported in their education, with widows and others who have come to FEBA for help, some of whose stories have been shared here. I am deeply grateful to each one and regret that you could not meet them all.

In 2016 Nassau Presbyterian Church provided a grant for English lessons to begin the leadership development of Maman Monique's colleagues. Woman, Cradle of Abundance, brought Maman Monique and Maman Antoinette to the United States for a tour with dual purposes: expanding North Americans' acquaintance with FEBA and enabling Maman Antoinette to get to know partners. The month of October was crowded with engagements. They spoke at two universities, two seminaries, two high schools, and six churches and visited two women's shelters (to gather ideas for work in Congo). In addition, I continued to record interviews with Maman Monique for this book, which I transcribed and translated in 2016–2017. She returned to Princeton in March

2018, again thanks to Princeton Seminary, to correct the manuscript and lecture for the conference my class sponsored. She approved the final corrections in the fall of 2019 when she was in North America as a speaker in the PC(USA) Peacemaking Program.

The New Women's Center

The two most important goals that Maman Monique and her colleagues requested of their US partners were assistance in getting an actual place, a headquarters and space for FEBA, and leadership development. An additional hope was for a new farm, in a better location where the political and military situation would not prevent the women from being able to grow food. Day-to-day needs continued, of course: salaries for teachers, sewing machines for graduates, support for school fees and medical needs, and more. Donations assist with these, and the North American partners also sell the beautiful products of the sewing school to help that project support itself.

To address the major project of a Women's Center, Woman, Cradle of Abundance, began a capital campaign in November 2013. There were some major donors; Susan Lidstone launched the campaign. The main fundraisers were concerts: the wonderful graciousness of five-time Grammy nominee Karrin Allyson brought the fantastic gift of jazz artistry to put this little nonprofit on the map. She gave three marvelous concerts, "Chansons pour Congo," in the autumns of 2013, 2014, and 2015. Board member Anna de Groot Preston organized her musical friends to present two lovely concerts of French music and women musicians in 2016. Shari Oosting created a 5K "#RunAgainstRape," and I spoke in many venues. By the summer of 2014 it was possible to buy a piece of property in Kinshasa. The prices were skyrocketing throughout the whole process (Chinese and Indian businesses were expanding in Congo, and merchants were competing for land), so estimates of costs were repeatedly revised. Building also had to be intermittent; concrete will not set in a downpour, and the regular rainy season has become more and more violent in recent years. Construction began in the 2015 dry season; the basic structure was completed in the summer of 2017. Early that year a J&J CaringCrowd funding project helped to provide furnishings.

In July 2018 the first floor of the Women's Center was ready for classes and monthly meetings. The sewing school moved in, the women gathered, and great was the rejoicing! Completing the residential second floor to serve as a dormitory for sewing students from a distance has taken another two years, with thanks to two other churches, The Presbyterian Church of Los Gatos, California, and Trinity Presbyterian Church, Cherry Hill, New Jersey. Furnishings for the counseling room and office for the organization and other equipment are still being gathered. The center is solid and durable, and very attractive. This house of learning and empowerment is here to stay, to provide a secure place to serve the next generation and beyond.

Other projects are also moving along, though more slowly. Leadership development has focused particularly on English lessons for Maman Monique's colleagues. She is the only one fluent in the language, which is a key tool—not only for contact with partners but also for purchasing trips to China and other places where French is not common. And, as you have heard Maman Monique tell, FEBA got its new farm thanks to Caryl Weinberg and First Presbyterian Church of Evanston, Illinois.

FEBA's Mentorships in Congo

Maman Monique has a large heart and a great vision of sharing. Some of that sharing is through encouragement and consulting, giving support for other groups of women and girls and children. This often means answering appeals for advice and mentoring. In chapter twelve she told about her impromptu lecture on the humanitarian situation in eastern Congo, which she was asked to repeat several times in Sweden. Through the Woman, Cradle of Abundance, in North America she also began an ongoing relationship with colleagues in a different part of the Kivu.

Kivu. In 2006 a group of Congolese activists in Uvira, Kivu, in eastern Congo, organized a nonprofit to address the situation of women and children in their war-torn region where militia of many allegiances had been fighting for a decade. They named their project The Center for Mentoring Children in Difficulties, with the French acronym CENEDI, and its main focus is education.

About the same time, Cheryl Ciaranca organized a club called Hands Across the Water (HAW) at her Community Middle School in Plainsboro, New Jersey, to enable her students to make contact with some counterparts in Africa. This began a connection between schoolchildren in Plainsboro and two villages near Uvira: first as pen pals and then, as the North Americans

learned more about the situation of their new friends, as fundraisers to help
the Congolese students pay school fees. By 2018, thirty-two young men and
women in eastern Congo had graduated from secondary school with some or
full assistance from HAW. In 2014, Hands Across the Water became a branch
of Woman, Cradle of Abundance. Maman Monique and Mr. Innocent Nunda
wa Nunda, the current head of the Uvira project, met virtually and began a
parallel conversation, which led to a mentorship between their nonprofits.

Now linked to Woman, Cradle of Abundance, the Uvira nonprofit expanded its activities to give more attention to the women of the community.
The numbers of women and girls—as young as eight—who have been raped
in recent years in these two small villages is heartbreaking—over one hundred.
Maman Monique has sent money, counsel, and clothing made by the sewing
school; North American partners have sent money for medical care and food.
In 2013 in the conflict between Rwanda and Congo there was a terrible
bombing of the city of Goma, North Kivu, which left the streets full of orphans. In 2015 CENEDI started a primary school for them, and the youth of
HAW are continuing to support that ministry, as well as efforts to find work
for graduates in Uvira. When the survivors of rape in the villages near Uvira
needed a new means of support, Maman Monique shared her wisdom, and in
2020 Woman, Cradle of Abundance, was able to provide them with a farm
with the help of another J&J CaringCrowd fundraiser.

Kasai. FEBA has another mentor relationship in the Kasai province. At
Tshikaji, just outside the capital of West Kasai, Kananga, the Congo branch of
ROW (Mission: Hope), led by Jimmy Shafe, was asked to start a sewing school
for unwed mothers. The project began about 2006, with three women leaders:
Maman Beki, Maman Rose Ngalula, and Maman Marthe. (In 2010, shortly
after seeing Maman Monique, my husband and sister and I visited the school.)
A number of classes of young women graduated and received sewing machines
to begin their own careers. Jimmy also sold some of their products in the
United States.

After some years, however, it became apparent that improvements were
needed. With all their good will, the teachers did not themselves have the
training needed to make the school able to contribute to its own support, or
to enable the students to make high-quality items. In 2016 Maman Beki spent
three weeks at the FEBA school in Kinshasa. Then she and her colleagues

asked Maman Monique to go to Tshikaji to do a workshop. This was delayed for a year by the Kamuina Nsapu war in the Kasai, but in July 2017 Maman Monique and Maman Jeannette did a week's intensive training for the women at Tshikaji. These women have persisted, through continuing effects of the military conflict, through internal reorganization in 2019, with some mediation by Maman Monique. In the midst of great suffering, sisters are still reaching out to help sisters.

Does this sound like coming full circle? Maman Monique's adult ministry has been in Kinshasa, but she has repeatedly reached out to those in her old home through the programs of the National Federation of Protestant Women, through mentoring women to increase their capacity, and through acting as a consultant for a new women's secondary school in the Kasai. She is passing on what she has learned to help others have a more abundant life by empowering women and fighting systemic poverty.

ACKNOWLEDGMENTS

MAMAN MONIQUE SPEAKS:

We thank the Lord for his gift, which cannot be compared with any other gift, his gift who speaks, whom all the world sees, a gift who gives life to many, many people who are marginalized and excluded: those people find a place.

We say thank you, thank you with all our hearts to all the people who have contributed and helped us to have our Women's Center. We say thank you, thank you with all our hearts to Princeton Theological Seminary and its president, to the leaders of the many congregations, to our sister Professor Elsie, and to all her colleagues who have invited us to talk about our ministry and to talk about women in Africa.

I would like to take this occasion to thank Witherspoon Street Presbyterian Church in Princeton, the congregation of my dear sister Elsie McKee. They invited us to speak. The members bought our sewing school articles, gave us sewing machines, and helped in a variety of situations. We are very grateful for all their acts; we thank each person who did something, who prayed for us or thought of us, who gave advice or offered material support: may they know that this has helped us bring our work to the place it is today.

We say thank you, thank you with all our hearts to our sister and friend Caryl Weinberg and the pastors and all the members of her church, First Presbyterian Church of Evanston, who have contributed by their prayers and their gifts. It is thanks to them that we have our farm; may they find here the expression of our gratitude. We say thank you to Jan and Tom Sullivan and others who support education; that is a great contribution to our ministry. Thank you to Olga Ricketts-Peart and the Bible Study for Congo; we are very grateful for all you have done and are doing and continue to do for us.

We want to thank our African Presbyterian sisters in the organization Tumekutana, who gave us the order for one hundred wraps with the logo Tumekutana 2018 for the conference in South Africa. It was a great contribution to our ministry. Thank you, Caryl and the women of First Presbyterian Church of Evanston, who made it possible for me to travel to this conference. That trip also enabled me to see my mother, who was at the end of her days. We could attend her, God allowed me to talk with her before her death, she died before my eyes. Other friends of Woman, Cradle of Abundance, like Beverley Williams, enabled us to bring her body home to Congo to be buried with dignity. Thank you, thank you, thank you, my sisters.

We say thank you, thank you with all our hearts to our dear friends of Woman, Cradle of Abundance, and ROW (Mission: Hope) who have made possible so much, so much. Thank you, Shari, Lisa, Sandra, Gordon, Karen, Susan, Cheryl, Anna, Beverley, Alicia, John, Anjali, Patti, Jimmy. For all the amazing concerts, Karrin Allyson: you are the best. We are so grateful to you for all you have done, especially for our Women's Center. Thank you for all you have done also for the women in eastern Congo; we are very grateful.

Now in conclusion, I lack the words to thank my sister, my very dear sister, *muan'etu* (my sibling), *mulunda wanyi* (my friend), Elsie Tshimunyi, and her husband, John, who have accompanied us in doing this work, who have made great sacrifices to support our ministry, even to create Woman, Cradle of Abundance, to seek out friends to work with her and to raise consciousness about our work. Her house has been transformed into a FEBA store, she wears FEBA, she talks FEBA at the seminary, in schools, in churches. Elsie, we the women of FEBA are very grateful; we do not have words to express our thanks. We say thank you to our sisters Beth, Katherine, Charlene, and our (your) late mother, Anne, who helped us with her legacy. Thank you, thank you to the whole family.

We say thank you to all of you, our sisters. Thank you to all of you our brothers who have contributed, all who have held out a hand, who have prayed. Thanks to all of your sacrifices, the women who serve FEBA can have a salary at the end of the month and the children can study and learn. When there have been very difficult times, you have helped: with illness, with death. When our graduate Bethye died, you enabled us to bury her properly. Thank you, thank you.

We think that now everyone can know our story through this book. Thank you, Dr. Jon Boyd, for helping us to publish it. We are very grateful. We say thank you to every person who reads this book, and we ask everyone to be a person who brings joy to children, who does not discriminate between girls and boys, who works for justice, who strives to create a world of love, joy, and no discrimination.

I wish to end by thanking God the Almighty, the everlasting God of hosts, who gave us parents who showed us his way, who loved us, who did not discriminate, who did not allow themselves to be controlled by the tradition: to that God alone be glory. We say thank you to God; we say thank you to the Presbyterian mission that taught our father and that we benefit from today. Many women, many young girls, many children have benefited. Thank you, eternal God of love, to you be all glory.

Elsie speaks:

Thank you so much, *tuasakidila wa bungi, muan'etu, mulunda wanyi,* Maman Monique. It is a privilege and joy to know you, and I am deeply grateful to you, my very dear sister, for the gift of sharing your story with me, for the honor of giving me a place in your heart and your ministry. This has been one of the great blessings of my life.

With Maman Monique, I say thank you so much to all who have contributed to making her story known and bringing this book to fulfillment. Special thanks to Princeton Theological Seminary for multiple research trips, for inviting Maman Monique to Princeton, and for making available technological facilities. Thanks to Samuel Yenn-Batah for several semesters of work on photos and audio-visual materials. Thank you to the many individuals who encouraged and helped in so many ways, facilitating my African Women Extraordinaire conferences, making audio-visual and photographic records, welcoming Maman Monique to speak in classes and events: Jan Ammon, Barbara Chaapel, Joicy Becker-Richards, Eric Rasmussen, Barbara McTague, Raimundo Barreto, Jacqueline Lapsley, Yvette Martell, Sushama Austin-Connor, Craig Barnes, Catherine Ahmad, Lisa Bowens, Beth DeMauro, Nicole Pride, and more. Thank you from my heart to all my students, who welcomed Maman Monique and loved her and have done more than you know to bring this story to light. Thank you also to the PTS Class of 1955 for the generous award that has helped with publication.

I join Maman Monique in thanking all the special Woman, Cradle of Abundance, group, some of whom have read the story (Beverley, Gordon) and all of whom have labored to bring hope and support to her ministry. Thank you to my family: my parents and grandparents who "gave" Congo to me and me to Congo, who modeled the faith and friendships that have made me the daughter of Christ's church in the Kasai that I am. Thank you to my sisters, who wear FEBA and love FEBA. Thank you to my generous, patient husband, John McGlaughlin, for accompanying me to Congo, for helping to record interviews, and especially for welcoming all my FEBA friends into our lives.

With Maman Monique I repeat my thanks to Jon Boyd, the thoughtful peer-review readers, and all the wonderful team at IVP Academic for making this dream come true, putting into your hands this story of faith and courage, humor and wisdom, perseverance and grace.

The highest thanks go to the Lord who came to bring life abundant. *Tuasakidila wa bungi, Mukulenge Jesu Kilisto.*

KEY PEOPLE

Adiyo Jeannette: head of the FEBA sewing school

Agnes Anekumba Umadjela: one of the founders of FEBA; member of the General Council of the Methodist Church

Annie Ntumba: assistant to Maman Monique in her role as director of the CPK Department of Women and Families; later director of the department

Antoinette Muleka Tshisuaka: former secretary of the CPK Department of Women and Families; life-skills teacher and AIDS ministry staff with FEBA

Bishola Sarah: Maman Monique's aunt (her mother's younger sister)

Bitota Rosalie Ditshilualua: Maman Monique's mother

Etienne Tshisekedi: nonviolent opponent of President Mobutu; cofounded Union for Democracy and Social Progress (UDPS) party in 1982

Félix Tshisekedi: president of DR Congo beginning in 2019; son of Etienne Tshisekedi

Ilunga Paul: Maman Monique's uncle (her father's youngest brother)

Inge Sthreshley: PC(USA) partner of the CPK Women's Center

Jean Carbonare: a Frenchman involved with the International Federation of Human Rights Leagues

Jean-Etienne: a family friend of Maman Monique

Joseph Kabila: president of Congo, 2001–2018; son of Laurent Kabila

Kalala Gaston: Tatu Mukuna's younger brother

Kanda Kaja: Tatu Mukuna's younger brother

Katuku Paul: Maman Monique's first husband

Kazadi Ngoie Philip (Nsenji): Maman Monique's paternal grandfather

Kibadi Nzeyi Henriette: school children and AIDS ministry staff with FEBA

Laurent Kabila: president of DR Congo from 1997 to 2001; forced Mobutu from power

Maman Mesu: first director of the Department of Women and Families of the Presbyterian Church of Kinshasa (CPK)

Marie-Jeanne Kapinga Kayuwa: one of the founders of FEBA; pastor in the Church of Christ Light of the Holy Spirit in Congo

Mbaya Tshibalabala (Simon): Maman Monique's maternal grandfather

Mbuyi Kaleka Mbaya (Marthe): Maman Monique's maternal grandmother

Misenga Mudile Marthe: Maman Monique's paternal grandmother

Mianda Kashala Ernestine: literacy teacher for FEBA

Mme Kabila: wife of Laurent Kabila, mother of Joseph Kabila

Mukuna Tshilobo Lukusa Constantin (Tatu Mukuna): Maman Monique's second husband

Ngoie Tshiamanyangala Kazadi Moses: Maman Monique's father

Nsakadi Jean: Maman Monique's uncle (her father's younger brother)

Pastor Nzeba: director of the Department of Women and Families of the Church of Christ in Congo (CCC); elected executive secretary of her presbytery in 2019

Pauline Mfulu: one of the founders of FEBA; national secretary of Baptist women

Sese Seko Mobutu: president of DR Congo from 1965 to 1997

Setri Nyomi: general secretary of the World Alliance of Reformed Churches

Tshijuka Louise: Maman Monique's aunt (her mother's older sister)

Tshimenga Joseph: Maman Monique's older brother

Tshimungu Mayela Joseph (Pastor Tshimungu): first general secretary/president of the Presbyterian Church of Kinshasa (CPK)

Interviews

General FEBA—June 22–27, 2011

Place: Kinshasa, DRC

Type and Personnel: Videotapes (all in French or translated to French), by Elsie McKee

Monique Misenga Mukuna (multiple)—founder

Marie Jeanne Kapinga Kayuwa   founder

Agnes Anekumba Umadjela, in Lingala with Maman Monique translating—founder

Antoinette Muleka Tshisuaka—FEBA staff

Suzanne Olowe, in Lingala with Maman Monique translating—FEBA member

Monique Misenga Mukuna

Date and Place: May 2013, in Princeton, NJ; a visit sponsored by Woman, Cradle of Abundance

Type and Personnel: Videotape (French-English), by Matthew Anderson, David Brendan, and Crawford Watson, friends of FEBA board member Karen Oleri

Date and Place: March 2014, in Princeton, NJ; a visit to speak at Princeton Theological Seminary for the African Women Extraordinaire conference

Type and Personnel: Videotape (English), by PTS Communications Office: Barbara Chaapel, Eric Rasmussen

Audiotape (English), by Alison Fraser Kling, PTS student

Various audios (French), by Elsie McKee

GENERAL FEBA—JULY 30–AUGUST 13, 2015

Place: Kinshasa, DRC

Type and Personnel: Audiotapes (all in French or translated to French from Lingala or Tshiluba), by Elsie McKee and John McGlaughlin. Here grouped by category, in alphabetical order.

FEBA Staff

1. Adiyo Woto Jeannette—sewing teacher
2. Kibadi Nzeyi [sometimes written Nzey] Henriette—schoolchildren and AIDS ministry
3. Mianda Kashala Ernestine—literacy teacher
4. (Monique Misenga Mukuna—president)
5. Muleka Tshisuaka Antoinette—life skills teacher and AIDS ministry
6. Ngombe Sakisa Denise—pastoral counselor (until 2018)
7. Nsimba Nlandu Fifi—assistant sewing teacher

Sewing Graduates

8. Boyata Jeannette
9. Gode Kabangu
10. Mundeke-Odito Eve—now FEBA seamstress
11. Sita Yollande

Sewing Students

12. Chantale Musawu
13. Kabica Leaba Kendra
14. Kapinga Ntumba Dina
15. Kongo Sarah
16. Likopala Esperance
17. Makongolo Dina
18. Mashiabu Marie
19. Muyiya Salima
20. Pambu Loriane

FEBA Members, Families, Orphans

21. Badiana Charlotte—elderly widow member of FEBA

22. Ngomba Mukala Mado—FEBA leader, widow

23. Odette Kalanga—widow member of FEBA

24. Kabombo Marie—elderly widow member of FEBA

25. Mpinguyabu Daniel—elementary student supported by FEBA, grandson of Kabombo Marie

26. Kamuleta Rose Ntumba—member of FEBA (mother of four, adopted two nephews)

27. Meta Kabanga Daniel—high school graduate supported by FEBA, nephew of Kamuleta Rose

28. Ntumba Mpoyi Joel—high school student supported by FEBA, son of Kamuleta Rose

29. Papy Mayimona Santu—high school graduate supported by FEBA

Other

30. Théophile Ngalamulume Mbombo—lawyer for FEBA

31. Ndelela Nkamba Sharon—Scholarship student, completed MD with FEBA sponsorship

MONIQUE MISENGA MUKUNA AND ANTOINETTE MULEKA TSHISUAKA

Date and Place: September–October 2016, various places in New Jersey

Type and Personnel: Audiotapes (French), by Elsie McKee

The two FEBA leaders were in the United States for a tour of about six weeks sponsored by Woman, Cradle of Abundance. Elsie accompanied them and made tapes as time permitted.

MONIQUE MISENGA MUKUNA

Some conversations March 2018, when Maman Monique visited Princeton to correct the book manuscript and speak at the African Women Extraordinaire conference at Princeton Seminary.

Various conversations, some by phone, some in person during August–October 2019, when Maman Monique was in the United States for a tour sponsored by the PC(USA) Peacemaking Program. These were mostly to fill in details or clarify points, or bring the discussion up to date.

Further conversations by phone over the period of final revisions.

General Index

SCRIPTURE INDEX